From Metaphysical Representations to Aesthetic Life

SUNY series in Chinese Philosophy and Culture

Roger T. Ames, editor

From Metaphysical Representations to Aesthetic Life

Toward the Encounter with the Other in the Perspective of Daoism

MASSIMILIANO LACERTOSA

Cover photo: Massimiliano Lacertosa.

Published by State University of New York

© 2023 State University of New York

All rights reserved

Printed in the United States of America

No part of this book may be used or reproduced in any manner whatsoever without written permission. No part of this book may be stored in a retrieval system or transmitted in any form or by any means including electronic, electrostatic, magnetic tape, mechanical, photocopying, recording, or otherwise without the prior permission in writing of the publisher.

For information, contact State University of New York Press, Albany, NY
www.sunypress.edu

Library of Congress Cataloging-in-Publication Data

Name: Lacertosa, Massimiliano, author.
Title: From metaphysical representations to aesthetic life : toward the encounter with the other in the perspective of Daoism / Massimiliano Lacertosa.
Description: Albany : State University of New York Press, [2023] | Series: SUNY series in Chinese Philosophy and Culture | Includes bibliographical references and index.
Identifiers: ISBN 9781438493640 (hardcover : alk. paper) | ISBN 9781438493664 (ebook) | ISBN 9781438493657 (pbk. : alk. paper)
Further information is available at the Library of Congress.

10 9 8 7 6 5 4 3 2 1

To Miodrag and Maitreya

Contents

Preface ix

Acknowledgments xi

Note on the Text xiii

Introduction 1

1. Toward the Encounter with the Other 11

2. From Worldview to Metaphor 29

3. From Metaphor to Ethics 49

4. From Ethics to *Ziran* 自然 77

5. From *Ziran* 自然 to Aesthetics 111

Returning to the Beginning (by Way of Conclusion) 135

Notes 157

References 177

Index 193

Preface

This book analyses some fundamental differences between the philosophical tradition of Plato-Descartes and the so-called philosophical Daoism. One might be tempted to consider this book a comparative study of Western and Chinese philosophies if these terms were not so controversial. Indeed, what does "Chinese philosophy" mean and translate?

My thesis is that Chinese philosophy is a definition and, therefore, it functions as an interpretation. To regard a Chinese text as "philosophical" means that one applies an interpretative filter to it. This, however, cannot be a naïve approach. Although it is necessary to adopt a philosophical language in order to deploy a philosophical analysis—at least if one wants to be published in journals of philosophy and communicate to the academic circle of philosophy—this does not mean that the translation of concepts from Chinese to, in this case, English has to blindly use the Western philosophical structure.

In this book I argue that if Chinese philosophy wants to interpret Chinese concepts into well-established and comfortable Western categories, this interpretation has the limit of self-repetition. If, on the contrary, Chinese philosophy translates the attempt to interpret and assimilate what is not familiar, then the idea of philosophy itself can be broadened or even changed.

Chinese philosophy does not need to fit into the narrow paths of Western logic, ontology, metaphysics. Quite the reverse: philosophy needs to adapt its language to provide an adequate interpretation of Chinese texts. Through the analysis of key passages from the *Daodejing* 道德經 and the *Zhuangzi* 莊子, I show how Chinese philosophy interprets something that is not necessarily present in Western philosophy. This means that terms such as "aesthetics," "ethics," and "philosophy" itself need to expand their meanings to address the context in which they are employed.

Yet how can this extension of meanings be possible? I am convinced that it is possible through comparison. The definition of a "philosophy of comparisons" proposed in this book is in line with such an endeavor. I conceive of a philosophy of comparisons as a philosophy that stems from its critical examination of itself. Therefore, this book is not just an analysis of key concepts in Western and Chinese philosophies but also a reflection on how this analysis is conducted. In other words, the comparison is not an end but a means to formulate a mutual understanding that is first and foremost a self-understanding. Thus, the comparative process becomes the path through which one can productively philosophize on one's own tradition and on the tradition of the other.

The philosophies of Friedrich Nietzsche and Martin Heidegger can help us to proceed on this path by showing the importance of self-critique in the process of self-understanding. Indeed, both philosophers—in their own ways—criticized the Western metaphysical tradition and its implicit assumptions. This self-reflective methodological aspect is fundamental to prepare the ground for the comparative analysis.

Consequently, the aim of this book is not to propose equivalences between the philosophies of Heidegger and Laozi or between those of Nietzsche and Zhuangzi. The aim is to reevaluate the philosophical traditions of Plato-Descartes and Daoism in a dialogue that pushes at the boundaries of entrenched conceptual frameworks. My intention is not to merely analyze two different ways of doing philosophy, but to move forward the philosophical discourse itself through this dialogue.

My hope is to take the readers on a trajectory of new insights, from language and world, to the nature of existence, knowledge, ethics, and finally to the transformative processes toward an aesthetically fulfilled life.

Acknowledgments

There are several people that I need to thank for helping me directly and indirectly during the years in which I wrote this book. First of all, I would like to express my immense gratitude to Arnaldo Picchi for showing me how to find new possibilities through improvisation. I am very grateful for the guidance and help I receive from Diarmuid Costello. I thank Fabienne Peter, Quassim Cassam, Daniele Lorenzini, David Bather Woods, Guy Longworth and the entire Department of Philosophy at the University of Warwick for supporting and valuing my research in Chinese philosophy. Special thanks go to Cosimo Zene, Johan Siebers, Tania Tribe, and Zhang Zheng for their mentorship. I am particularly indebted to Graham Parkes, Robin Wang, and Antonello Palumbo for their precious comments on an early draft of this work. I would like to express my profound gratitude to Karyn Lai, Ma Lin, Hans-Georg Moeller, and Steven Burik for their attentive reading of the book and thoughtful suggestions. I am also grateful to Roger Ames for believing in my research and to James Peltz for guiding me through the process of publication.

I am indebted to the Confucian Institute for the Fellowship that allowed me to spend two years in Beijing. The Beijing Normal University provided a welcoming and stimulating environment for my research. In particular, I thank Zhao Chang for his kindness and support during my staying at the Beijing Normal University. But most of all, I thank my friends in Beijing for helping me to better understand Chinese philosophy and culture.

Finally, I want to thank my family for the loving support that led me to this outcome. In particular, I thank Marianna for seeing and thinking what I do not. And I thank my two sons for letting me discover a new world every day. This book is for them.

Note on the Text

Chapter 1 is a new elaboration of the article "For a philosophy of comparisons" (*Asian Philosophy* 27, no. 4 (2017): 324–339) and the book chapter "Interpreting *Dao* (道) between 'Way-making' and '*Be-wëgen*'" (in *Ancient and Modern Practices of Citizenship in Asia and the West: Care of the Self*, edited by Gregory Bracken, 103–120 (Amsterdam: Amsterdam University Press, 2018)).

Chapter 5 further develops the article "The Ethical Stance of the 'Qiwulun (Discourse on Corresponding Things)'" (*Dao. A Journal of Comparative Philosophy* 18, no. 2 (2019):183–196).

Unless otherwise indicated, translations from Chinese are by the author. Emphasis in quotations is always from the original.

Introduction

The main aim of this book is to describe a path that goes from the theoretical constructions of metaphysical representations to the ethical implications of an aesthetic life. Before proceeding in this direction, however, it is crucial to define the starting point of this journey by explaining how I use some terms in relation to their etymology. I believe that this is necessary (1) pedagogically and (2) methodologically.

(1) It is necessary pedagogically, because it offers the possibility to compare the origin of these terms with their subsequent or contemporary meanings. This is not to say that etymology gives the *true* meaning of a term, but only that it gives additional information worth appropriate consideration. (2) It is necessary methodologically, because words are not neutral and can refer to different conceptual assumptions in different times and in different contexts. This entails that a precise definition of how terms are used can avoid misunderstandings, especially when the aim is a redefinition and revaluation of concepts—as I shall discuss soon.

Hence, the analysis of these terms should be seen as a starting point and not as an end in itself. I consider "ethics" and "aesthetics" here and discuss "philosophy"—along with some important Chinese terms—in chapter 1.

At the beginning of the second book of the *Nicomachean Ethics* (1103a), Aristotle specifies that the ethical derives its name (*ēthikḗ* ἠθική) from *ēthos* (ἦθος) "character," which is formed by a variation of the word *éthos* (ἔθος), meaning "habit," "custom," "disposition." Michel Foucault (1987, 117) explains that, for the Greeks, *ēthos* referred to a way of being and to conduct oneself; it was "a certain manner of acting visible to others." Before any moral philosophy, before any differentiation between what is good and what is bad, what is right and what is wrong, ethics needs to pay attention to this way of being that is first and foremost a disposition toward the world.

In this sense, "ethics" does not necessarily have a positive or negative connotation if it is conceived as *ethos*, that is, if it defines a habit and not a normative set of moral standards. The contemporary philosopher Jacques Rancière (2010, 184) rightly holds that, before referring to a domain of moral values, the word *ethos* stands for two things: "dwelling" and "way of being"—the way of living that corresponds to this dwelling. Thus, according to Rancière, ethics is "the kind of thinking in which an identity is established between an environment, a way of being and a principle of action." More than an "identity," I will consider the possibility of thinking ethics as a *relation* between an environment and a principle of action that *results* in a way of being.

This relation—and its consequent way of being—cannot be stable in the sense of a normative moral standard because while a principle of action can be fixed, an environment is always in transformation. This relation, therefore, cannot be static because actions and environments need to find a constant reciprocal adaptation. Yet, to find a balanced adaptation, one needs to be aesthetically attuned to the world. This means that, prior to any moral theory—and prior to any environmental ethics as well—it is crucial to understand how ethics is linked to aesthetics as a specific disposition toward the world in which one comes in contact with the other at large.[1] But what does "aesthetics" mean here?

The term "aesthetics" derives from *aísthēsis* (αἴσθησις), which refers to the perception of the senses (from *aisthánomai* αἰσθάνομαι "to perceive"). As a specific category for the "theory of liberal arts" (theoria liberalium artium), the word was conceived by Alexander Gottlieb Baumgarten in the middle of the 18th century. In *Aesthetica* (1961, §1), Baumgarten defines it as "the science of sensory cognition" (scientia cognitionis sensitivæ) and specifies that aesthetics is a "lower knowledge" (gnoseologia inferior). In this formulation, aesthetics pertains to sense perception and, as a lower faculty of cognition, is related but distinct to logic, the higher faculty of cognition.

Immanuel Kant radicalizes the distinction between faculties.[2] In the first introduction to the *Critique of Judgment* (20: 223), he asserts that "judging (that is, objectively) is an action of the understanding (as the higher cognitive faculty in general) and not of sensibility." Thus for Kant the expression "aesthetic judgment" is contradictory because "an objective judgment is always made by the understanding, and to that extent cannot be called aesthetic" (20: 222). This implies that aesthetic judgment "affords absolutely no cognition (not even a confused one) of the object, which happens only in a logical judgment" (5: 228).

It is not my intention to offer an overview of Kant's *Critique of Judgment* here. I neither want to analyze how Kant justifies the subjectively universal validity of judgments of taste, nor consider how for Kant "taste, as a subjective power of judgment, contains a principle of subsumption, not of intuitions under concepts, but of the faculty of intuitions or presentations (i.e., of the imagination) under the faculty of concepts (i.e., the understanding), insofar as the former in its freedom is in harmony with the latter in its lawfulness" (5: 287).[3]

Nor yet am I interested in the historical development of aesthetic as theory of beauty.[4] Although I shall consider a specific idea of art in relation to Friedrich Nietzsche, my main intention is to understand, on the one hand, the role that the sensible/supersensible distinction plays in ethics and, on the other hand, the ethical implications of different approaches to sense perception.

Hans-Georg Gadamer (2004, 36) pointed out that "we are influenced by Kant's achievement in moral philosophy, which purified ethics from all aesthetics and feeling." I assume that "we" refers to the Western philosophical tradition. I will argue that the purification of ethics from aesthetics has a long history in Western metaphysics prior to Kant. This leads me to the question: how is the relationship between ethics and aesthetics in other traditions? In this respect, Daoism can be a valuable element of comparison.

The term "Daoism" (or "Taoism") refers to the concept of *dao* (or *tao* 道), which is generally translated as "way." As shall be seen in the next chapters, the concept is far more complex than this. For now, however, suffice it to say that one of the most significant appearances of *dao* in Chinese philosophy is in the *Daodejing* (or *Tao te ching* 道德經), also known as *Laozi* (or *Lao-tzu, Lao-tze* 老子), from the name of the sage who was supposed to be its author.[5] Although the term "Daoism" is of Western coinage, the idea of a cultural tradition that refers to *dao* can be traced back to Sima Tan 司馬談 (died 110 BCE), who conceived the term *daojia* 道家 (literally "*dao* family").

Besides the *Daodejing*, the other book that is commonly regarded as the foundation of Daoist thought is the *Zhuangzi* (or *Chuang-tzu* 莊子). Similarly to the *Laozi*, the *Zhuangzi* is not the work of a single author. To refer to Zhuangzi as the author of the *Zhuangzi* is only a convention that I sometimes retain for the sake of brevity or to define the character that appears in the book.[6] Due to the common philosophical ground shared by the *Laozi* and the *Zhuangzi*, some scholars refer to them as *Lao-Zhuang* 老莊. This term first appeared in the last chapter of an important text of the early

Han dynasty (206 BCE–220 CE)—the *Huainanzi* 淮南子 (139 BCE)—and shows how the books were linked together very early on in China.[7]

I shall use the term "Daoism" interchangeably with *Lao-Zhuang*. This, however, does not mean that these texts represent a defined school of thought already formed in the Warring States (475–221 BCE). It only means that they propose a similar approach to the world.

Harold Roth (1999, 6) criticizes the idea of a *Lao-Zhuang* philosophy, which is not the only philosophical Daoist tradition, the other being the *Huang-Lao* 黃老 (Yellow Emperor and Laozi), "an early Taoist philosophical lineage with Legalist tendencies that was previously known only through historical writings." With "previously," Roth refers to the excavated texts discovered in Mawangdui 馬王堆 in 1973. According to him, these discoveries "have led scholars to question the exclusivity—and even the very existence—of a 'Lao-Chuang' school of Taoist philosophy in the late Warring States and early Han." This, however, does not settle the problem and, as Roth himself critically affirms, "some scholars still think in terms of a Lao-Chuang philosophical school that influenced a later Huang-Lao philosophical school."

Chad Hansen (1992, 371) reverses the problem and argues that it was the *Huang-Lao* dogmatic interpretation of Daoism that came to affect the historical image of the *Lao-Zhuang*. For Hansen, the "superstitious dogmatic ideology" of the *Huang-Lao* became "the ancestor of both religious Daoism and the ruling interpretation's inherited view [the mystical view] of philosophical Daoism."

Regardless of the existence of a philosophical school in the Warring States and the elusiveness of the *Lao-Zhuang* Daoism, the *Laozi* and the *Zhuangzi* offer an idea of humanity-world relationship that is worth analyzing. Indeed, the *Lao-Zhuang*'s vision of duality is interestingly divergent from the Platonic structure of Western metaphysics.

As discussed in detail in chapter 1, chapter 5, and the last chapter, an important part of Western metaphysics is based on an onto-theological representation of the world in which the sensible and the supersensible are radically divided. On the other hand, in the *Lao-Zhuang* there is an aesthetic approach to the world in which the dualities are corresponding. In the latter, "because of the absence of . . . religious, spiritual pillar and the lack of abstract, metaphysical speculation, nature comes to encompass all things, including God, so that one can simply allow the spirit to rest in nature, as opposed to struggling to transcend it" (Li 2010, 101). This is a problematic statement, and I will discuss its content throughout the book. Only a brief consideration is necessary here.

Although I will not go into the specific debate that questions whether the *Daodejing* and the *Zhuangzi* are religious texts, my intention is to tackle the problem more directly by considering the issues of theology and onto-theology in relation to them.⁸

The analysis of Martin Heidegger's philosophy is crucial in this respect insofar as it offers one of the most refined critiques of onto-theology in Western metaphysics. This, however, does not mean that I will consider Heidegger's connections with Asian thought here. This is not only because there are already important books on the topic,⁹ but also because I am suspicious of whether this is a viable comparison.

The problem with the comparative analysis of some scholars is that they see the dialogue between the later Heidegger and Chinese thought as a genuine dialogue. Their argument is mostly based on the assumption that Heidegger was influenced by the reading of the *Daodejing*. And this seems to allow scholars such as Katrin Froese to reinterpret Daoist philosophy through the Heideggerian lenses—and more specifically through the idea of nothingness. Although I appreciate Froese's efforts to propose and expand the idea of comparative philosophy, I find her methodology misleading.

First of all, I do not think "there is a strong affinity between Heidegger's notion of Being and the idea of the Dao" (Froese 2006, 55)—even in the forms of *Seyn* and *Seiṇ*. Moreover, the supposed influence of Daoist philosophy on Heidegger's thought can hardly justify the interpretation of the *Daodejing* in Heideggerian terms. On this, I agree with Ma Lin, who offers the most lucid analysis of Heidegger's philosophy in relation to Asian thought. According to Ma (2008, 166), "Heidegger's interest in Asian words and verses is limited to the motivation of finding support for his own preconceived ideas," and this means that "Heidegger has never thought of modifying his central ideas in light of the insight from other traditions."

In chapter 2, I will show how the impossibility for Heidegger to genuinely engage in a dialogue with Chinese philosophy has roots in his conception of worldview philosophy (*Weltanschauungsphilosophie*). Indeed, more than the fact that for Heidegger the East-West dialogue is secondary to the dialogue with the Greek philosophy and "cannot enjoy the same status as the 'only one and first beginning' " (Ma 2008, 71; 213), we need to consider how Heidegger defines other philosophies as worldview philosophies.¹⁰

As a consequence, I am not convinced by comparisons such as the one offered by Steven Burik—who proposes, however, a much stronger and more coherent analysis of both Heidegger's thought and Daoism than Froese's. Burik (2009, 147) avoids the pitfall of overlapping Being and *dao* by suggesting that "the notion of *Ereignis* (appropriation, event, happening) . . . could compare well with the idea of *dao*." While it is true that *Ereignis* avoids the *direct* reference to Being, this does not mean that *Ereignis* avoids metaphysical implications.

For Heidegger (2012, §4), the question of Being remains his "*unique* question," "the question of all questions," the question that points to "what is *most unique*," and this is more problematic than it seems—as I shall discuss in chapter 3. I am not saying that Heidegger does not offer a useful possibility of thinking Western philosophy under a different light. Nor am I suggesting that one cannot find any similarity between Heidegger's philosophy and the *Lao-Zhuang*. My idea is that, by *twisting* (in the sense of *Verwindung*)[11] Western metaphysics, Heidegger offers an excellent example of philosophical self-critique that can help to prepare the ground for the encounter with the other.

And yet, because of this *Verwindung*, Heidegger's thought retains some fundamental structures of not only metaphysics but also monotheistic theology—even though one can interpret his *Sein* as more akin to becoming than an unchanging substance.[12] This implies that the overall Heideggerian philosophical project is embedded in a tradition that is considerably divergent from that of Daoism—despite some alleged similarities.

I do not believe that the primary task of a comparative analysis is the definition of equivalences between philosophies, and this book does not proceed in that direction. On the contrary, comparisons should advance the idea of philosophy itself and produce a modification in the understanding of both the self and the other. Thus, the critical study of Heidegger's philosophy is not an end in itself for the comparative analysis but a means to produce such an understanding. This, along with the interpretation of the *Lao-Zhuang*, can lead to a shift of perspectives in the philosophical discourse. And this shift does not mean a mere modification of concepts, but it proposes a different ethical understanding of *being the world*—and not simply *in* the world. We shall see how this ethical understanding is possible thanks to the aesthetic gesture of the corresponding other.

The encounter with the other becomes in this way an ethical endeavor that requires a specific aesthetic attitude not only toward the world at large but also toward one's own self. In this context, therefore, the self is not by any means a synonym of "subject" because the self does not ground any epistemological certainty—as will become clearer in chapter 2. Besides, the other is not bound to the metaphysical alterity of the Other (*l'Autre*), where "L'absolument Autre, c'est Autrui" in Emmanuel Levinas's terms (1990, 28),[13] but it encompasses the corresponding other of the *Zhuangzi*—discussed in chapter 5. Thus, the self–other relationship needs to be considered from the aesthetic standpoint on the experience horizon of the other human being and the world at large—in both the subjective and objective meaning of the genitive.

To see this different perspective, it is necessary to step out of the anthropocentric standpoint and see the relation of the objects in the world under a different light—that is to say, to see humanity not as dominating the world but as corresponding with and to it. On the other hand, to achieve this shift of perspective, it is also crucial to overcome the limitations of the onto-theological nature of Western metaphysics and its hierarchical structure Being–beings, which entails the necessity of breaking the restrictions implied in its terminology.

As a result, a significant part of the book is dedicated to this deconstructive endeavor. That is to say, it is important to contextualize the Western metaphysical standpoint proceeding toward new ethical and aesthetic understandings of the world. The study of the *Daodejing* and the *Zhuangzi* will be possible only after this preliminary process. Indeed, the philosophical approach to these texts is not without problems.

The confrontation with other philosophical traditions is always a delicate process. This is particularly true in relation to early Chinese texts, which present significant differences in language and, therefore, in thought. For this reason, chapter 1 is dedicated to the definition of "comparison" along with the definition of a "philosophy of comparisons."[14] Prior to any possible attempt at understanding another standpoint, it is necessary to define the theoretical assumptions that this confrontation brings into play.

Since the issue of comparing concepts is of primary importance, one of the first tasks of this study is the analysis and definition of them. Chapter 1 starts by reflecting on problems of cross-cultural interpretations and translations analyzing how concepts are rooted in theories and philosophical assumptions. Inquiring into the concept of philosophy per se, the chapter discusses key works of Martin Heidegger, who offers one of the most interesting and controversial interpretations of philosophy. After the analysis of extracts from *What Is Philosophy?* (1958) and "What Is Metaphysics?" (1998b), I consider the related problem of the Chinese terms *you* 有 and *wu* 無. The point is that, to translate such terms, it is crucial to revise the onto-theological assumptions of Western metaphysics through which *you* and *wu* are often interpreted.

This revision triggers a process of re-grounding grounds with the consequent possibility of language transformation, which in turn activates new relations between cultural diversities. Thus, philosophy itself becomes an eminently comparative dialogue between cultures. Without setting a single method for all these problems, the chapter argues that comparisons themselves call for necessarily different methodological approaches. Hence, while Daoism helps to illuminate these issues defining one of the possibilities that a philosophy of comparisons entails, this same reasoning opens a way for an ethical and aesthetic reading of the *Daodejing* and the *Zhuangzi*.

Thanks to this analysis, it becomes clear that a more precise definition of the theory for the approach to the other is necessary. Chapter 2 discusses this aspect by considering the problem of *Weltanschauung*[15] and by analyzing how one interprets the language and the perspective of the other. The introduction of this concept, however, brings into discussion serious issues, including the doubt that this term—like any other—is not neutral. Although many scholars use the concept of worldview, they employ it uncritically. Considering that there is no substantial study on it, an important part of this book is assigned to its analysis.

The chapter shows that if one uses a tool such as the one of worldview, one also needs to justify this use. In other words, as soon as one defines the other, one needs to clarify how this definition has been possible. This means that if one attributes to the other a vision of the world, this same concept needs to be contextualized and justified. My thesis is that every time one tries to move toward the other one constantly falls back on oneself, which means that the definition of the other is, ipso facto, a definition of oneself. In this sense, the analysis of the concept of *Weltanschauung* leads to a more attentive definition of the Western metaphysical standpoint. Hence, in this chapter I discuss the concept of Being in detail.

The analysis of *Weltanschauung* has the other important consequence of introducing the problem of aesthetics. The idea of worldview is closely related to the concept of world picture (*Weltbild*), which already implies a proto-aesthetics. While chapter 2 lays down the premises of the final conclusions of this book, its section regarding the world picture considers how aesthetics has a connection with the way the world is perceived and is described. As a result, I discuss the concepts of subject and object, as well as the problem of representation.

If chapter 2 introduces the issues of representation, chapter 3 analyzes the problem of value. In order to do this, I consider the Heideggerian perspective in relation to the Nietzschean idea of becoming. This helps us to understand how the metaphysical hierarchical structure of Being–beings differs from the anarchical structure of becoming.[16] The analysis of becoming leads to the discussion of metaphor and its implicit questioning of the status of truth values, which also implies the possibility of a representation that does not distinguish between sensible and nonsensible. The analysis of metaphor becomes crucial to introducing the possibility of a representation that is not necessarily linked to metaphysical structures.

Chapter 3 concludes the self-evaluative and deconstructive part of the book by bringing to its final implications the issue of language and its relation to Being. But the chapter opens a new perspective as well. There, I propose a more precise idea of how values are embedded in metaphors and, therefore, how the comparative process is not only a matter of translating worldviews but also a matter of translating values. And this allows a more flexible approach to the *Lao-Zhuang* from a philosophical standpoint.

Chapter 4 analyzes the *Daodejing*. After the discussion of the problem of language and the question of metaphor, it is possible to better understand the perspective offered by this important book. The focus is on the question of naming. A more attentive analysis of the opening lines of the *Daodejing* introduces key concepts of early Daoism. Along with the discussion of these concepts, an ethical perspective starts to take shape.

Thanks to the analysis of important passages such as chapters 25, 37, and 64, I argue that the *Daodejing* offers a radical redefinition of the concept of value and reference systems. With this investigation it becomes clear that *dao* 道, far from any metaphysical substance, gives priority to the concept of *ziran* 自然 ("spontaneously" or, more literally, "so of itself").[17] The introduction of *ziran*, however, entails an important set of other concepts such as *wuwei* 無為, *wuming* 無名 and *wuyu* 無欲.[18] Their analysis brings to the fore not only a different perspective on ethics but also the possibility for a more aesthetic encounter with the world.

Chapter 4 concludes with the last of the *wu* terms, namely, *wuqing* 無情.[19] This, however, is a concept expressed by the *Zhuangzi*. With this term I introduce the issue of *shifei* 是非 as well.[20] In order to clarify the meaning of *shifei*, chapter 5 engages in the analysis of the "Qiwulun" 齊物論, one of the most important chapters of the *Zhuangzi*. With this part, I conclude the recognition of the ethical value of being part of the spontaneous transformation of things (*wuhua* 物化) by defining more precisely the aesthetic attunement to the world. The scope of this chapter is to redefine the idea of experiencing the self, the other, and the world so as to see how ethical values are not necessarily attached to norms but can be developed through a constant changing encounter with the other at large.

The concluding chapter reconnects all the passages of the study, returning to the meaning of the title and giving a precise account of the proposed shift from metaphysical representations to aesthetics life. In this part, I describe in more detail how the aesthetic experience of the world becomes the path through which one can acquire an ethical posture in relation to oneself, the other, and the world. My final aim is to show how the shift from the metaphysical representation of the world—divided in sensible and supersensible—to the aesthetic and undivided experience of the world entails the shift from the separation of subject/object to the spontaneous aesthetic gesture of the world that produces itself.

1

Toward the Encounter with the Other

1.1 The Problem of Translation in Comparative Studies

There is one major problem at the core of the discipline of comparative studies, a problem that every specific comparison needs to consider: is it possible to interpret across cultural boundaries? And the first obstacle that a comparison of cultures needs to overcome is usually a language barrier. Hence, interpretation across boundaries is mainly a problem of translation. This does not mean that the cultural issue is reduced to the linguistic one. In an academic context, however, it is not possible to avoid a certain degree of reductionism. The term "culture" itself is reductionist and the concept of culture per se is problematic.

Wolfgang Iser (1996, 300) holds that "cultures are not clear-cut givens, let alone holistic entities, their encounters inevitably result in mutual molding." For Iser, the "very fact that mutuality operates the interchange between cultures is due to the structure of culture itself, which is never a 'unified text,' but is something in the making" (301). It is clear that, if "cultures are not clear-cut givens," any comparison faces the linguistic problem of defining its subject from the outset. Thus, every time one mentions "Chinese culture," "Chinese thought," "Western standpoint," etc., one needs to remember that these terms are employed for the sake of argumentation, and they never refer to "unified texts." This also implies that, in this context, these terms cannot be regarded as essentialist tropes insofar as they always refer to pluralities of worldviews. This will become clearer in the next chapter. For now, let us continue the analysis of the comparative issue.

While interpretation across boundaries is mainly a problem of translation, it is conversely possible to consider translations as specific attempts to compare cultures.[1] Considering the extensive production of past and present translations, it seems natural to affirm that cross-cultural interpretations are possible. This possibility, however, should not be taken for granted.

If one wants to interpret across boundaries, it is necessary to understand from which standpoint one activates the interpretative process; that is to say, one needs to acknowledge that "all understanding inevitably involves some prejudice" (Gadamer 2004, 272). The scientific assumption is one of these prejudices. If the interpreter approaches other cultures only with the idea of understanding the other without considering and enquiring about *their own* understanding, they will continue to reproduce the same mistake of historicism, which, "*despite its critique of rationalism and of natural law philosophy, is based on the modern Enlightenment and unwittingly shares its prejudices.* And there is one prejudice of the Enlightenment that defines its essence: the fundamental prejudice of the Enlightenment is the prejudice against prejudice itself, which denies tradition its power" (Gadamer 2004, 272–273). In interpreting and translating, we employ judgments in two different directions. To understand other cultures, I move from my standpoint toward the other by transposing my system of thoughts to the other. On the way back, I translate what I consider meaningful in the other context into my system of thoughts. In both cases, I exercise judgment in choosing in which direction I move and which concepts I use for my translations. Consequently, I deploy a set of theoretical justifications in this two-way process.

Hopefully, this process produces a modification in my system of thoughts; indeed, what "may seem, in the beginning, like an attempt to understand another culture through our own, in the end may result in a shift in our fundamental way of understanding, which is, in the end, the only way to understand across cultures" (Allinson 1989b, 3). Still, to perform this shift and to produce the transformation that a philosophy of comparisons seeks, we need to understand how translations presuppose theories.

Chad Hansen (1992, 8) asserts that when we consult a dictionary—which is one of the first steps to approach another culture—we assume we are "learning *the* meaning of a term." This is misleading. According to Hansen a dictionary "is an inherited, piecemeal, fragmented interpretive theory." Dictionaries of the usage are no exception; they only show other theoretical stances.

See, for instance, what David Crystal (2009, ix) says in his introduction to Henry Watson Fowler's *Dictionary of Modern English Usage*. Fowler was revising his *Dictionary* for final publication in the early 1920s when he "plainly felt the tension between the traditional focus on a small set of words, pronunciations, and grammatical usages, as indicators of 'correct' linguistic behaviour, and the diverse and changing realities of the way educated people actually used language in their everyday lives." Fowler had to decide in which direction his dictionary should proceed. This clearly shows how any choice is always grounded in a specific and, more or less, acknowledged theoretical position.

Consequently, a translation of a passage "*presupposes* the translator's theory; it is not evidence for it" (Hansen 1992, 10). Besides, in translating, one translates not just words, expressions, or sentences, but concepts. If an expression or a sentence has a meaning, this is rooted in a broader context made of a constellation of concepts in relation to other clusters of constellations. The organization of these clusters is both the reference system that allows the emergence of meaning and the background information that allows translations.[2]

When Hansen states that a translation *presupposes* the theory of the translator, he means that, comparing two different cultures, the translator attempts to translate a concept from one system to another. Therefore, in translations—and more generally in comparative studies—one needs to consider the reference systems and the background information of both sides of the boundary. More precisely: on the one hand, it is necessary to compare the relations between meanings and background information at play *within* both sides of the boundary in order to *locate* concepts; on the other hand, one needs to compare these relations *between* the two sides in order to *translate* concepts.

Insofar as words are not just static abstractions but doors to clusters of concepts, it becomes clear that "the responsible exercise of comparative Chinese and Western thought requires a combination of philosophical and sinological skills" (Hall 2002, 17). This is true not only for the comparison of Chinese and Western thought. If the main problem of comparative studies is a problem of translation, and if in translations we compare not just words but concepts, then the most intimate aspect of this problem is a philosophical one. Yet this is not a solution. Quite the opposite.

The philosophical nature of comparisons opens an even more controversial problem: how can one consider philosophy a crucial device in comparative studies if it stems from the Western ground? Is the word "philosophy" not a specific concept derived from the Greek *philósophía* (φιλόσοφία) and therefore completely inscribed in the Western tradition? Would it not be another form of cultural imperialism to impose such a coercive theoretical approach?[3] The answers to these questions are the first necessary duty of the comparative analysis in philosophy.

Richard Rorty (1991, 8) warns us that "we should stay alert to the possibility that comparative philosophy not only is not a royal road to intercultural comparison, but may even be a distraction from such comparison. For it may turn out that we are really comparing nothing more than the adaptations of a single transcultural character type to different environments." The theoretical problem is precisely this: do adaptations play a necessary part in the process of understanding across boundaries? If it is true that "a translation is an interpretive adaptation of an idea in a foreign language" (Cua 2009, 46), it is fundamental to consider the presuppositions behind these adaptations. This clearly entails a philosophical analysis in the sense of a self-critique of philosophy itself. Therefore, it is of primary importance to define what "philosophy" is. Indeed, through a more accurate understanding of its ground, it is possible to define a specific standpoint that enables to sharply look at the other side of the boundary as well as to look back at the point of departure when the boundary is crossed.

1.2 Is Philosophy Just *Philósophía*?

In the previous section, we saw how comparative analyses face the problem of translation and how translations need to translate not only words but also concepts. This implies a philosophical analysis that can define the relations between concepts and background theories. The problem, however, is to understand if philosophy itself does not introduce cultural presuppositions. For this reason, we need to ask what philosophy is.

In *What Is Philosophy?* (1958, 35), Heidegger holds that when people formulate this question, not only *what* they question but also *how* they question is basically Greek in origin. More than on the word "philosophy," Heidegger focuses his analysis on "What is?" (τί ἐστιν). "What is?" poses the question and, at the same time, already gives an answer. The question is about the *essentia*, the essence of something and thus the *esse*, the Being, is already affirmed, already implied in the question. For Heidegger, this gives the possibility of the philosophy itself insofar as "the quiddity is determined differently in the various periods of philosophy" (37). In other words, "that which is asked each time by means of the clues of the τί, the *quid*, the 'what,' is to be newly determined each time" (37) and, concurrently, what *is* newly determined always affirms the *esse* of the new determination. For these reasons, the history of philosophy is, according to Heidegger, the history of τί τὸ ὄν: what is Being?

Therefore, Heidegger concludes: "The statement that philosophy is in its nature Greek says nothing more than that the West and Europe, and only these, are, in the innermost course of their history, originally philosophical" (31).[4] A few pages later, however, he states that his discourse does not want to set a fixed program. On the contrary, "it would like to prepare all who are participating for a gathering in which what we call the Being of being [*Sein des Seienden*] appeals to us. By naming this we are considering what Aristotle already says. 'Being-ness appears in many guises.' 'Existence is revealed in many ways [Τὸ ὄν λεγέται πολλαχῶς]'" (97). The original German text renders Aristotle thus: "Das seiend-Sein kommt vielfältig zum Scheinen" (1966, 31). Heidegger interprets τὸ ὄν with *das seiend-Sein*,[5] which refers to the difference between being as a determined entity and Being as such.[6] This forms the so-called ontological difference. When Heidegger translates τὸ ὄν with *seiend-Sein*, he presents a comparison that interprets in the direction of his own philosophy and, in particular, in the direction of the ontological difference. Consequently, Heidegger not only is crossing the boundary with his translation/interpretation, but is also *setting* the boundary. That is to say: he interprets τὸ ὄν through his idea of ontological difference in order to reconsider, realign, and explain the entire history of metaphysics as the oblivion of Being. Hence, philosophy becomes the history of metaphysics in his "unthought essence of *esse*" (Heidegger 1998e, 280).

And yet, *Sein* remains central: on the one hand, philosophy originates with the question τί ἐστιν and, on the other hand, the question of Being as such becomes "the encompassing question of metaphysics" (Heidegger 1998b, 95). This clearly delimits philosophy to a specific cluster of languages. Nevertheless, Heidegger (1998b, 96) also writes that "metaphysics belongs to the 'nature of the human being.' . . . As long as human beings exist, philosophizing of some sort occurs. Philosophy—what we call philosophy—is the getting under way of metaphysics, in which it comes to itself and to its explicit tasks." If philosophy is "the getting under way of metaphysics" and if philosophy as φιλόσοφία is a prerogative of Western culture, how is it possible that metaphysics and philosophy "belongs to the nature of the human being"? Someone can observe that between "What Is Metaphysics?" ([1929] 1998b) and *What Is Philosophy?* ([1956] 1966), another "*Kehre*" happened. Still, how should this "turn" be interpreted? Should philosophy be read retroactively as metaphysics that belongs to the nature of humankind enabling everyone to philosophize? Or should metaphysics be considered progressively as philosophy that, being expressly Greek in its root, enables only a delimited cultural group to think metaphysically?

I believe there is a third way. Surprisingly, Heidegger (1998c, 231) himself suggests this *other path*, asserting that the question "What is metaphysics?" "questions beyond metaphysics. It springs from a thinking that has already entered into the overcoming [*Überwindung*] of metaphysics. It belongs to the essence of such transitions that, within certain limits, they must continue to speak the language of that which they help overcome." If metaphysics can be overcome, then there is a thinking process outside metaphysics that does not need to be called philosophy or it will be called philosophy only conventionally, without a necessary reference to φιλόσοφία and to τὸ ὄν. If there is a path for philosophy outside metaphysics, then there is a possibility to think without being bound to the onto-theological nature of metaphysics. If this is possible now, it had to be possible also in the past—as it was for Heraclitus[7]—or in other places of the world—as it was in China. If one accepts this rationale, not only can the idea of philosophy be broadened but also the concept of metaphysics itself changes radically, enabling thus different perspectives. In other words, it becomes possible to encounter the Chinese thought without the restrictions of the Western understanding based on the grounding *subiectum* and its onto-theological nature, as we shall see soon.

The choice to confront the Western thinking tradition with the Chinese one—and in particular with Daoism—is an opportunity to understand if metaphysics is a necessary category for philosophy at all—and not just to overcome it.[8] Thus, Daoism "may represent a way, not so much of denial of the possibility of philosophical knowledge as such, but rather of letting go of a traditional Western way of thinking in order to reveal an altogether different mode" (Clarke 2000, 175). Daoism may represent "an alternative way of doing philosophy, one that is 'self-transformative' and 'orientative' rather than truth-seeking or certainty-seeking" (Clarke 2000, 175). If Daoism offers the possibility to conceive a different way of thinking, the re-grounding of grounds that a philosophy of comparisons seeks emerges precisely from these differences, not as a simple assimilation but as a reciprocal transformation. And yet, even if this transformation is possible, from where can one start the comparative process in order to understand not only Daoism but also one's relation to it? To answer this question it is necessary to consider the problem of translation for *you* 有, *wu* 無, and *dao* 道.

1.3 The Meaning of *You* 有, *Wu* 無, and *Dao* 道

In the previous section, we started considering some specific features of Western philosophy. Through the Heideggerian analysis of philosophy we have seen how one of the central elements of Western metaphysics is the ontological difference between Being and beings. It is now time to consider how this has consequences in the translation of some important Chinese concepts.

1.3.1 *You* 有 and *Wu* 無

The basic issue that every scholar inevitably faces dealing with early Chinese thought is that the verb "to be," which is one of the peculiarities of the Indo-European languages, has no precise correspondence in classical Chinese. In his translation of the important work of Zhang Dainian, *Key Concepts in Chinese Philosophy* (2002), Edmund Ryden writes, "The Chinese language does not have any word that correspond to the Greek εἶναι, which is both a grammatical copula and an affirmation of existence. The closest to the verb 'to be' is '*you*' [有] which equally well means 'to have'" (150). Despite these premises, Ryden translates *you* and *wu* as "being" and "beingless." Therefore, when Zhang quotes chapter 40 of the *Daodejing*, Ryden translates it thus: "Reversal is the motion of the Way [*dao*]; weakness is the use of the way. The myriad things under heaven [天下 *tian xia*] are generated from being [*you*]. Being is generated from beingless [*wu*]" (151). Leaving aside the first part of the text and its relative problem of *dao* for the moment, I want to focus on the overall tone of the passage. Although there are many ways of understanding Chinese philosophy, and although each translator certainly considers very carefully the reasons for and against their choices, I find Ryden's translation misleading. This is not only because it follows the inveterate habit to use being and nonbeing for *you* and *wu* but also because it renders *tian xia* 天下 as "under heaven," giving to the sentence an even more pronounced metaphysical flavor.[9]

Since the fundamental analysis of Angus Graham ([1960] 1986), it is clear that the verb "to be" and the verb "*you*" refer to two different reference systems. This, however, has not become a well-rehearsed fact in the studies of Chinese philosophy. Charles Wu (2016), for instance, offers a new translation of the *Daodejing* in which *you* and *wu* are rendered as "Being" and "Nonbeing." Similarly, John Minford (2019) translates them

18 | From Metaphysical Representations to Aesthetic Life

as "Being" and "Non-Being." But this is not only a problem of translators. Even an attentive scholar such as Katrin Froese (2006, 142) conceives of *wu* as "non-being" or "nothingness" and, following Alan K. Chan, affirms that "*wu* has a fundamental substance" which is "prior to 'being.'"

A study of Chinese philosophy cannot avoid a careful analysis of fundamental concepts such as *you* and *wu* precisely because translation of Chinese thought with Western metaphysical concepts is highly problematic. By overlooking this central issue, one can fall into misinterpretations and cultural impositions. This is not to say that early Chinese thought could not conceive any metaphysical perspective. It only means that metaphysics—as conceived in the Western traditions—was not the main focus of classical Chinese language and thought. And yet, one needs to be wary not to fall on the other side of the problem by denying to Chinese philosophy any possibility of abstraction.

Zhang Longxi (1998) voices this danger.[10] He opposes an "image of China that is nothing but a cultural myth of difference" (110). This is undoubtedly important; one needs to avoid simplistic oppositions such as "the West and the rest." Differences are present not only within the same tradition but also within the same author or work. For Zhang, "difference is a matter of degree, not of kind" (111). Still, even if differences are a matter of degree, sometimes this degree is so significant that it is close to a difference of kind. This is particularly evident in relation to *dao*.

1.3.2 *Dao* 道

Let us briefly consider the first line of the *Daodejing* from the common version of Wang Bi 王弼 (226–249 CE):

Dao ke dao, fei chang dao

道可道，非常道[11]

This is one of the most problematic passages of the *Daodejing*. I shall discuss it in more detail in chapter 4. Only two aspects are worth mentioning here. The first one is the clear difficulty in interpreting the concept of *dao* per se with its undefined number and gender and its double function of noun and verb.

In general, the most common English and German translations of *dao* are respectively "way" and "Weg." The first problem with the English translations is the common capitalization of the term "Way"—in German this problem is not so apparent because of the capitalization of all nouns. This practice has a historical motivation. *Dao* was translated for the first time into Western languages by missionaries who rendered it as "Lex" or as "Ratio" (Couplet 1687, xxiv) in a metaphysical sense.¹²

In *The History of the World* (1829, 102), Walter Raleigh links the eternal law to God. He considers natural law and human law as deriving from divine law and states that "the eternal and divine law differ only in consideration." In *Summa Theologiæ* (I–II, q. 93, a. 1–3), Thomas Aquinas explains how "all laws proceed from the eternal law" (omnes leges a lege æterna procedunt) and clarifies that "the eternal law is nothing else than the *ratio* of divine wisdom" (lex æterna nihil aliud est, quam ratio divinæ sapientia). In this sense, both *Lex* and *Ratio* are emanations of the divine wisdom. It comes as no surprise when Philippe Couplet (1687, xxiv) states that one thing is certain, Laozi had some notion of a first and supreme deity ("una res tamen certa est, primi ac supremi cujusdam Numinis habuisse notitiam").¹³

Similarly, in one of the first translations of the *Daodejing* in Latin—probably written by Jean-François Noëlas—*dao* is conceived as "*Ratio*" or, more precisely, as "*æterna Ratio*." The first line goes: "Ratio quæ potest ratiocinando comprehendi, non est æterna Ratio" (Collani, Holz, and Wegmann 2008, 96). In English this becomes "The reason that can be grasped by reasoning is not the eternal Reason." Clearly the "*æterna Ratio*" that cannot be comprehended is the law and wisdom of God. We shall come back to this in relation to Descartes. For now, suffice it to say that this *Ratio* is just another way of referring to the utmost Being and its mandate.

As openly expressed by James Legge (1891, xiii) in relation to the Jesuit's translation of the *Daodejing*, "the chief object of the translator or translators was to show that the 'Mysteries of the Most Holy Trinity and of the Incarnate God were anciently known to the Chinese nation.'" Legge refers to Figurists such as Jean-François Fouquet, who, in the *Problème théologique* (1718), directly affirms that "the character 道 *dao* means the God worshipped by Christians" (Le caractère 道 *Tao* signifie le Dieu qu'adorent les chrétiens) (Chan 2015, 514).¹⁴

Although translators have progressively abandoned the direct reference to God, the issue of the capitalization of the noun remains. Moreover, the problem does not change by the use of the character's Romanization, which is often rendered as "the Dao." In Chinese, however, there is no number for nouns, nor is there anything that can correspond to the article "the." Thus, the use of the definite article along with the capitalization of the noun clearly echoes the previous translations, giving to "the Dao" a metaphysical taste.

The other problem of the first line of the *Daodejing* is the character *chang* 常. In his "attempt to discover what the book meant when it was first written," Arthur Waley (2005, 13) renders "The Way that can be told of is not an Unvarying Way." Here, not only is the concept of *dao* singularized and capitalized as "the Way" but *fei chang* 非常 is also translated with the capitalization of "Unvarying." These choices clearly proceed in a transcendent direction. Even if it were possible to accept the capitalization of "Way" as a conventional form for concepts, the decision to use a capital letter for an adjective shows a precise intention. It is evident that Waley considers *dao* to be a nominal concept defined by eternal and absolute attributes.

This vision resonates in many other translations such as Lin Yutang's. Although Lin avoids the problem of translating *dao* by using its Romanization, he remains totally inscribed—and probably even more flagrantly—in an onto-theological mind-set. His version (2009) abandons any precautions defining *dao* as "Absolute" in what one can consider the climax of the metaphysical interpretations of the *Daodejing*: "The Tao that can be told of is not the Absolute Tao." This choice is even more striking if one considers that, in the introduction to his translation, Lin is against the metaphysical interpretation of early Chinese thought.

Probably differences are a matter of degree, but it is hard to see a degree of difference in these translations. If one precludes the possibility of plurality, one is left only with assimilation. And the translations of *dao* as "the Dao," *chang* as "Absolute," *you* and *wu* as "Being" and "Nonbeing," are the assimilation of the Chinese thought to Western metaphysics. There is neither understanding nor learning in this process, only repetition.

On the other hand, if one distinguishes between Western metaphysics and Chinese philosophy, this does not undermine the concepts of *dao*, *you*, *wu*, etc. Quite the opposite. The best example in this direction is the one offered by Jacques Derrida (1982a, 199) when he asks, "Is there a 'metaphysics' outside the Indo-European organization of the function 'to be'?" He replies that "this is not in the least an ethnocentric question. It does not amount to envisaging that other languages might be *deprived* of the surpassing mission of philosophy and metaphysics but, on the contrary, avoids projecting outside the West very determined forms of 'history' and 'culture.'" One can conclude that translations such as Ryden's or Lin's are highly questionable. It is of little use to acknowledge differences in grammatical structures without considering the concepts and reference systems to which they are linked; it is contradictory to warn that the Chinese language does not have any corresponding word to the Greek εἶναι if, afterwards, the very concept of εἶναι is applied to interpret the *Daodejing*. This is misleading with respect to both sides of the boundary. Thus, one misses the main purpose of translation and fails the comparison between different concepts.

The automatic repetition and application of unquestioned structures of thought in the comparative analysis misses the opportunity to learn from the other and, consequentially, to change ossified standpoints by re-grounding grounds. On the other hand, the acknowledgment, preparation, and transformation of philosophical grounds are prerequisites and consequences of crossing boundaries. This does not avoid the "ontological relativity" of Quine (1969) but helps to thematize it as background theory. In this sense, the Heideggerian "*be-wëgen*" (1985, 186) and Ames-Hall's "way-making" (2003) try to interpret *dao* transforming their own languages and grounds, overcoming limitations in both directions. This does not mean that these translations are unproblematic.

1.4 Translating *Dao* 道

In the previous section, I defined the historical reasons for the misleading translations of the term *dao*. In this section, I will evaluate the advantages and limits of translating *dao* as "way-making" and "*be-wëgen*."

1.4.1 *Dao* 道 as "Way-Making"

It is well known that, in Chinese, nouns can have a verbal function depending on their position in the sentence. Roger Ames and David Hall (2003, 57) solve the problem of the nominal and verbal function of *dao*, interpreting it as "primarily gerundive, processional, and dynamic: 'a leading forth.'" Their rendering of the first line of the *Daodejing* goes: "Way-making that can be put into words is not really way-making."[15]

This translation is in opposition to the absolutization of *dao* imposed by transcendent perspectives and implies that as soon as we define *dao* we stop experiencing and acting it. In other words, the determination of *dao* in absolute terms misses the procedural aspect that the verbal meaning of the character entails. Against any essentialization, Ames and Hall also coherently eliminate capitalizations. Finally, "way-making" is not determined by any article: there is no "the" for way-making, which suggests not only a constant action but also a plurality of possibilities.

Although the translation of *dao* as "way-making" gets rid of the prevailing metaphysical interpretations, one cannot adopt it without some precautions. I have two reasons to be cautious: first, it is impossible to neglect the affinity of "way-making" with Nelson Goodman's concept of "worldmaking";[16] second, the term "way-making" has a direct connection with Heidegger's "*be-wëgen.*" These concepts refer to different perspectives that need to be carefully analyzed. Let us consider the notion of worldmaking first.

In *Ways of Worldmaking*, Nelson Goodman (1978, 7) faces the question of "how worlds are made, tested, and known." In trying to escape from the essentialist perspective, Goodman (1976, 265) proposes a theory that envisages a plurality of worlds fabricated by human beings. Considering that Ames and Hall (2003, 57) regard way-making as "forging a way forward" or "road building," the affinity between worldmaking and way-making becomes evident. These two concepts emphasize the procedural aspect of the human relationship with the world, overcoming in this way its essentialist and nominalist interpretation.

In doing so, however, they seem to put the entire weight on the human being, with the danger of reducing the world to an object present-at-hand. This is not far from the modern Western understanding of the subject as *subiectum*, which in turn is the grounding substance (*sub-stare*, "to stand under") that objectifies the world—that I will discuss in the next chapter. Although Goodman rejects this objectification as the only "One" reality and favors a plurality of productions, he considers humanity the *subject* in this process. Therefore, the concepts of both worldmaking and way-making are too close to the modern assumption of the *creative mind*. This idea clashes with the concept of *dao*, which is not simply a production of humans.

Consider this passage of the *Xici* 繫辭—also called *Dazhuan* 大傳, the *Great Commentary* of the *Yijing* 易經—(A5.1): "the revolving process of *yin* and *yang* refers to *dao*" (*yi yin yi yang zhi wei dao* 一陰一陽之謂道).[17] *Dao* is related to *yin* 陰 and *yang* 陽, the two complementary and mutually entailing aspects of a process of constant change. Similarly to night and day, *yin* and *yang* constantly transform into each other. This process does not pertain exclusively to human beings but involves all the myriad things (*wanwu* 萬物).

If the revolving process of *yin* and *yang* refers to *dao*, then *dao* as way-making—and, by extension, as worldmaking—is not the subject's product, but the process stemming from and depending on the relationship between different aspects of the world—in which humankind is only *one* of its manifold components.

This will become clearer with the analysis of the *Zhuangzi*. For now, it is necessary to balance the concept of worldmaking and its subjective humanism. To do so, it is useful to turn to Heidegger and his idea of *dao*.

1.4.2 *Dao* 道 as "*Be-wëgen*"

It is true that Heidegger refers to *dao* as "*Weg*" (way). His interpretation of the Chinese character, however, lies in the concept of "*be-wëgen*." In "The Nature of Language" (1971b, 92) he affirms that the word *dao* has been superficially understood as "a stretch connecting two places." Heidegger, therefore, considers *dao* as what "gives way" (*be-wëgt*) and explains that "We hear the words 'give way' [*Be-wëgung*] in this sense: to be the original giver and founder of ways."

According to Heidegger, *dao* is the origin and founder of ways insofar as it *be-wëgt*, it gives way. He mentions that, in the Alemannic-Swabian dialect, the etymology of *be-wëgen* and *Be-wëgung* is the verb *wëgen*, which means "to clear a way," for instance across a snow-covered field. Heidegger clarifies that "This verb, used transitively, means: to form a way and, forming it, to keep it ready. Way-making [*Be-wëgen*] understood in this sense no longer means to move something up or down a path that is already there. It means to bring the way . . . forth first of all, and thus to *be* the way" (1971b, 130).[18] It is interesting that Peter Hertz translates *be-wëgen* as "way-making." Ames and Hall do not refer to Heidegger anywhere in their translation, but it is unlikely that they were unaware of this important Heideggerian passage. Be that as it may, we need to consider an important aspect of this verb.

Gail Stenstad (2006, 80–81) analyzes the term, explaining that it is not a standard German word because it is not *Bewegung*, which properly means "movement." For Stenstad the hyphen and umlaut stand for something different. She argues that, by emphasizing the prefix, "Heidegger may be suggesting that we are not to understand *be-wëgen* as a transitive verb in some typical subject-object structure," which implies that this "way" is not an object for a subject. Rather, this way is what "gives and makes ways *in* way making." According to Stenstad, "Way-making makes way in such a way that 'it is' the way, that is, all there 'is' is way-making movement. The movement moves, and that is all. It gives way in self-withdrawing, in yielding way. Such giving way clears the way for saying, for the self-showing of whatever is freed into the clearing or opening of the way." Stenstad's analysis is impeccable. Yet, if there is no "way" already *there* somewhere, just waiting to be discovered and followed, if *be-wëgen* is a verb without a subject-object structure, thereby denying any subjective grounding, and if all there "is" is way-making movement, the question becomes: who or what is responsible for this movement, who or what *gives* way?

Stenstad suggests that *be-wëgen* gives way in self-withdrawing. Still, if we equate *be-wëgen* with self-withdrawing, we equate it with the ontological difference and, therefore, with *Sein* (Being). And yet, Stenstad is right, this is the direction in which Heidegger points. It is not by chance that Heidegger emphasizes the word "to *be (sein)*" at the end of the aforementioned passage. Here lies an important aspect of Heideggerian philosophy which I will analyze more attentively in the next chapter, and will only briefly touch on here.

In his attempt to reduce the subjectivist interpretation of *Dasein* (literally "being there"; more properly "existence"; in Heidegger's understanding, it refers to the being of humans), Heidegger conceives Being as *es gibt*, "there is" (literally, "it gives"). In "Letter on 'Humanism'" (1998d, 254–255), he openly asserts that we can grasp the ontological difference only if we comprehend that "es gibt das Sein" ("there is Being," "it gives Being," "il y a l'Être"), provided that "the 'it' that here 'gives' is being itself."[19] In trying to escape the metaphysical danger of the rational mind that grounds itself reducing the world to an object present-at-hand, Heidegger falls into the opposite trap of the impersonal metaphysical assumption—or, to use the words if Emmanuel Levinas (1979, 298), "the philosophy of the Neuter."[20]

This becomes even more evident in relation to *dao* when Heidegger (1971b, 92) affirms that "Tao could be the way that gives all ways."[21] Katrin Froese (2006, 46) interprets the passage as "the Dao may be the all-moving way," giving to *dao* a marked sense of *primum movens*.[22]

We are back to square one: *dao* is equated with *Sein*.[23] It is evident that this vision of *dao* as a self-withdrawing Being is as misleading as the concept of worldmaking.

1.4.3 Interpreting *Dao* 道 between "Way-Making" and "*Be-wëgen*"

If one wants to consider *dao* as "way-making" or "*be-wëgen*," it is paramount to search for a compromise between the subjective creation of "worldmaking" and the impersonal given/self-withdrawing of "*es gibt*." In order to proceed in this direction, I propose to consider a passage from Paul Ricoeur's *The Rule of Metaphor* (1978, 360; 362).

In trying to answer the question "do we know what is meant by world, truth, reality?" Ricoeur asserts that "we must . . . dismantle the reign of objects in order to let be, and to allow to be uttered, our primordial belonging to a world which we inhabit, that is to say, which at once precedes us and receives the imprint of our works. In short, we must restore to the fine word *invent* [*inventer*] its twofold sense of both discovery and creation." "Invent" (from *inventus*, past participle of *invenire*) means "to find," "to discover while searching," but also "to arrive somewhere." Indeed, *invenire* is composed of *in* and *venire*, literally "to come in (a place)." Ricoeur's words help clarify that, in dealing with the world, one is constantly mutually entailing with it: the world always precedes and conditions humans and, at the same time, humans discover and make sense of the world in many ways.

If we understand the concepts of way-making and *be-wëgen* not as creation or *Sein* but as invention, then we reintroduce the relational aspect of the term, by which it is implied that one neither creates a world *ex nihilo* nor is totally determined by it. Rather, one walks in the middle of these two extremes. That is to say: it is possible to discover a place by making space for it in one's own conceptions. *Dao* as way-making/*be-wëgen* needs this discovering process.

Nevertheless, what is discovered is not an objective place but something in constant transformation, which constantly reshapes and is reshaped. One finds a space in the world by making a space for this process as part of the world, which in turn opens and limits this space. *Dao* is not something inside or outside humankind; it can neither be created nor be given. *Dao* is closer to becoming than any foundational substance, *subiectum*, or *Sein*, and humankind participates in it as any other part of the world.

Tu Wei-Ming (1985, 38–39) reminds us something similar in declaring that in the classical Chinese thought the "issue was not the eternal, static structure but the dynamic process of growth and transformation. To say that the cosmos is a continuum and that all of its components are internally connected is also to say that it is an organismic unity, holistically integrated at each level of complexity." We need to keep this in mind; it will be one of the crucial points in the analysis of the *Zhuangzi*. For now, it is possible to conclude that, if we embrace this perspective, we can better understand the *boutade* of Ames and Hall (2003, 14) when they assert, "As a parody on Parmenides, who claimed that 'only Being is,' we might say that for the Daoist, 'only *beings* are,' or taking one step further in underscoring the reality of the process of change itself, 'only *becomings* are.'" It is difficult to say if "only *beings* are" as well as if any "only" can define what is supposed to exist. But this is a parody and ought to be considered as such. Sure enough, it does not mean that everything goes. On the contrary, conceiving a world of becoming implies that it itself needs to be acted while it simultaneously affects us, constantly. The process metaphor of *dao* needs such a relation. This suggests that one participates in this process with the world and the others, but also through them.

Dao is not a normative principle that can be defined and followed, because this would not be the constant process of *dao*. If one accepts this interpretation of the first line of the *Daodejing*, it becomes evident that, more than any substance or Being, *dao* indicates the possibility of always *inventing* anew the relations between the self, the other, and the world at large—thus opening a space for a comprehensive dialogue that goes beyond the anthropocentric perspective without transcending to metaphysical hypostases.

1.5 The Problem of *Philósophía* as Pseudo-Problem

From the previous analysis, I have suggested that, in order to enter in dialogue with the other, it is of primary importance to allow mutations in concepts and languages, activating processes of self-transformations. Similarly, in approaching Daoism, it is necessary to create a space for new words and new concepts in order to welcome other understandings. If this is the basic layer of the comparatist's approach, then the problem of philosophy is a pseudo-problem. Although it is always possible to refer to *philósophía* as a specific idea developed in a specific time and place, it is also possible to broaden the use of the word "philosophy" to embrace new concepts. There is no prescription to preserve a word only in its etymology and, although it is necessary to consider the ground where concepts were born, there is no need to freeze a language in an etymological vision. It is imperative to think of philosophy not as a pseudo-problem but as a possibility for comparisons and transformations. This is a necessary step to change its language.

Therefore, if philosophy is not a specific result of a determined cultural group, but a possibility for critically enquiring both the self and the other, then philosophy can open a space for a dialogue between concepts and between systems of reference. This does not mean that, when opened, it will be sufficient to fill this aperture with a few ideas. It is exactly the opposite: the encounter with new concepts is necessary to keep this opening open.

Through this metaphor, not only is it possible to accept the dialogue with other metaphors, but the dialogue itself allows for the transformation of concepts. In a mutually propulsive double movement, the dialogue opens a space in language for other concepts; and new configurations of reference systems open possibilities for further dialogue. And so on.

This is not by any means a mere idealistic process. The point is not to formulate a conceptual abstraction from reality. Quite the reverse. The point is a constant adaptation to the changing circumstances of reality. As I will discuss at length in relation to the *Zhuangzi*—which is quite critical of fixed norms—a reference system is always in a reciprocal and co-determined relationship with the experience of the world, participating in its process of aesthetic transformation. After all, dealing with the transformation of the myriad things (*wanwu zhi hua* 萬物之化) (*Zhuangzi*, 9/4/33) is a matter of being part of it. Indeed, "the myriad things and I are continuous" (*wanwu yu wo wei yi* 萬物與我為一) (*Zhuangzi*, 5/2/52).[24]

This becomes even more relevant in relation to the second chapter of the *Daodejing*, where it is said that "something and nothing are mutually engendering" (有無相生 *youwu xiangsheng*). Here, "nothing" (*wu* 無) is not the metaphysical and absolute nothingness but what is yet to come or no longer. In this sense, the mutual engendering process of *you* and *wu* refers to forming and un-forming. This implies that not only everything is relational but also that everything is in the constant process of revolving transformation. In other words, the mutual engendering process of the myriad things constantly revolves on itself producing simultaneously something and other than something, that is, forming and un-forming.

The *Zhuangzi* (4/2/35–36) explains that things are not only in constant formation but are also constantly dividing because their formation is dissolution and vice versa. In its fragmented dissolution, a thing contributes to the formation of a new one and the constitution of this new thing includes the element of the former dissolved one (Chen 2008, 218). In this sense, physics and metaphysics are overlapping, provided that the "meta" of metaphysics recovers the meaning of a temporal "after"—which implies a "before"—and discharges the transcendent "beyond"—which implies an "in itself." Fragmentation, formation, and dissolution are all parts of a continuous process inherent to something (*you*) and other than something (*wu*)—as both no longer and not yet. That is to say: they are part of a revolving transformation of simultaneous forming un-formed and un-forming formed.

Humans participate in this process by being in relation to the myriad things. *Dao* can be considered as a stream that constantly streams and is streamed where everything actively and passively takes part to it. As we shall see in the analysis of the second chapter of the *Zhuangzi*, the "Qiwulun"

齊物論, *dao* suggests a double movement in which the myriad things find, reach, and transform each other.

If such a concept of *dao* can be conceived, this is the first step on an ongoing process that incessantly needs to be prepared in order to be active. The concept itself is the invention, the *in-venire*, of a space that allows its self-positing. This concept belongs to a dialogue with the other that is intrinsically also a dialogue with oneself: a dialogue intended philosophically as self-positing and self-transforming through the other.

By means of this theorizing, the cross-cultural endeavor can be undertaken without the bias of having no biases but with the precise intention to open them, use them, and make them significant. Employing the fore-structures as pillars of one's system of reference, one can enter in a philosophical dialogue with the other side of the boundary trying not only to understand the two different reference systems but also to transform the relations between them.

Consequently, philosophy becomes an eminently comparative dialogue between cultures, that is, a philosophy of comparisons. From this perspective, the dialogue with Daoism fosters an aesthetic reconfiguration of concepts, which in turn allows the *in-venire* of other language and other understanding. This is the process of re-grounding grounds inherent in the philosophy of comparisons that this book proposes, a transformation that constantly defines and redefines itself through the encounter with the other and the world.

2

From Worldview to Metaphor

2.1 Worldviews and Language

In the previous chapter, along with the concepts of *you* 有, *wu* 無, and *dao* 道, I introduced other important terms such as *Sein*, object present-at-hand, and *subiectum*. I argued that, in the process of comparison, it is necessary to consider the reference systems and the background information of both sides of the boundary. Indeed, in crossing boundaries, a set of theoretical justifications are deployed when one sets out and when one returns. We have seen some of these theoretical problems when one translates *you* and *wu* from a Western metaphysical perspective and we have evaluated some possibilities for the translation of *dao*.

In the introduction, however, I mentioned that the aim of this book is to examine the ethical implications that a different concept of aesthetics can provide. Before proceeding in this direction, it is crucial to start from the critical analysis of the inquirer's fore-structures, that is to say, the inquirer's positions and background theories in relation to aesthetics.

To do so, this chapter will focus on the philosophy of Heidegger, not because of its link with Daoism, but for its idea of universal ontology and its critique of Western thought. My focus here is on the concept of worldview. I believe that if one wants to understand the representations of the world offered by other cultures, it is paramount to define more clearly what representations are and if they have the same function as worldviews.

Yet, to understand what a representation is, one must consider the idea of language in general. This is necessary not only because I am *writing* about representation but also because language is one of the most important means to represent reality. After a reconsideration of the representational idea, it will be possible to define more clearly the dialogic process of differentiation and assimilation of values implicit in the ethical understanding of aesthetics.

2.1.1 Language as Interpretation of the World

A good point of departure is the famous essay "The Task of the Translator," in which Walter Benjamin (1968, 80–81) quotes a passage of Rudolf Pannwitz's *Die Krisis der europäischen Kultur*. For Pannwitz, translators start from wrong premises when they try to turn a foreign language into their own instead of turning their language into the foreign one. This means that the "basic error of the translator is that he preserves the state in which his own language happens to be instead of allowing his language to be powerfully affected by the foreign tongue." To avoid this error, the translator "must expand and deepen his language by means of the foreign language."

It is difficult not to agree with Pannwitz—and with Benjamin who quotes him.[1] Translations ought to be a matter of allowing the concepts present in the foreign tongue to affect one's own language. But how can this be possible? Wilhelm von Humboldt can help to clarify this aspect.

According to Humboldt (1997, 18), "the differences between [languages] are not those of sounds and signs but ultimately of interpretations of the world [*Weltansichten*]." In his works, Humboldt uses both *Weltansicht* and *Weltanschauung* to express how language is a means to understand the world. According to him, language is "the impression of the intellect and of the world-view of the speakers" (1907, 23; trans. Manchester 1985, 2).[2] Thus, one can consider language as a trace that shows the implicit concepts of the speaker. Humboldt himself uses the term trace (*Spur*) to describe what he means by *Weltanschauung* when he states, "A language carries traces that have been produced in its development, especially from sensual intuition of the world or from the inner realm of thoughts, where that world intuition was already influenced by the intellect" (1907, 23, trans. Manchester 1985, 101). Language, on the one hand, influences the formation of concepts and, on the other hand, bears the traces of these formations. This means that language has the double function of interpreting the world and, simultaneously, making its interpretations explicit.

It is paramount to bear in mind this double orientation of language which does not *re-present* the world as it is but only presents worldviews.[3] To say it differently: the worldviews are not representations of the world in itself—representations of the objective world—but only interpretations. The objective world is already a worldview—already an interpretation. Hence, the term "worldview" is not a mere "vision of the world" that objectifies the world but, more properly, an "interpretation of the world" that allows an interaction with it.

If language offers interpretations as worldviews and if these worldviews become traces of these interpretations, these traces enter in the realm of the interpretable, which implies that they can be *traced back* in their development and can be interpreted in their turn. Thus, worldviews become the means to understand themselves through language.

This tracing back allows the worldviews to be simultaneously the interpretative tool and the interpreted outcome. This is not a vicious circle but what constitutes language as a process. Every time one tries to have a critical stance toward the world—either tracing back or comparing concepts—one *uses* and, at the same time, *produces* worldviews through language.

2.1.2 The Fusion of Worldviews

In the previous section, I introduced the concept of *Weltanschauung* to understand Pannwitz's idea that the primal elements of the foreign language should expand and deepen the translator's own language. These primal elements are the traces of worldviews expressed by these languages. Someone, however, might say that differences between languages constitute the very obstacles that threaten the possibility of tracing back these worldviews and, therefore, the possibility of translation itself. Let us see what this means in more detail.

In *Truth and Method*, Gadamer (2004, 389) admits that translation "is an extreme case of hermeneutical difficulty." He believes, however, that this task is not only possible, but is also the proper means for an expansion of the worldviews. Gadamer's position is coherent with his idea of "fusion of horizons." The translation allows a fusion in which two visions of the world can meet and can expand reciprocally. Being an interpretative activity, translation can increase the possibilities of the translated language, thus bringing the worldview of this language on a different ground. At the same time, in interpreting the foreign language, one needs to welcome the different horizon that its worldview offers by expanding one's own vision of the world.

This means that, through worldviews, one can achieve not only a better understanding of the other but also a better self-understanding. This is the position of Richard Kearney (2006, xix), who affirms that "there is no self-understanding possible without the labour of mediation through signs, symbols, narratives and texts." According to Kearney, the self of this self-understanding is an "engaged self which only finds itself after it has traversed the field of foreignness and returned to itself again, this time altered and enlarged, 'othered.'" I believe that, insofar as it is possible to be "othered" by the other, one can also understand the other *otherwise*, enabling an endless interpretation of both sides.

The result is a movement of constant exchange between the parts that activates a mutual expansion. This movement, however, is not by any means a *positivistic* progression. It is fundamental to put aside any teleological expectation of knowledge. If "understanding is always understanding-differently" (Gadamer 1989, 96), there is no ending to this differential process. The text—in the widest meaning of the word—"speaks differently as its meaning finds concretization in a new hermeneutical situation and the interpreter for his part finds his own horizons altered by his appropriation of what the text says" (Linge 1977, xix). This produces a progressive shift that cannot stop at one definite point.

If one considers the hermeneutical circle in this manner, then the text speaks differently not only in relation to different interpreters but also inside the process of each interpreter's reading. If the horizon is altered by the "appropriation of what the text says," the interpreter, in his or her proceeding, is a mobile standpoint that constantly reads what the text *is saying*. The expansion is mutual insofar as both interpreter and text have a constant reciprocal influence.

Therefore, in this cyclical return of the hermeneutical activity, both parts open themselves toward the other, allowing a fusion exactly where the extension of their own world pictures takes place. Similarly, this process happens in translation since movement is its inherent element. It is not by chance that the word "translation" comes from the Latin *translatio*, which in turn was the translation of the Greek *metaphorá* (μεταφορά, from *metaphérō* μεταφέρω, literally "carry across"). Both *translatio* and *metaphorá* imply the movement of carrying something from one place to another.

In this sense, the word "'translation' is already a metaphor for the process of translation" (Guldin 2016, 20). This means that the idea of translation itself depends on one's own worldview: it depends on how the relations to the others, the world, and the worlds of the others are conceived. This in turn depends on how one understands the relation between language and world.

It is worth underlining that when Gadamer (2004, 447) tries to elucidate the relation between language and world—the "verbally constituted world"—he feels the need to specify that "Our verbal experience of the world is prior to everything that is recognized and addressed as existing. *That language and world are related in a fundamental way does not mean, then, that world becomes the object of language*. Rather, the object of knowledge and statements is always already enclosed within the world horizon of language. That human experience of the world is verbal does not imply that a world-in-itself is being objectified." The world is not reduced to simple presence by language, it is not objectified and cannot be used, disposed, controlled as if it were an object. In this passage, Gadamer defends himself against every potential critique regarding the possibility of reducing the world to a *presence-at-hand*. He directly refers to this by stating that the "verbally constituted experience of the world expresses not what is present-at-hand, that which is calculated or measured, but what exists, what man recognizes as existent and significant" (452).

Language expresses only interpretations and not things in themselves as present-at-hand. Still, is this not also a worldview, an interpretation? Yes, it is, and here lies the main point. Through this interpretation one is able to account for a plurality of worlds that are existent and meaningful in relation to the languages that express them. Thus, the world as objective and present-at-hand is the result of a specific use of language.

Nevertheless, we cannot take this for granted. It is not a coincidence if Gadamer spends several pages on this problem. He refers to Heidegger's philosophy and to one of the most important themes of Western philosophies related to the concept of worldview. Let me consider this issue more closely so as to explain how it is possible to define one's position in relation to the world, to the other, and to the concept of translation.

2.2 Worldviews and Ontology

So far, we have seen how translation is a form of fusion of horizons in which different worldviews find a reciprocal influence and expansion. The idea of worldview, however, can lead to an objectification of the world. To see this problem more clearly, it is useful to consider the Heideggerian critique of *Weltanschauung*. This will help us to understand whether the concept of worldview is a useful tool for philosophical comparative analysis.

2.2.1 Heidegger's Critique of *Weltanschauung*

Although the position of Heidegger regarding the concept of worldview is clear, its development is not linear. In *The Basic Problems of Phenomenology* (1982, hereafter BPP), a lecture course that Heidegger gave in 1927, he presented a brief history of the concept of *Weltanschauung*.[4] This history is at the very beginning of the book and serves the scope of proposing, by contrast, Heidegger's aims: on the one hand, Heidegger distances himself from "any contemporary tendency in phenomenology" (BPP 3) and, on the other hand, he refuses the idea of a philosophy of *Weltanschauungen*.[5] Thus Heidegger wants to propose a philosophy that is alternative to both Edmund Husserl and Wilhelm Dilthey.[6] Leaving aside the problem of phenomenology for the moment, I shall concentrate on the second term of the critique and in particular on Heidegger's proposal of a "scientific philosophy" in contrast to a philosophy of worldviews.

After his etymological analysis of the term, Heidegger claims that what is meant by *Weltanschauung* "is not only a conception of the contexture of natural things but at the same time an interpretation of the sense and purpose of the human Dasein and hence of history" (BPP 5). Heidegger not only links *Weltanschauung* to *Dasein* but goes so far as to affirm that "philosophy has as its goal the formation of a world-view" (BPP 7). What's more, "in its very concept philosophy is world-view philosophy [*Weltanschauungsphilosophie*]" (BPP 6).

Not only is Heidegger favorable to the concept of *Weltanschauung*, he also gives to this concept a pivotal function in the philosophical activity. Even more, the formation of *Weltanschauung* is the philosophical activity itself. Why, then, does he suddenly change direction and affirms that "the notion of a world-view philosophy is simply inconceivable"? Why does he withdraw all the positive words spent in its favor and dismiss worldview philosophy as "an absurdity" (BPP 12)?

To answer these questions, we need to consider Heidegger's philosophy in its entirety. The appraisal of the concept of worldview is only a rhetorical device that Heidegger uses to clarify and highlight *his* philosophy. The entire argumentation about *Weltanschauung* has only one scope: to demonstrate that "*being is the proper and sole theme of philosophy*" (BPP 11). Heidegger explains that philosophy "is the theoretical conceptual interpretation of being, of being's structure and its possibilities. Philosophy is ontological. In contrast, a world-view is a positing knowledge of beings and a positing attitude toward beings; it is not ontological but ontical" (BPP 11). Heidegger defines two philosophical attitudes here: on the one hand, the proper ontological approach, which interprets Being as such and, on the other hand, the misleading ontical approach of worldview, which interprets beings forgetting their essence, to wit, forgetting *Sein*.

In Heidegger's interpretation, *Weltanschauung* needs to be avoided because it deflects from the proper scope of philosophy. According to him, "philosophy, as science of being [*Wissenschaft vom Sein*]," cannot "adopt specific attitudes toward and posit specific things about beings" (BPP 12). In adopting a specific stance toward reality, one does not propose any kind of philosophical reasoning but only and merely a vision of the world.

Heidegger wants to show that philosophy is something more *original*, in the sense that its origin precedes any worldview, any positing of a specific entity. In this line of thought, worldviews are derivative, they do not deal directly with the Being as such that they presuppose. Only philosophy, properly intended in the Heideggerian sense, deals directly with Being.

Should one infer that there is only one possibility for philosophy to be proper and that this philosophy does not produce any worldview? Are *Weltanschauungen* mere descriptions of beings? Furthermore, if a worldview is a positing knowledge of beings without relation to Being, is this knowledge a counterfeit compared with the ontological one? Does it mean that proper knowledge comes only from a proper philosophy?

First and foremost, it is necessary to comprehend whether, after the Heideggerian critique, the concept of *Weltanschauung* is still functional or if it became an absurdity. The sole fact that Heidegger makes use of it—although in a negative way—seems to exclude the latter. Indeed, Heidegger cannot renounce completely to this concept. On the contrary, he needs it because he wants to demonstrate that philosophy has always been a worldview philosophy. Always, before him, of course. Let me follow his argument to make this point more explicit.

Heidegger distinguishes between worldviews as the *production* of philosophy and worldviews as the *object* of philosophy. He suggests that philosophy cannot avoid considering the formation of worldviews—not even his philosophy—because of its essential relation to *Dasein*. Yet, as ontological science, philosophy must not propose any kind of worldview: it cannot engage in any specific formulation of worldview.

This means that if one considers the hermeneutical context in which this thought arises, philosophy, in Heideggerian terms, must deal with the interpretation of the world as such without proposing any specific one. The moment philosophy puts forward a specific interpretation of the world, that moment it abandons the essence of the interpretation and turns to specific beings, thus becoming a vision of the world. For Heidegger, an ontic *Weltanschauung* cannot be an ontological science because it fails to consider the universal component of its determination, that is, it fails to acknowledge the ontological difference.

This is also the main critique Heidegger addresses to Karl Jaspers and his *Psychologie der Weltanschauungen* (1919). In "Comments on Karl Jaspers's

Psychology of Worldviews" ([1919–21] 1998a), Heidegger already presents the differentiation between specific and general worldviews. The only difference is that, in this case, he refers to the *psychology* of worldviews—the subject of Jaspers's book. Heidegger makes two main points here.

The first is methodological. There is no mere observation resulting in a mere description. In describing something, one interprets it, employing preconceptions and, therefore, worldviews. It is worth nothing that *Weltanschauungen* are not an issue per se. The real problem is to neglect that one always uses them. In other words, Heidegger suggests that Jaspers cannot be deceptive regarding his interpretations, he needs to present them in connection with his preconceptions and worldviews—from which they derive.

This leads directly to the second point concerning the philosophical critique. With his method of mere observation, Jaspers fails to reply to the real challenge of philosophy; that is, he fails to enter in the radical, general, and infinite questioning process that questions itself. Such questioning needs to understand how its process takes place; it needs to problematize its same understanding. Only in this way can it preserve itself in its questions.

The two critiques Heidegger addresses to Jaspers converge to the same focal point. It is, after all, in both cases a matter of making explicit the interpretative and epistemological stances used in one's description of the world by means of their thematization.

Yet Heidegger suggests something more. In this infinite hermeneutical process, one discharges the description of the world as worldview and starts describing the process of worldview's formation. In the same way, in trying to establish the universal science of Being, Heidegger ceases to conceive beings and commences to conceive Being—believing that this would not have proposed an additional worldview.

2.2.2 Worldviews versus Universal Ontology

In the previous section, we saw how Heidegger grounds his critique of worldviews in his idea of ontological difference. This allows the generalization of the philosophical process, giving to Heidegger the possibility to establish a philosophy that legitimates "by its own resources its claim to be universal ontology" (BPP 12). At least this is his intention. But what are the consequences of this position in the context of a philosophy of comparisons?

According to Heidegger, the ontological difference—the differentiation between Being and beings—is not an arbitrary distinction. Rather, "it is the one by which the theme of ontology and thus of philosophy itself is first of all attained" (BPP 17). The concept of *Weltanschauung*, therefore, is a perfect tool in Heidegger's hands to demonstrate, by contrast, what a universal ontology ought to be.

The questions then become: in approaching the others and their worldviews, should one adhere to the Heideggerian project, which seems to give us a universal authority? In other words, should one believe that the Heideggerian methodology has a superior gaze because it does not propose any description of specific beings but analyzes the essence of these descriptions? This leads to a provisional, final question: is this philosophy the only proper one and are all the other systems of thought mere *Weltanschauungen* unable to aspire to any universality?

For Heidegger, the answer to all these questions would probably be "yes," with no hesitation. According to him, although the scientific nature of philosophy—as science of Being or universal ontology—is implied in its very concept, all philosophies in the course of history miserably failed to accomplish what their essence demanded. Heidegger affirms his philosophy twice: on the one side, he interprets philosophy from his point of view by considering it the science of Being and, on the other side, he implies that he is the only one who has fully unfolded the essence of philosophy. Therefore, *his* philosophy is the proper one; all the others failed their task and became worldviews.

The history of the historical worldviews is, in Heidegger's thought, the history of metaphysics—to wit, the history of *Sein*'s oblivion. This idea became more defined in the following years when Heidegger's philosophy started to be synonymous with the overcoming of metaphysics.

To avoid the same mistake of the previous thinkers, universal ontology must not be a specific interpretation of the world; it must not posit knowledge of specific entities. Instead, it must be the universal interpretation of all interpretations; it must deal with Being as the essence of all beings. Universal ontology interprets, through the ontological difference, the essence of all worldviews and the entire history of metaphysics—trying to overcome it.

One can conclude that, in his critique of worldview, Heidegger wants us to think that *his* philosophy, as the philosophy *par excellence*, is not a philosophy of worldviews because it does not posit what *is*, it does not define a world. On the contrary, his philosophy takes into account for the first time the Being of beings, which *gives* the possibility of all possibilities, the possibility of all beings and all *Weltanschauungen*. That is to say, it gives the interpretation of all interpretations. Heidegger refuses to consider his philosophy as one philosophy among others and suggests that if one does not understand his philosophy, the essence of the world and human life cannot be understood. Universal ontology is, therefore, synonymous with Heidegger's philosophy.

Although Heidegger progressively abandons the rhetoric of a universal science of philosophy, he does not change the basic assumption of his thought. With the elimination of the concept of scientific philosophy, Heidegger can definitely dissociate himself from Husserl and can openly affirm the task of his philosophy.[7] It is possible to have confirmation of this in the lecture course *The Fundamental Concepts of Metaphysics: World, Finitude, Solitude* (1995), which he gave in 1929–30.

The title of the first subsection of the course is already revealing: "The incomparability of philosophy." Heidegger's intention is to radicalize his philosophy to the extent that it can stand by itself without any counterpart. For this reason, he changes his previous position and affirms philosophy as "neither science, nor the proclamation of a worldview" (1). Philosophy becomes something that *"can be determined only from out of itself and as itself—comparable with nothing else"* or, more plainly, "something that *stands on its own, something ultimate"* (2).

Heidegger abandons the concept of scientificity, disjoining his position from everyone and everything. The ontological difference allows his thought to be ultimate, to "stand on its own." Heidegger draws a precise line between his thought and the rest of philosophy both as science and as worldview. This position is held at least until 1936–38, the period of *Contributions to Philosophy* (published in 1989), where he states, "The distinction between 'scientific philosophy' and 'worldview philosophy' is the last scion of the philosophical bewilderment of the nineteenth century" (31).

How can one relate with this radical position? Does Heidegger leave any space for a dialogue with him? Does he not completely overturn the concept of *Weltanschauung* and dismiss any other conceptual formulation within a worldview and outside the ontological difference? Does this not result, *de facto*, in the impossibility of establishing any comparison and, therefore, any dialogue?

Unfortunately, this seems to be the outcome of Heidegger's radical revision of philosophy—at lease for the time being, as affirmed in "A Dialogue on Language" (1971a, 3).[8] Does this mean that, in order to pursue a philosophy of comparisons, it becomes necessary to dismiss Heidegger or, following his example, one must abandon any attempt to establish a philosophy of comparisons? I believe there is another, more fruitful solution.

It is imperative to consider and dissociate two different aspects of Heidegger's thought. One is its overall enterprise that aims to establish an overarching philosophy of Being. The other is its critique of Western philosophy through the ontological difference. These are two different aspects of the same reflective thought. If one can accept Heidegger's meta-position not as establishing an absolute explanation of the entire possibility of reasoning but as a tool for questioning and evaluating one's own standpoint, a self-revaluation or, even better, a constant self-revaluation becomes possible. In this sense, the process of re-grounding grounds can be initiated not only to open one's own assumptions to self-enquiry but also to open the self to the dialogue with the other.

The discourse on worldview, therefore, was already a first comparative exercise that has shown how philosophy can be considered not only as an investigation into its own forms of productions but also as a specific attempt to define the world. In a philosophy of comparisons these two positions need to be kept together as self-re-evaluative tool and dialogic access to the other respectively.

Then the problem is not Heidegger's revision of metaphysics or his attempt to overcome it but his aim, what he wants to obtain with this overcoming, namely, his ontology. This means that it is possible to consider Heidegger's *perspective* on the fundamental ontology as *one* of the possible consequences of his critique of worldview. Hence, one does not need to dismiss any aspect of his philosophy. On the contrary, it is possible to consider Heidegger's philosophy as a part of the Western tradition and as part of the premises for a dialogue with Chinese philosophy—or with the other in general. Still, if one wants to assimilate this critique, one also needs to observe it where it is more profound.

2.3 Worldviews and Representations

In the previous section, I sketched the opposition between worldviews and universal ontology in Heidegger's thought. We have seen how, when taken to its final consequences, this position leads to the "incomparability of philosophy." Indeed, universal ontology is a metatheory that explains the production of worldviews without dealing with any specific worldview. I concluded the section underlining that, although problematic in the context of a philosophy of comparisons—as I will discuss in more detail in the next chapter—Heidegger's philosophy is extremely useful in its critique of

Western metaphysics. Consequently, in this section, I want to consider more attentively the problem of representation. To do so, I will analyze some of Heidegger's main arguments in relation to the concept of *Weltbild* and the subject/object dichotomy.

2.3.1 *Weltbild* and the Subject/Object Dichotomy

In "The Age of the World Picture" ([1938] 2002b, hereafter AWP), Heidegger delivers the most striking offensive against the concept of *Weltanschauung*. Yet this is only a secondary target; the first one is the philosophy of Descartes, which is responsible for reducing the world to a picture, to a *Weltbild* (literally "world picture"). It is "in the metaphysics of Descartes that, for the first time, the being is defined as the objectness of representation [*Vorstellens*], and truth as the certainty of representation." As a consequence, the "whole of modern metaphysics, Nietzsche included, maintains itself within the interpretation of the being and of truth opened up by Descartes" (AWP 66). I will discuss Nietzsche in the next chapter.

For the moment, it is important to consider that, in Descartes's philosophy, representation is truthful and objective only insofar as there is a subject who represents it. The world as *Weltbild* is the consequence of the subject/object separation. In other words, the world picture is the result of the process that subjectifies the subject and, simultaneously, objectifies the object. Let me first clarify the subjectification of the subject.

The word "subject" derives from the Latin *subiectus* (neuter *subiectum*), which means "lying under" (past participle of *subicere* "to place under," composed of *sub* "under" and *iacere* "to place," "to throw"). As the translation of the Greek *hypokeímenon* (ὑποκείμενον), *subiectum* is for Heidegger the metaphysical concept of "that-which-lies-before, that which, as ground, gathers everything onto itself." As such, it does not have a direct relation to humans. Nevertheless, with Descartes human being "becomes that being upon which every being, in its way of being and its truth, is founded." Thus humanity "becomes the referential center of beings as such" (AWP 66–67).

It is paramount to underline that *subiectum*, as that which "lies at the basis as ground," is ground insofar as it *gives* ground, it grounds itself in itself, it takes upon itself the authority to determine and define beings. To say that humanity becomes *subiectum* means that it becomes the authority that establishes the truth. This truth, in turn, gives the ground to define beings. Humanity as *subiectum* establishes the objective truth through which every being is defined as object. The objective truth *represents* beings as objects from the point of view of the subject as *subiectum*. This clearly produces a strong anthropocentric perspective, as we shall discuss later in more detail.

For Heidegger, the subject that offers the certainty of an unshakable ground is the Cartesian *cogito*, in which thinking "is representation, setting-before, a representative relation to the represented" (AWP 82). Through this representation, humankind grounds the epistemological framework that allows its knowledge to be certain: objective knowledge and, therefore, knowledge of the objective world. Thus, the world becomes an object, a *Weltbild*, a world picture.

The subject/object separation is allowed by and takes place in a representation that objectifies the object from the viewpoint of the subjectified subject. To say it in Heidegger's words, as soon as "the world becomes picture the position of man is conceived as worldview [*Weltanschauung*]" (AWP 70). This means that the worldview is the representation that the representative human being represents.

Heidegger conceives *Weltbild* and *Weltanschauung* as specific products of modernity. These came to the fore as consequences of the new humankind's representation—in the double meaning of the genitive. Thus, "that the world becomes picture is one and the same process whereby, in the midst of beings, man becomes subject" (AWP 69). *Weltanschauung* and *Weltbild* are the direct counterparts of the dichotomies subjectified–subject and objectified–object made possible by the modern representation of entities.

This representation is the target of Heidegger's critique. Jacques Derrida (1982b, 310) explains that, for Heidegger, the characteristic of the modern epoch is "the interpretation of the essence of what is as an object of representation." This interpretation is, for Heidegger, no longer the Greek's "self-disclosure for . . . but rather the laying hold and grasping of . . ." (AWP 82). But what does this mean?

The representation as *repræsentatio* is the act of re-presenting (*Vor-stellen*), that is, of putting something before oneself at one's disposal. This is the opposite of *Anwesen* "presencing," which for Heidegger (2000, 64) derives from the Greek *parousía* (παρουσία). Heidegger holds that *parousía* is not the German *Substanz* that comes from the Latin *substantia* (substance), which in turn is what sustains and is grounded by the *subiectum*. Consequently, *Anwesen* is what comes to appearance without being an object for a subject. In opposition to *Anwesen*, the act of re-presenting means "to bring the present-at-hand before one as something standing over-and-against, to relate it to oneself, the representer, and, in this relation, to force it back to oneself as the norm-giving domain. Where this happens man 'puts himself in the picture' concerning beings. . . . Man becomes the representative [*Repräsentant*] of beings in the sense of the objective" (AWP 69). We have finally reached the concept of present-at-hand introduced in section 2.1.2. For Heidegger, the present-at-hand is the world as an object that subjects represent in front of themselves. Yet the problem now is: how could this modern representation be possible? How did it take place?

Heidegger explains that Descartes was responsible for this "positioning" of human being: he secured this position by taking up on himself the fundamental ground that allows this positioning. With Descartes humankind becomes the *Repräsentant* (as *subiectum*) of beings (as objects). Thus, Heidegger's essay "The Age of World Picture" is a specific attack against Descartes, against the concept of representation as *cogito*, and against its norm-giving domain.

The Cartesian *cogito* makes human being the *preeminent* being, the "*subiectum* which, in respect of the primary true (i.e., certain) beings, takes precedence over all other *subiecta*" (AWP 83). Beings are certainly true on the ground that the *cogito* secures itself as *subiectum*. On the one hand, the "fundamental certainty is the *me-cogitare* = *me esse* which is, at all times, indubitably representable and represented" and, on the other hand, this is "the fundamental equation of all calculating belonging to self-securing representing." Therefore, in this "fundamental certainty, man becomes certain that, as the representer of all representation, the setter-before of all setting-before . . . he is securely established—which means, now, that he *is*" (AWP 82–83). The representation defined by the *cogito* determines what *subiectum* is and, therefore, what objects are.

This is patently the opposite of Heidegger's philosophy and his attempt to give back to *Sein* the function of *Anwesen*, presencing. As explained before, for Heidegger Being cannot be understood as *a* being, as *something that is*. Being gives itself and is given by itself. Through this giving the unconcealment is possible. Being withdraws and conceals itself in order to unconceal all beings.[9] This is the unconcealed truth (*alḗtheia* ἀλήθεια) that cannot be a *subiectum* or a representation as *cogito*. Yet how literally should one take these ideas?

2.3.2 Representations as Metaphors

Although one can be impressed by Heidegger's argumentation, a doubt persists that the critique of representation is self-defeating. Does one not always represent something as a concept formulated through language?

Does Heidegger himself not represent a concept when he introduces, for instance, S̶e̶i̶n̶, the Being crossed out? On the other hand, should one consider the representation of concepts as a necessary objectification—as if only an objective world could be represented? Does this entail that, in any language and culture, a representation of world, God, or any other abstract concept is always intended as an object within a worldview? This is hardly justifiable. Believing this would mean to believe that one understanding is the explanation for everything. Would this belief not result exactly in an objectification of the other?

It is evident that Heidegger pushes his critique against representation and against Descartes to consolidate his position. Although it is possible to agree with many aspects of Heidegger's analysis—in particular with the dangerous consequences of distinguishing between the subjectified–subject and the objectified–object—one cannot generalize these concepts and assume that this is the unavoidable outcome of all representations.

What's more, does the opposition of *Vorstellen* and *Anwesen* not describe two different experiences of Being, two modalities of being-in-the-world with different approaches to the subject/object problem? One cannot avoid asking if Heidegger employs the concept of *Weltbild* as a metaphor that explains his interpretation of the modern human being. This would imply that *Vorstellen* and *Anwesen* are also metaphors employed to interpret how different experiences of the world are expressed through language. The suspicion then arises that, regardless of his critique, Heidegger writes from inside the age of the world picture. After all, does he not define what the experience of Being in Greek thought *is*? Does this not result in a representation and crystallization of that experience?

This does not merely mean that Heidegger still needs the metaphysical language for his philosophy—something that he would have accepted as we have seen in chapter 1. It means that Heidegger produces a picture of the Greek's world that derives from his philosophy.[10] Heidegger (2008, 165) argues that all "philosophy of culture is worldview philosophy. It freezes definite situations in the history of the spirit and wants to *interpret culture*." Does he not do exactly this? Or is Heidegger's interpretation a different one, an interpretation with a different *status*?

As discussed before, Heidegger tries to establish an interpretation of interpretation, a meta-metaphor that is all inclusive and without standpoint—as if it were possible to employ a concept of the world that is not already a *vision* of the world. I believe that one ought to resign oneself to the evidence that worldviews, with their degree of crystallizations, are unavoidable when the other is considered—whether another human being or the world at large.

Nevertheless, this is not necessarily a negative limitation, provided that it is acknowledged. If limitations are recognized, then one can *propose* to the other an interpretation as a *limited interpretation*, which needs the other to be revivified. This is the strength of Nietzsche's definition of world as will to power that I shall discuss in the next chapter.

Interpretations are part of the human experience: one is one's own language and one's own interpretations. As a consequence, through interpretations, one offers to the other one's own limitation and, in doing so, one strives to be changed and revivified by the other. The first step toward this process is to accept that one always uses and produces worldviews, even when one tries to establish a metatheory. And while a meta-discourse can help to problematize the questioning process itself—that is to say, to question questions—this will never dissolve one's own standpoint.

Despite his metatheory, Heidegger regards Greek thought—and any thought—from a specific perspective which can be seen as *objectively* representing it. This is what Derrida suggests when he asserts that "it will be difficult to avoid the question whether the relationship of the epoch of representation to the great Greek epoch is not still interpreted by Heidegger in a representative mode, as if the couple *Anwesenheit/repraesentatio* still dictated the law of its own interpretation, which does no more than to redouble and recognize itself in the historical text it claims to decipher" (1982b, 322). Derrida has a good point; this component is present in Heidegger's interpretation of Greek philosophy. Yet this is only one aspect of the problem.

In the previous chapter, I maintained that, in the process of comparison, one needs to consider philosophy as both an investigation into its own forms of productions and as a specific attempt to define the world. This means that it is necessary to contemplate both the function and the content of the specific perspective analyzed. In other words, one needs to pay attention not only to the meaning of a metaphor but also to its function as metaphor.

If one considers the meaning of *Anwesen*, this is about the coming to appearance of something; however, if we consider its function as metaphor, this describes how beings are conceived. In other words, *Anwesen* as metaphor *shows* how world and beings are understood as "presenting themselves." This reveals how the function of language is always a description, an understanding through meanings—which is what I meant when I defined worldviews as interpretations of the world implicit in language.

One needs to be aware that it is not possible to step out of language: in defining concepts, one relies on language and produce something that is allowed by this same language. This is the central issue of translation. For Derrida (1982b, 297–298), translatability is a problem of representation and, simultaneously, representation itself is subject to interpretation.

Concepts are representative of a specific experience of the world and even the concept of *Vor-stellen* is metaphorical, representing one of the modalities of this experience. When it comes to translation this representative aspect of concepts becomes problematic exactly because one needs to take into consideration the different meanings of the words translated as functions of different representations. To translate words means, on the one hand, to translate concepts and, on the other hand, to interpret them as representation of world experiences.

Nevertheless, this also is an argumentation that takes place inside language and as such is metaphorical: it shows a way of understanding and, therefore, a way of representing the experience of the world. In this sense, metaphors are used to represent experiences of the world—which can involve the tangible, the intangible, and even the so-called non-concepts such as *différance* (Derrida 1982a, 7)—and to expand these same experiences.

It must be clear that I do not suggest going back to Descartes's position and its anthropocentric perspective. Representation—as well as *Weltanschauung*—is not defined by the subject as *subiectum* or by the human's absolute power of representation. Rather, it is defined by its content and function as metaphor. This implies that representational activities do not automatically ground a *subiectum* producing an objectification of the world. On the one hand, linguistic activities always have a metaphorical nature through which the experience of the world is interpreted; on the other hand, the metaphors embedded in language do not necessarily ground an objective knowledge.

Even if it is possible to agree with Heidegger that philosophy should not propose a unique worldview, people cannot avoid constantly using and producing worldviews through their language activities. Insofar as worldviews are interpretations of the world implicit in language, they are constantly used and produced in one's linguistic activities, even if the intention is to avoid a *specific* worldview.

In chapter 5, I will consider how this can become an ethical approach to the other. Indeed, the interpretations of the others—in the double sense of the genitive—bear the consequences of these interpretations as worldviews without the assumption that these visions are absolute, definitive, or ultimate. Interpretations seek the others so as to proceed in their linguistic activity. To say it differently, interpretation needs comparisons with other worldviews to be at the same time a determination and a limitation of one's own enquiring.

This means that, even if the aim is not to define a static world of beings, words always name entities and worldviews statically. This is obviously a problem, one of the most significant in other traditions as well—as the *Daodejing* will show it very clearly. Thus, to escape the petrifying constriction of the naming activity, one enters in conversation with the other and proceeds in the linguistic interpretative process. This implies that one approaches the other not to repeat oneself but to be transformed by the other.

Although the aim is not to produce a *Weltanschauungsphilosophie*, it is not possible to deny that a dialogue needs words, concepts, representations, worldviews, metaphors. Moreover, one needs new concepts to expand the horizon of expectations and to *comprehend* the other. This also implies that, the conversation with the other can help to see the pre-assumptions implicit in one's own interpretations and to make them not only apparent but also relevant.

In this sense, the extension of language can take place as the explication of what is silent in one's language. If it is possible to make pre-assumptions speak, then it is also possible to listen to them and change them. The *Zhuangzi* will help us in this direction: one needs to forget the self-centered perspective to have more space for listening to the other and to oneself. In this sense, the dialogue with the other is always also a dialogue with oneself.

Yet am I not caught again in metaphors? Undoubtedly. Even more importantly, it is precisely this circle of metaphors that allows the process of re-grounding one's own ground. The essential is that, as far as metaphors are considered as such, one will be able to recognize that there is no grounded knowledge in them and the truth established by them is valid only within them. *Alétheia* itself—as well as *subiectum, Vorstellen, Anwesen,* etc.—is not any kind of meta-metaphor but only another way of making sense of one's relation to the world.

Humans are not just a picture in the world, neither as *subiectum* nor as object. Worldviews and metaphors are formulations that one, as part of the world, employs in the attempt to embrace and comprehend oneself and the other in relation to the world. Even the concept of truth as unconcealment stems from this relation and—although for Heidegger it has a different generality in its manifold historical determinations—it responds to the same interpretative process.

Truth as unconcealment does not have any different value from any other concept of truth. Even more, it does not have value at all, like all other concepts of truth. Value starts to be applied to truth only when one forgets its metaphorical origin. Truth acquires value insofar as it is considered literally. The same applies to metatheories. They do not have a higher status. They need to be considered in their metaphorical function and content as any other theory.

2.3.3 Metaphors and Metatheories

As a consequence of the previous analysis, we can provisionally conclude that Heideggerian thought is extremely useful, provided that we acknowledge its metatheoretical nature. While the hermeneutical approach can interpret and explain how one is historically and linguistically determined, it is not possible to neglect that this interpretation is totally inscribed in the theoretical framework that hermeneutics itself sets. As soon as one tries to impose this framework as *the* interpretation that includes all the other interpretations, one affirms a second-level theory that pretends to see everything from outside, "without a standpoint." Consequently, the theory grounds its general validity through the foundation of its same ground.

Conceived as such, this overarching theory is not far from the Western modern desire of establishing a unified explanation of its relation to the world. The main issue is that even though hermeneutics seems to accept plurality, if one conceives it as a metatheory and not as just another perspective—as Nietzsche does—we keep subordinating plurality to a superior and unified system.

The problem is not the hermeneutical approach per se but its determination as a metatheory that is only another formulation of the *subiectum*'s grounding. Probably for this reason Heidegger abandoned the hermeneutical standpoint and focused his later philosophy on the structure of Being and its possibilities. However, this does not change his basic assumption that one concept can explain all the others.

If one wants to proceed toward the confrontation with other philosophical traditions, this assumption is not acceptable. Philosophy cannot be reduced to "the theoretical conceptual interpretation of being, of being's structure and its possibilities" (BPP 11). This would preclude the understanding of different worldviews. Philosophy cannot interpret the other without positing this same interpretation as *a* theoretical interpretation and not *the* only one. Moreover, precisely because this hermeneutical approach is *an* interpretation, *a* metaphor, one needs to compare it with other interpretations and metaphors. Here lies the main component of both the theoretical and methodological proposition of a philosophy based on comparisons: the proposition of a philosophy that is able to define itself through comparisons and not a philosophy that explains everything through its metatheory.

Steven Burik (2009, 4) implies this when he states that "the interlocutors *of* the comparative dialogue to a large extent dictate the guiding theory behind that particular dialogue." Burik, however, remains captured in the basic mistake of the phenomenological approach. According to him, in "comparative philosophy . . . with regard to language it is crucial to 'shatter' our own presuppositions in translating a work from a different culture" (32). The idea itself of shattering one's presupposition is only an illusion or, at the best, just another presupposition. The point is precisely to make the presuppositions speak—without them one would have nothing to change.

If one allows oneself to be guided by the specific conversation—giving up the illusion to guide it—this clearly removes any possible formulation of a prefabricated, overarching theory. A philosophy based on comparisons is, therefore, first and foremost a proposition that undermines the same concept of meta-concept, this being one of the most dangerous faults of metaphysical assumptions.

Contrarily to the Heideggerian position, metaphysical statements are grounded not in the Being's oblivion but in unifying, reflective, and self-asserting metatheories.[11] For this reason one needs to be cautious to accept tempting metatheory of *dao* such as the one proposed by Heidegger when he affirms that "Tao could be the way that gives all ways" (1971b, 92). This is just a metaphysical, autoreferential, and metatheoretical affirmation.

I have already commented on *dao* in the previous chapter, and I shall come back to it in chapter 4. In the meantime, I shall see if Nietzsche can offer a different perspective and a different theoretical approach to establish a dialogue with Daoism. Before this, however, I will conclude the discourse on language and define more precisely the idea of metaphor. Only after this step can I proceed toward the redefinition of an aesthetic encounter with the other. As mentioned at the end of chapter 1, the concept itself should be seen as the *in-venire* of a space that allows its self-positing and self-transforming through the other. I shall discuss how this concept is nothing but a metaphor that, because it does not turn in an absolute truth, can keep open the space for a dialogue with the other. This also means that, through metaphor, it will be possible to understand the aesthetic experience of the world described by concepts such as *dao*, *wuwei*, *wuming*, etc.

3

From Metaphor to Ethics

3.1 The Language of Being

In the previous chapter, I approached the problem of translation. Following the suggestion of Humboldt that differences between languages are not simply of sounds and signs but, more radically, differences of interpretations of the world, I considered the concept of worldview. This analysis showed how one constantly uses and produces worldviews through language. I argued that translations need to consider and compare the worldviews used and produced by different languages. Through these comparisons it is possible to expand and deepen one's own language, and to be positively affected by the foreign tongue.

This is the preliminary theoretical effort that one needs to put in place in the attempt to encounter the other. Nonetheless, it is imperative to take into account the epistemological implications of this encounter. Proceeding toward the dialogue with the *Daodejing* and the *Zhuangzi*, it is fundamental to consider the ground from which the comparison is approached. As seen, if the dialogue with the other presupposes the task of translation and if the translation needs to be a comparison of worldviews, then it is crucial to consider one's own understanding of worldview. The very idea of translation depends on worldview and, consequently, on how one defines the relation with oneself, the others, the world, and so forth. For this reason, I proposed the definition of *Weltanschauung* as an interpretation of the world implicit in language.

This definition requires some precautions, as the Heideggerian critique clearly showed. Indeed, one cannot neglect the relation that the concept of worldview has with the representational thinking and, therefore, with the metaphysical foundation of the *cogito*. This does not entail a complete agreement with Heidegger's critique. Rather the opposite.

We have seen so far that Heidegger's philosophy is particularly useful in its deconstructive process of analysis that questions its own tradition. Yet this philosophy is affected by the desire of establishing the universal science of Being as "universal ontology." Although Heidegger constantly changes his terminology—progressively abandoning the ideas of phenomenology, hermeneutics, worldview philosophy, and science of Being—his focal point remains always the same: the self-disclosure and self-withdrawing of *Sein*. To express this double movement of Being/being, Heidegger tirelessly tries to find new words and new concepts in an endless work of revision.

It is important not to underestimate this aspect of his philosophy, which is probably the most significant. Heidegger constantly rectifies and broadens his terminology as if only through this process he could express the proper essence of *Sein*. The downside of such a process is that the ontological difference becomes the touchstone for everything else. In an extremely sophisticated grammar game, Heidegger constantly reproduces—always the same and always differently—the unchangeable pattern: whatever language names, this *is* something, in particular when language names Being as such.

According to Heidegger, however, *Sein* cannot *be* something. Consequently, through language, *Sein* proffers itself as being and simultaneously self-withdraws as Being. This ontological double movement becomes for Heidegger the criterion to judge the representational thinking and the entire onto-theological history of metaphysics.

While it is possible to agree that the linguistic activity constantly defines and limits the horizon of one's experience, through the same process it is also possible to find new metaphors and expand one's own worldviews. Heidegger's philosophy is an admirable example in this respect. The real problem that I want to discuss in this chapter—before proceeding with the analysis of the *Laozi* and the *Zhuangzi*—is whether the representational aspect of linguistic activities, with its formation of worldviews and metaphors, is itself metaphysical.

This becomes even more relevant if one does not want to define *something* but wants to describe *processes*. It is evident that a process cannot be conceived as something. I shall see how this applies, for instance, to the concept of sitting and forgetting (*zuowang* 坐忘) in the *Zhuangzi*. Still, I am not ready to directly engage in this discourse yet. I need to prepare the ground in order to understand what a *process* means.

While the analysis of Heidegger was central to question the Western philosophical standpoint and in particular the problem of the subject/object dichotomy, it is time now to consider how the theoretical centrality of *Sein* in his philosophy is a serious limitation, in particular for its tight relation to language.

3.1.1 Heidegger's "Essential Translation"

Heidegger considers the history of philosophy as the history of *Sein*'s oblivion and needs the Indo-European grammatical structure to develop his theoretical discourse. Outside this structure—outside the centrality of being—his philosophy would dissolve. This has important repercussions on the present study.

Since the outset, I underlined how one of the main issues one faces in the attempt of encountering the other is the problem of translation. This same problem is the weakest point of Heidegger's philosophy. It is possible to synthesize the Heideggerian idea of translation—and consequently his opposition to the concept of worldview—with this passage from *The Principle of Reason* (1991a, 97; hereafter PR): "in any given epoch of the *Geschick* of being, an essential translation responds to the manner in which a language speaks in that *Geschick* of being."[1] Let me first consider the idea of *Geschick*.

The term becomes increasingly important in Heidegger's later works and, as rightly stated by Michael Inwood (1999, 68), it "has to do with being rather than Dasein." This indicates already a shift of perspective. Fornero and Tassinari (2002, 740–741) summarize the so-called Heideggerian turn (*Kehre*) as a different attitude toward the problem of Being, a turn that is an overturn of the analysis of Being and an inverted modality to deal with it. Heidegger no longer considers Being in relation to humanity but, after the turn, humanity is considered in relation to Being. This entails that Heidegger, instead of comprehending Being from an existential point of view, comprehends existence from the point of view of Being.

Although the idea of *Dasein* is not completely dismissed, it becomes almost marginal compared to the increasing prominent role of Being in its multifarious configurations: not just *Sein* but also *Seyn* and *Sein*. Concepts such as *es gibt*, *Ereignis*,[2] and *Geschick* become predominant by virtue of their strategic role played in relation to *Sein*.[3] Indeed, Heidegger can indirectly define *Sein* through these concepts. This is particularly evident with *Geschick*, which replaces and radicalizes the concept of *es gibt*. Inwood (1999, 68) explains that Heidegger derives *Geschick* directly from *schicken* as 'what is sent,' often writing *Ge-Schick*. . . . Metaphysics, in the sense of surmounting or transcending beings, is a *Geschick* in that it is 'put, i.e. sent [*geschickt*] on the path of its prevalence.' What sends? Being. Heidegger associates being's sending with the phrase *es gibt Sein*, 'there is being,' but literally 'it gives being'—a convenient way of avoiding saying that being 'is.' What does *es*, 'it,' denote? Being itself. Hence being gives, i.e. sends, itself or its own truth or lighting.

More than any literal understanding of *Geschick*, one needs to conceive it in relation to *Sein* and *es gibt*. Compared with *es gibt Sein*, the concept of *Geschick des Seins* has the additional advantage, from the Heideggerian perspective, of avoiding any implication of what *is there* as something. *Geschick* defines *Sein* as what *is given* in entities without being something. Thus, the "history of being is the '*Geschick*' of being that proffers itself to us in withdrawing its essence" (PR 61).[4] Similarly, *Ereignis* defines the same possibility of *Sein* as presencing. According to Heidegger (1971c, 127), one can think the appropriating event as "the giving yield whose giving reach alone is what gives us such things as a 'there is [*es gibt*],' a 'there is' of which even Being itself stands in need to come into its own as presence."[5] In other words, *Sein* needs *Ereignis* to be given as *Geschick*. Therefore, *Ereignis* and *Geschick* are two complementary concepts that define *Sein* in its modalities of proffering and withdrawing: in its appropriating event, *Ereignis* produces that presencing that culminates in *Geschick* as the self-withdrawing of Being. One concept mirrors the other and, simultaneously, needs the other.

And yet, they are not sufficient. They need to be named; they need the sound of language (*Sprache*). Only through language can *Sein* be given and the event of appropriation be appropriated by itself granting *Geschick* as history of Being. For Heidegger (1971c, 128), "We can give a name to the appropriation that prevails in Saying: it—Appropriation—appropriates or owns [*Es—das Ereignis—eignet*]. When we say this, we speak our own appropriate already spoken language."[6] The Heideggerian "essential translation" takes place in this appropriating event that language allows. The only problem is that this "appropriate already spoken language" is the language of Being.

3.1.2 Being and Sayers

If we go back to the quotation concerning the problem of translation, what is at stake here should be more visible. Let me consider it again: "in any given epoch of the *Geschick* of being, an essential translation responds to the manner in which a language speaks in that *Geschick* of being" (PR 97). New questions immediately arise.

First of all, what is an essential translation and how can we distinguish it from a nonessential one? Should one consider *Geschick* as the *métron* μέτρον, the measure of all things, the only guarantor for a correspondence of meanings and for meaning itself in general? Would this not imply that what is spoken in every language is always and constantly *Sein*? Or should we consider the way language speaks as diverse, innumerable and regard the *Geschick* of Being as *a* metaphor, just one metaphor among others? And if *Geschick* is a metaphor—one of the many possible explanations of one's relation with oneself, the world, and the other—would it not function as any other worldview?

The problem is that not only does Heidegger oppose the idea of worldview, he also refuses the idea of metaphor *tout court*, asserting that the "metaphorical exists only within metaphysics" (PR 48). If one cannot conceive the *Geschick* of Being as a metaphorical vision of the world, the other option is to regard it as a normative, unified, and unifying disposition of language. This means that, despite all the differences between languages, *Sein* is the immutable norm that pertains to language in its entirety. Indeed, for Heidegger (PR 96) "language speaks [*Die Sprache spricht*], not humans."

In commenting on "*Die Sprache spricht*," Herman Philipse (1998, 205) observes that this "is not the structuralist doctrine that language as a structure is prior to the individuals speaking that language, these individuals being raised in a common culture and into a preexisting language." Heidegger "rather claims that Being speaks to us through language, so that language in its primary essence (*Wesen*) is the Word of Being."[7] What does happen, then, when "being" is not a central grammatical part of a language? It should not come as a surprise that Heidegger (2000, 86) himself posits this question. He replies that without Being as a component of language there would be no language at all. According to him, without Being, "We ourselves could never be those who *say*. We would never be able to be those who we are. For to be human means to be a sayer. Human beings are yes- and no-sayers only because they are, in the ground of their essence, sayers, *the* sayers." Although it is possible to agree that humans are sayers, this does not necessarily result in a positive connotation. In the next chapter, I shall argue that Daoism has a more critical approach toward language. Moreover, it is difficult to conceive the saying of the sayers being dictated by only one concept. Here it is not even a question of Being or *Sein* or *Geschick*. The issue is the absolute restriction of every language and every conception of the world to one normative expression of this very possibility of language.

It seems that the configuration of *Sein* in the Heideggerian philosophy becomes a simple complementary support of his theoretical endeavor. Even the words of Derrida (1982a, 199) do not dispel these doubts. According to the French philosopher, Heidegger's thought cannot be regarded as ethnocentric. Derrida's reasoning, however, is not convincing when he says, "If we recall that elsewhere Heidegger distinguishes the sense of 'Being' from the word 'Being' and the concept of 'Being,' this amounts to saying that it is no longer the presence in a language of the word or (signified) concept 'Being' or 'to be' that he makes into the condition for the Being-language of language, but an entirely other possibility which remains to be defined." If it is neither a matter of signified nor a problem of concept, how can one understand the "sense" of Being? Moreover, if the concept of Being is not an issue, why does Heidegger—as well as Derrida—retain it as a *Grundwort*, a fundamental word, instead of replacing it with another one linked to its "sense"?

Derrida, faithful to his philosophical enterprise, keeps deconstructing the Heideggerian thought without proposing any way out, any "definition" of this "entirely other possibility." Hence, this possibility remains only an illusory promise. This confirms the suspicion of a monolithic and authoritative idea of Being, not only for its one-sided linguistic derivation, but also for its applicability as a possibility to come.[8] The visible danger is to reduce everything to just *one* possibility.

A clear example in this direction is the one of Gregory Fried (2001, 141–142), who quite timidly suggests that "Heidegger is almost certainly wrong in saying that *only* German and Greek can 'speak' philosophy because only in these two languages does the language itself intersect so forcefully with Being to engender the *question* of Being." Fried then adds that "for Heidegger's questions to be taken seriously as anything more than the parochial products of certain Indo-European languages, it must be shown that the 'matter for thought' that stands forth in his question of Being can be translated, as it were (and not by finding exact equivalents for *Sein* in other languages, for these equivalents do not exist), into a question that makes sense *in* and *about* all language." Without any doubt Fried has the best intentions. And yet, it is evident that this goodwill results in a unidirectional approach.[9] Not only is the possibility to translate the question of *Sein* just one aspect of the matter—the other is to see if this is relevant in the other context—but also it is not clear why this question must make sense "*in* and *about* all language."

Is it not contradictory to say that there are not equivalents of *Sein* in other languages if the scope is to find a universal sense "*in* and *about* all language"? Would this not result in a cultural imposition anyway? Why should the question of *Sein* be translated in something all-encompassing? Or should one think that *Sein* can be translated *only* into something all-encompassing? This would mean that the essence of *Sein* is to be all-encompassing. This is a legitimate interpretation but not necessarily relevant in other cultural traditions.

3.1.3 Being as a Metaphor

There is nothing wrong with absolute Being, provided that this vision can be discordant with a pluralistic or non-metaphysical one. The issue of translation is the opposite of the one proposed by Fried: it is not a matter of allowing Being to be translated in a "question that makes sense *in* and *about* all language" but to allow Being to be questioned and even contradicted by other languages. In this perspective, Being, *Geschick*, and *Ereignis* are all different formulations of an all-encompassing metaphor that sounds as absolute as it is undebatable.

I refer here to Hans Blumenberg's idea of absolute metaphors. In the Heideggerian context, however, this concept acquires a negative tone insofar as it refuses to acknowledge its very status of metaphor. Blumenberg (2010, 13) asserts,

> It is self-evident that metaphors like that of the power or impotence of truth *do not admit of verification*, and that the alternative already decided in them one way or the other is *theoretically* undecidable. Metaphors are unable to satisfy the requirement that truth, by definition, be the result of a methodologically secure procedure of verification. They therefore not only fail to say 'nothing but the truth,' they do not say anything truthful at all. Absolute metaphors 'answer' the supposedly naïve, in principle unanswerable questions whose relevance lies quite simply in the fact that they cannot be brushed aside, since we do not *pose* them ourselves but find them already *posed* in the ground of our existence.

These metaphors are posed in the ground of one's existence because they are strictly related to language, not language in general but one's own language. Without acknowledging the metaphorical nature of concepts—and in particular of grounding concepts—the *sense* conveyed in them becomes rigid, normative, undebatable. In "The Way to Language" Heidegger (1971c, 127) expressly states this unquestionable aspect of *Ereignis*.

Going back once more to the aforementioned passage—"in any given epoch of the *Geschick* of being, an essential translation responds to the manner in which a language speaks in that *Geschick* of being" (PR 97)—we can conclude that if what a language speaks is always the language of Being, then what is spoken in this language is a monophonic monologue. From a wider perspective, "the well-known theses of Heideggerian philosophy—the preeminence of Being over beings, of ontology over metaphysics—end up affirming a tradition in which the same dominates the other" (Levinas 1979, 53). Yet *Sein* can be part of a polyphonic conversation if one regards its normative character as metaphorical—that is to say, the normative character of Being is a metaphor and not a norm in itself. As a metaphor, it pertains to a worldview that can be compared to others.

Nevertheless, the purpose is not to find equivalences or differences but to see how convergences and divergences can stimulate each other, fostering other metaphors toward other meanings. Consequently, a philosophical comparison translates concepts as metaphors—being translation itself regarded in its metaphorical function. This means that, if in linguistic activities one uses and produces worldviews, which in turn are based on constellations of metaphors, then the comparisons involved in this discourse are translations of metaphors that refer to worldviews. Thus, the encounter with the other becomes a metaphorical and translational activity that pushes the limits of the comprehension of one's relation with oneself and the world.

I have already mentioned the relation between the word "translation" and *metaphor*. The movement implied in these terms is not only the movement of meanings but also one's own movement: one is always and constantly in movement, in translation, insofar as the very idea of self is metaphorical. It is time now to clarify more precisely this concept of metaphor and proceed finally toward the encounter with the *Daodejing* and the *Zhuangzi*.

3.2 Nietzsche on Truth and Metaphor

Contrary to the Heideggerian belief, the metaphysical tradition forgot not Being as such but the metaphorical formulation of its truth. According to Nietzsche (2000, 56), truths are metaphors that after long usage became fixed and binding: "Truths are illusions which we have forgotten are illusions;

they are metaphors that have become worn out and have been drained of sensuous force." Nietzsche, on the one hand, openly attacks the concept of truth and, on the other hand, implicitly defines metaphor as an illusion—which, in his terms, equals interpretation.

This is not by any means a negative evaluation of metaphor. On the contrary, the problem resides in truths and not in metaphors. Truths are just weak metaphors that have lost their original interpretative power. When the primary function of a metaphor fades away, the literal sense becomes preeminent and the original creative interpretation becomes the normative truth. Thus, Nietzsche also performs a reversal of the classical relation between concept and metaphor.[10]

3.2.1 The Relations between Concepts and Metaphors

Contrary to the Aristotelian tradition in which metaphor is referred to concept, Nietzsche overturns the relation of the two terms. While for Aristotle metaphor carries the concept from a "proper" place to a figurative one, for Nietzsche there is no "proper" place for concepts because they are always metaphorical. In Nietzsche's philosophy, metaphors are interpretations of the world insofar as the concept itself is metaphorical and is not given *a priori*.

We need to keep this in mind if we want to resist the fossilization of meanings resulting in normative truths. To avoid the crystallization of truths it is necessary to preserve and constantly renew the metaphorical nature of concepts—genealogically return to and revivify them. Blumenberg (2010, 5) holds that metaphors "have a history in a more radical sense than concepts, for the historical transformation of a metaphor brings to light the metakinetics of the historical horizons of meaning and ways of seeing within which concepts undergo their modifications." Considering the Nietzschean idea of truths as "movable host of metaphors," it becomes clear that his genealogical process is precisely a tracing back of these metaphors as historical horizons—that is to say, as worldviews.

Nietzsche suggests that one can avoid the infiltration of the literal and "proper" meaning into metaphors by acknowledging that there is no "essence" that grounds the world and things in themselves: "we believe that we know something about the things themselves when we speak of trees, colours, snow, and flowers; and yet we possess nothing but metaphors for things—metaphors which correspond in no way to the original entities" (Nietzsche 2000, 83). Sarah Kofman (1993, 82) explains that the proper "is such only because it is the fruit of a unique perspective . . . in the sense of an appropriation of the world by a specific will." As a consequence, the question of essence "is itself already an imposition of meaning, an interpretation" (84). Still, this "proper" pushes many to consider metaphor a metaphysical concept. The argument is that the transposition of metaphor from the proper to the figurative is the same transposition that in metaphysics turns the sensible into intelligible.

3.2.2 Does the Metaphorical Exist Only within Metaphysics?

This is the vision proposed by Heidegger in *The Principle of Reason* (1991a, 48): "The idea of 'transposing' [*übertragen*] and of metaphor is based upon the distinguishing, if not complete separation, of the sensible and the nonsensible as two realms that subsist on their own. The setting up of this partition between the sensible and nonsensible, between the physical and nonphysical is a basic trait of what is called metaphysics and which normatively determines Western thinking." Thus, Heidegger can affirm that "the metaphorical exists only within metaphysics."

In order to evaluate this position, it is of absolute importance to verify if the "meta" of the metaphor has the same function as the one of metaphysics. That is to say: should one consider the movement of the metaphor in Nietzschean terms as interpretation of the world that does not divide the proper from the figurative, the sensible from the nonsensible, or in Heideggerian terms, where this separation is necessary? In other words: is the "meta" of the metaphor a transposition—as for translation—or is it a going beyond—as for transcendence?

In Nietzschean terms, the metaphor is employed as a translation that does not refer to an original or proper text—the "original" being already a metaphor. With his idea of metaphor, Nietzsche wants to escape the restrictions of metaphysics and its drive to go beyond, to transcend. Still, if a metaphor is an interpretation and if the metaphysical vision of the world is itself metaphorical, the "meta" of metaphor can assume both an immanent and a transcendent connotation.

This means that the function of a metaphor depends on the vision of the world established by the metaphor itself. This is not a mere vicious circle as long as one is able to see how the metaphor positions itself in relation to the circle. The issue is to see if the metaphor is inside or outside the circle—that is to say, if it purposely depends on itself or if it posits its "reason" over and beyond itself.

3.2.3 The Circularity of Knowledge

As we have seen, contrary to the metaphysical tradition in which metaphor is a derivative concept, in Nietzsche the concept is a metaphor. When the priority of the concept is posited, the natural consequence is that the metaphysical dualisms of proper and figurative, sensible and nonsensible arise. This duality avoids the circularity of interpretation that always returns on itself as another interpretation *ad infinitum*.[11] In positing something outside the interpretation as *the proper* that can be the guarantor of its existence, the concept escapes an infinite regression. Therefore, for Nietzsche—who embraces the circularity of interpretations—the concept is necessarily a metaphor. Conversely, for the metaphysical thinking—that considers itself as producing representations of a proper reality—the metaphor is a concept that shifts from its literal meaning.

Derrida (1982a, 219) argues that, in defining metaphor, one needs the concept of metaphor, and if the concept is metaphorical, then the metaphor returns on itself as a metaphor of metaphor. Ricoeur (1978, 287) comments that, for Derrida, the "theory of metaphor returns in a circular manner to the metaphor of theory," implying that there can be "no principle for delimiting metaphor, no definition in which the defining does not contain the defined."[12] Yet this is not just the problem of metaphor. This is the problem of knowledge in general.

As soon as the proper meaning that gives authority to its representation vanishes, the knowledge that depends on this separation loses its ground, collapsing necessarily on itself. Therefore, if knowledge does not have a proper reality or a literal meaning to which it can refer, it cannot find a ground outside itself and becomes circular. A theory of knowledge that is not grounded from the outside needs to establish how a theory can be formulated without having a previous knowledge, which is impossible. Hence, the circularity is not a specific problem of the metaphoric but of the thinking process *per se*.

Nietzsche uses the metaphoricity of concepts to show that all the theoretical formulations are circular. Only the *belief* in the separation between the giver and the receiver of knowledge can stop this circle, which implies that only a metaphysical explanation of knowledge can be linear and not circular. The impossibility of stopping the infinite regression of metaphoricity makes a metaphor not metaphysical. Therefore, the circular "meta" of metaphor is radically different from the transcendent "meta" of metaphysics:

the former is a centripetal movement that returns on itself *ad infinitum*; the latter is a centrifugal movement that tries to escape the circle and to be saved from it by an external authority.

According to Nietzsche, there is no salvation; truths are worn out metaphors and all knowledge is metaphorical. This, however, does not mean that Nietzsche has a humanistic perspective. The metaphor does not ask for a grounding justification either outside or inside its circularity. The metaphor simply dispels reason—reason being its product and not a reality in itself—avoiding thus the formation of another dichotomy, namely, the subject/object dichotomy.

In *Twilight of the Idols* (1998, "Reason in Philosophy" 5), Nietzsche is clearly against reason as *subiectum*, which "believes in the I, in the I as Being, in the I as substance, and *projects* the belief in the I-substance onto all things—only then does it *create* the concept 'thing.'" In this sense, the so-called Nietzschean perspectivism is not humanistic.

Therefore, metaphor is not grounded in and does not ground the subject—the latter being just another interpretation that reflects a "proper object" only metaphorically. The metaphorical process does not ask for and does not want to ground reason because its function is the displacement of grounds. Contrary to the "meta" of metaphysics, which requires a ground that is never present, the "meta" of metaphor is the constant displacement of the possibility for a grounding reason.

It is not possible to ground the metaphor in a metaphorical theory and it is equally impossible to ground an interpretational one. The circularity is present in both cases. What is more, the metaphor cannot be regarded as a meta-metaphor: its circularity does not end up being metatheoretical and all-inclusive. Rather, this circularity exposes itself and shows its limit, undermining every possible all-inclusivity that tries to restore the univocal truth of an all-encompassing explanation. And yet, even the all-inclusive interpretations have their rights to be themselves, provided that their metaphorical nature is not forgotten. Regardless of its content, a metaphor is so insofar as it is not taken literally.

The circularity of the metaphor shows its nonliteral and not transcendent nature: "Metaphysics has often revealed itself to us to be metaphorics taken literally; the demise of metaphysics calls metaphorics back to its place" (Blumenberg 2010, 132).[13] Thus, it is possible to reverse the Heideggerian position, stating that metaphysics exists only within the metaphorical: "it is not metaphor that carries the structure of Platonic metaphysics; metaphysics instead seizes the metaphorical process in order to make it work to the benefit of metaphysics" (Ricoeur 1978, 294).

As long as one can recall its origin, the idea of absolute—as well as *Sein*, God, *subiectum*, etc.—can be appreciated as what it is, a fascinating metaphor. Therefore, the metaphysical reasoning is just one of the possibilities of the metaphorical process, the one that tries to retreat from its circular nature.[14]

Nonetheless, one important problem emerges from the previous discourse. If there is no proper meaning and if metaphor is circular, how can one define values?

3.2.4 Inside and Outside the Metaphorical Circle

To fully appreciate the role played by Nietzsche in challenging the idea of truth with the one of metaphor, it is necessary to consider his philosophy of value. According to Gilles Deleuze (1983, 1), "Nietzsche's most general project is the introduction of the concepts of sense and value into philosophy." It is with the idea of God's death that Nietzsche introduced, *de facto*, the problem of value into philosophy. If the *primum movens* of value is no more, it is necessary to find new values to make sense of the world. At the same time, without a *superior reason* it becomes possible to evaluate values from a different standpoint. With the death of God, it is possible to confront and evaluate what was a given value, a dogma, an axiom.

According to Nietzsche, this has become not only possible, but necessary. In *On the Genealogy of Morality* (2007a, "Preface" 6) he states that "we need a *critique* of moral values, *the value of these values should itself, for once, be examined.*" Deleuze (1983, 1) comments that "the problem of critique is that of the value of values, of the evaluation from which their value arises, thus the problem of their *creation*." In Deleuze's words, the problem of circularity is presented very clearly. Still, how is it possible to evaluate values? What is the value used to evaluate these values?

Before attempting to answer these questions, it is worth noting that, while Nietzsche wants to revaluate values, this does not mean that he seeks a complete destruction of values and their origins for the sake of devastation. He attacks these values and their origins not to leave ruins behind himself but to illuminate them, to understand them, and to change them. This is evident if one considers his position in *On the Genealogy of Morality* (III 9).

The main point there is to avoid the castration of the intellect with concepts such as "pure reason," "absolute spirituality," and "knowledge as such." Far from a blind *vis denstruens*, Nietzsche tries to *see* problems without covering them with an omni-comprehensive absolutism that restricts the possibilities of the intellect. To affirm the plurality of visions, Nietzsche deploys the concept of multiple interpretations. More precisely, he affirms that vision can only be perspectival; hence, there is only "perspectival knowing." This, however, does not result in a static relativism where every interpretation is equal to another. Rather, Nietzsche contrasts the imposition of a single interpretation by employing a confrontation of "interpretative powers." For him "the *more* eyes, various eyes we are able to use for the same thing, the more complete will be our 'concept' of the thing."

Nietzsche wants the multiplicity of visions, the richness of values, not the static object in itself. In aphorism 556 of *The Will to Power* (1967; hereafter WP), Nietzsche expressly affirms: "A 'thing-in-itself' just as perverse as a 'sense-in-itself,' a 'meaning-in-itself.' There are no 'facts-in-themselves,' for a sense must always be projected into them before there can be 'facts.' The question 'what is that?' is an imposition of meaning from some other viewpoint. 'Essence,' the 'essential nature,' is something perspective and already presupposes a multiplicity. At the bottom of it there always lies 'what is that for *me*?' (for us, for all that lives, etc.)." It is important to underline the last part of this passage. Nietzsche does not stop at the question "what is that for *me*?"—which implies the question of what that is for each human being—but continues saying "for us, for all that lives, etc." This means that he contemplates perspectivism not only from the point of view of the self but also from the point of view of the community and of all living things. Nietzsche considers perspectivism from all possible perspectives, even non-human ones. In this sense Nietzsche wants the confrontation of "interpretative powers" instead of a castrated intellect.

To understand the value of these interpretative powers and concepts such as "pure reason," "absolute spirituality," and "knowledge as such," Nietzsche resorts to genealogy. This becomes evident when he addresses the problem of Kantian categories in *Beyond Good and Evil* (2002, 11; hereafter BGE). Here Nietzsche refers to the general issue of the *Critique of Pure Reason* (B19), where Kant states, "The real problem of pure reason is *now* contained in the question: How are synthetic judgments *a priori* possible?"

Nietzsche sees that, in justifying synthetic *a priori* judgments, Kant falls into a vicious circle: "How are synthetic judgments *a priori possible?* Kant asked himself,—and what really was his answer? *By virtue of a faculty,* which is to say: *enabled by an ability*" (BGE 11). The problem, therefore, becomes: is it possible to avoid this collapse into a vicious circle? Or, to say it differently: when people theorize on intellectual abilities, do they not always need to employ intellectual faculties? And also the other way around: do they not always employ intellectual abilities to build the tools to analyze their intellectual faculties? According to Nietzsche, the time has come to reformulate the basic question "How are synthetic judgments *a priori* possible?" with the question "Why is the belief in such judgments *necessary*?" In doing so, he tries to shift the attention from the *validation* of intellectual processes to the *value* of these processes.

Nietzsche is not interested in undermining the Kantian explanation of synthetic *a priori* judgments for its circularity. He is more interested in understanding why, despite this circularity, one needs to believe in these judgments. Nietzsche does not avoid the obstacle of circularity but goes directly to its center, striving to see the problem from a closer standpoint. He tries, on the one hand, to look at the production of values and, on the other hand, to understand the value of these productions. This is the task of the genealogist philosopher.

In fragment 516 of *The Will to Power*, Nietzsche asks whether "the axioms of logic" are adequate to reality or they are "a means and measure for us to *create* reality, the concept 'reality,' for ourselves." This is a genealogical question. Nietzsche's reply is that, in the axioms of logic, there is "no *criterion of truth*, but an *imperative* concerning that which *should* count as true." This statement, however, is not an end but a means to achieve something else—inasmuch as, in general, genealogy is not an end in its critique but a means for a transvaluation of values. Nietzsche affirms that "if we do not grasp this, but make of logic a criterion of true being, we are on the way to positing as realities all those hypostases: substance, attribute, object, subject, action, etc.; that is, to conceiving a metaphysical world, that is, a 'real world.'"

For Nietzsche, the problem is not the circular interpretation per se but the *value* one gives to its circularity. By forgetting that everything is interpretation, one confuses what should count as truth—within the circle—with the metaphysical truth—outside the circle. This means that one confuses the interpretation of logic with *the* logic; the interpretation of truth with *the* truth; the metaphorical with the literal. Consequently, an interpretation that makes the world understandable becomes the metaphysical world, the *true* world.

For all these reasons, one should refrain from understanding the Nietzschean philosophy with absolute metaphysical categories. His philosophy must not be taken literally. Nietzsche himself expresses this with the clearest words in *Beyond Good and Evil* (22). In replying to the objection of opposing an interpretation with another one, he asserts, "Granted, this is only an interpretation too—and you will be eager enough to make this objection?—well then, so much the better." Nietzsche is fully aware of the nature of his interpretation; he does not reject the objection that his interpretation is as valid as that of anyone else—rather, he welcomes any objection of this sort. But why does he reply "so much the better"? Why does he seem to be so eager to receive this objection? There are at least two answers.

A basic answer is that if someone recognizes that Nietzsche's interpretation is only another interpretation, one will necessarily acknowledge that any other understanding of the world is an interpretation. This is the first step of Nietzsche's transvaluation of values: no longer a domination of a singular understanding but a confrontation of "interpretative powers."

The second, much more important answer—and at the same time, second step of transvaluation of values—is that, in being interpretative, the Nietzschean metaphor is not only consistent with but also necessary for the interpretation that it proposes. Nietzsche's philosophy does not exist outside this metaphorical process and outside his circle.

And yet, this metaphorical process does not become a metatheory, a normative meta-metaphor; it only opens itself to the confrontation with other metaphors showing that values are such only in relation to their reference systems. Consequently, even to say that "everything is subjective" is interpretation: " 'The subject' is not something given, it is something added and invented and projected behind what there is" (WP 481). Nietzsche openly asks if it is "necessary to posit an interpreter behind the interpretation," thus questioning his same metaphor. His reply is simultaneously a self-affirmation as interpretation and a self-negation as absolutization. Indeed, even the metaphor of "an interpreter behind the interpretation" is just "invention, hypothesis." According to Nietzsche "In so far as the word 'knowledge' has any meaning, the world is knowable; but it is *interpretable* otherwise, it has no meaning behind it, but countless meanings.—'Perspectivism' " (WP 481).

It is now possible to conclude with the words of *Beyond Good and Evil* (36) that "the world seen from inside, the world determined and described with respect to its 'intelligible character'—would be just this 'will to power' and nothing else." This is the scope of the transvaluation of all values: the world seen, described, and determined from inside—that is to say, from inside its metaphors, from inside its metaphorical circles, from inside its wills to power.

Through this process, the transvaluation does not try to substitute old values with new ones but introduces a new modality to see, describe, and determine values. The will to power that determines itself as world—an interpretation affirmed inside the interpretative world—is the circle that posits its values inside itself in opposition to the circles that posit the values outside themselves. This is the Nietzschean transvaluation of values.

Contrary to the Heideggerian opinion, Nietzsche is not the last of the metaphysicians, not because there are others after him or because he is the first of the postmodernists. In Nietzsche, there is no need to overcome metaphysics because it has been neutralized. Internalized and incorporated in the metaphorical circle, metaphysics becomes one of the many ways of understanding.

"The eternal joy of becoming" expressed in *Twilight of the Idols* ("What I owe the ancients" 5) is the transvaluation of all values where nothing is suppressed and everything has legitimate existence in the confrontation of "interpretative powers." A confrontation that does not make all the interpretative powers the same but gives them the same dignity of affirmation or negation. The world as will to power is a metaphor that proceeds toward other metaphors. Hence the possibility to see how values function in relation to their systems of references posited by the values themselves inside the metaphorical circle.

From this standpoint, it is finally possible to enter in dialogue with the *Laozi* and the *Zhuangzi* with a more open and comprehensive set of possibilities. This does not entail that one has freed oneself from fore-structures or pre-assumptions. Quite the reverse. This perspective gives the precise measure of how, inside the metaphorical circle, interpretational values mirror systems of references and vice versa. Thus, in analyzing concepts, one uses pre-assumptions to see how these refer to and constitute reference systems. I started by saying that, in the linguistic process, one always uses and produces worldviews. I hope it is clearer now how these worldviews are used and produced through metaphors. Nonetheless, one last question needs to be asked: is it possible to evaluate the value of the world as will to power?

3.3 The Ethical Implications of Nietzsche's Metaphors

One of the most common objections made to Nietzsche is that the world conceived as will to power is a metaphysical concept. I discussed how the idea of metaphor itself can be considered metaphysical. This is a legitimate position if one seizes the problem of metaphor from a Platonic position. It is less acceptable if one considers it from a Nietzschean one. The same can be said for the concept of will to power as world but also for other concepts outside the Western tradition—in this context, the reference is to *dao*, the myriad things (*wanwu* 萬物), the transformation of things (*wuhua* 物化), etc.

I mentioned that Heidegger and Ricoeur have contrasting positions in relation to metaphor. Heidegger sees the problem from a Platonic perspective, which implies a radical transfer from the proper to the figurative, from the sensible to the intelligible. This is precisely a metaphysical conception: it interprets metaphor with metaphysical categories as Ricoeur has explained. If one accepts Heidegger's formulation, every concept can be regarded as metaphysical. Should we consider, therefore, any discourse on time, emotions, dreams, etc. metaphysical?

Heidegger (1991a, 48) is right when he says that the setting up of the separation between the sensible and nonsensible is "a basic trait of what is called metaphysics and which normatively determines Western thinking." However, one also needs to consider the scope of this separation: if it affirms a realm of truth from which one believes to grasp the essence of reality, then this is surely a metaphysical endeavor. On the contrary, if someone, like Nietzsche—or Zhuangzi, as I will argue—affirms the impossibility of such an essence, the metaphysical stance is refused from the outset.

John Richardson (1996, 3) summarizes that "philosophies are (broadly) metaphysical, by being organized systematically around a (more narrowly) metaphysical core." According to him, this core "consists in an account of the 'essence' or 'being' of things, so that 'metaphysics' is equivalent to 'ontology.'" As a result, "metaphysics claims a (1) *systematic* (2) *truth* (3) about *essence*." If one accepts this definition, then metaphor cannot be conceived as metaphysical, especially in Nietzschean terms. For Nietzsche metaphor is the opposite of a systematic truth about essence. Truths are only illusions which one has forgotten are illusions.

Still, how should we take Nietzsche's affirmations about the world and about becoming? Does Nietzsche not define what the world as will to power *is*? Is becoming not the essence of this world? In many places Nietzsche refuses this idea. I mentioned how, in fragment 556 of *The Will to Power*, he opposes both ideas of thing-in-itself and essence. For Nietzsche there is no ultimate metaphysical essence because there is no ontological category that can ground it. And this has important ethical implications.

3.3.1 The Metaphor of the World as Will to Power

According to Alexander Nehamas (1985, 80), the will to power is not metaphysical because "it provides a reason why no general theory of the character of the world and the things that constitute it can ever be given."[15]

This is true not only because a thing-in-itself is just an interpretation among others, but also because the will to power has an effect on and is affected by all the other quanta of power. This relational process allows things to be what they are: neither objects present-at-hand for a subject nor things in themselves.

Nietzsche is particularly clear on this when he states that "the properties of a thing are effects on other 'things': if one removes other 'things,' then a thing has no properties, i.e., there is no thing without other things, i.e., there is no 'thing-in-itself'" (WP 557). Let us keep these important considerations in mind while I proceed to the text where Nietzsche gives the best definition of these relations in the world as will to power.

Fragment 1067 of *The Will to Power* opens thus: "And do you know what 'the world' is to me? Shall I show it to you in my mirror?" In this mirror the world is a "monster of energy" that constantly transforms itself, although not as a monolithic essence but as "a play of forces and waves of forces, at the same time one and many." Continuing with the metaphors of sea, waves, and ebbs, Nietzsche describes this world as "eternally changing, eternally flooding back" in a way that entails both space and time: a movement that produces "tremendous years of recurrence," a recurrence that is obviously an eternal recurrence. The relation of forces, therefore, is not just a relation in space but also a relation in time.

Then Nietzsche changes tone and introduces a different note to describe this cyclical relation, which goes "out of the play of contradictions back to the joy of concord." It is crucial to consider this movement as playful and, even more importantly, as joyful. The central figure of the passage is Dionysus, which defines the world as eternally self-creating and self-destroying. This Dionysian world describes the world as will to power, a world that is "beyond good and evil," "without goal" and "without will." And yet, how can the world as will to power be without will? The reason is that, faithful to his cyclical logic, Nietzsche can only conceive of a will that wills itself.

It is not by chance that Nietzsche introduces this aphorism with the metaphor of the mirror: he is showing this world to us (the readers) in *his* mirror. The question is: who or what is reflected in this mirror? Nietzsche was certainly able to see this world in his mirror, otherwise he would not have shown it. Are we also able to see it? Are we capable of seeing Dionysus in that mirror? Is it possible to see the reflection of a will that wills itself there?

Nietzsche wants us to see this world that is a continuous flux of waves of energy, eternally changing and eternally returning on itself. He wants us to see in his mirror this world as will to power because we ourselves are this will to power and nothing besides. There are at least two possible readings for this conclusion. One is the metaphysical understanding of Heidegger that sees here an affirmation of the essence of the world as will to power. The other sees it not as a problem of essence but as a problem of value. I am more inclined toward the latter.

Nietzsche does not affirm any metaphysical essence for the world. Rather, Nietzsche describes a world as void of essence, a world that can absorb all the possibilities of change. There is no univocal direction for this world that has no goal and no will because the directions can be many. It is not possible to define the world univocally because it is in constant transformation and, therefore, it is constantly undetermined. More precisely, the world is constantly determined by its single components and, simultaneously, undetermined in its entirety. Each force, each perspective determines a world from its own interpretation, but the world has no goal. For this reason, the world as will to power is eternally self-creating and eternally self-destroying. Here lies the most interesting aspect of Nietzsche's ethical perspective.

In this process of self-creation and self-destruction, everything is part of this self-transformation. Even more importantly, for Nietzsche there is no ontological difference in this world: everything has the value of affirming itself beyond good and evil. Heidegger could not accept that the Nietzschean idea of the world as will to power is an ethical interpretation and not an ontological one, with the consequence of misinterpreting Nietzsche's understanding of becoming as the fundamental essence of reality, i.e., as Being. Yet, in Nietzsche, there is no ontological difference, no separation between ontical and ontological, because there is no Being that unconceals itself in beings. This Being remains unthought in Nietzsche because he tries to get rid of metaphysical thinking. Nietzsche is more concerned with the value of what becomes than with the essence of Being.

But what is the revaluation that Nietzsche is attempting with the world as will to power? Why does he show this world in a mirror? What can this view offer more than others? What is its value? Nietzsche gives a simple reply that can be puzzling at first glance: his is an "anti-metaphysical view of the world—yes, but an artistic one" (WP 1048). In order to understand the value of the world as will to power, it is crucial to define the value of art and how it relates to becoming.

3.3.2 Art as Child's Play

Before trying to understand what this artistic view of the world entails for Nietzsche, I need to consider the important fragment 617 of *The Will to Power* and the related problem of the Being/becoming dichotomy: "To impose [*aufzuprägen*] upon becoming the character of being—that is the supreme will to power" (WP 617). Two points are essential here.

The first one is that Being needs to be imposed upon the becoming as a specific will—the utmost will. As the construction of a dam that is meant to contain the constant flowing river, Being is a construction upon the fluid process of events. An impossible task that Nietzsche clearly criticizes: "Twofold falsification, on the part of the senses and of the spirit, to preserve a world of that which is, which abides, which is equivalent, etc." (WP 617)

The second point is that this same construction is a process. Nietzsche does not define how things ought to be. Rather, he critically describes the relation between will to power and becoming. This supreme will to power is just another element inscribed in becoming. The supreme will to power is the supreme illusion to crystallize becoming.

It is not surprising that Nietzsche continues the aphorism, affirming, "That *everything recurs* is the closest *approximation [Annäherung] of a world of becoming to a world of being*:—high point of the meditation" (WP 617). It is well known how important the idea of eternal recurrence is for Nietzsche. This means that he is not only critical toward himself but also extremely lucid. If the affirmation of the supreme will to power is an imposition on becoming—an imposition of Being on becoming—then the eternal recurrence—as Nietzsche's interpretation of time—is also an imposition, which results in the "closest *approximation of a world of becoming to a world of being.*" One can infer that the supreme will to power expressed by Nietzsche through the eternal recurrence of the same is this approximation; that is to say: the eternal recurrence is an expression of the will to power. Should one, therefore, consider this recurrence as another falsification?

Nietzsche is aware that every interpretation results in a crystallization and that every definition of the world is a metaphor that can become a truth. For him, "knowledge-in-itself in a world of becoming is impossible." Knowledge is only possible as "error concerning oneself, as will to power, as will to deception" (WP 617). The will to power is, therefore, the process that not only creates metaphors but also crystallizes them in stable truths.

Nietzsche, on the one hand, defines this twofold process inscribed in interpretations by means of the supreme will to power and, on the other hand, proposes his own interpretation by means of the eternal recurrence of the same. And yet, Nietzsche is constantly against the idea of Being, and the concept of eternal recurrence itself is described as becoming. In *Ecce Homo* (2007b, III "BT" 3) he is explicit on this: "The affirmation of passing away *and destruction* that is crucial for a Dionysian philosophy, saying yes to opposition and war, *becoming* along with a radical rejection of the very concept of 'being.' . . . The doctrine of the 'eternal return,' which is to say the unconditional and infinitely repeated cycle of all things."[16] For Nietzsche, the imposition of the character of Being upon becoming can result only in an *approximation*—even if the closest—of a world of becoming to a world of Being. Just an approximation, because Nietzsche is conscious that this is not an ontological affirmation but a metaphor with ethical implications. "Becoming does not aim at a *final state*, does not flow into 'being' " (WP 708).

Becoming is in opposition not only to Being but also to some aspects of the will to power. Becoming corrodes any attempt to the crystallization imposed by the will to power. Becoming suggests an ethical attitude, an *ethos* toward "invention, willing, self-denial, overcoming of oneself: no subject but an action, a positing, creative, no 'causes and effects' " (WP 617).

It is clear that Nietzsche proposes different typologies of will to power. Some follow the *ethos* of becoming, others move under the influence of Being. The concept of art helps us to understand this plurality of wills to power. Nietzsche sees art in relation to becoming "as the will to overcome becoming, as 'eternalization,' but shortsighted, depending on the perspective: repeating in miniature, as it were, the tendency of the whole" (WP 617). Art, in other words, describes the general tendency of the struggle between the creation of an illusory stability and the eternal change of becoming.

In this sense Nietzsche's vision of the world as will to power and eternal return of the same is an artistic and anti-metaphysical view of the world. Art for Nietzsche does not surrender to the creation of stability. This stability, however, exposes itself as a creation of value and not as an ontological "fact." Conscious that it is impossible to eliminate the desire for stability, Nietzsche tries to destabilize this stability. He tries to remove from interpretations the comforting security of a metaphysical ground.

In *The Gay Science* (2001, 347), he argues that some people still need metaphysics as a foothold. This demand for a metaphysical support is "the instinct of weakness that, to be sure, does not create sundry religions, forms of metaphysics, and convictions but does—preserve them." The problem is not the productive proposition of metaphors, with its creations of religions or metaphysics, but their preservations or, to say it better, the stabilization of what was originally the active process of the will. The consequence of this preservation is *faith*—regardless of what is preserved as religion, metaphysics, politics, etc.

Nietzsche continues the passage, affirming that faith is the result of a lack of will. Consequently, "the less someone knows how to command, the more urgently does he desire someone who commands, who commands severely—a god, prince, the social order, doctor, father confessor, dogma, or party conscience." This clinging nature of faith on truths implies that the original imposition of will as metaphor becomes the stable principle to ground the meaning of the world.

Nietzsche sees this desire of faith as a fossilization of a specific kind of will, a "will to truth" which is "a making firm, a making true and durable" (WP 552). Truth, however, is "something that must be created and that gives a name to a process, or rather to a will to overcome that has in itself no end." Nietzsche conceives of this truth as a "*processus in infinitum*, an active determining—not a becoming-conscious of something that is in itself firm and determined" (WP 552). This process is the will to power that imposes itself upon becoming. But this process has no end. Therefore, truth ought to be not an absolute determination but a constant revaluation that adapts to changing circumstances. The question is: how is it possible to imagine a command that does not want to stabilize its determination? Nietzsche seems to exclude this possibility when he affirms that stability is the "goal" of humanity: "Man projects his drive to truth, his 'goal' in a certain sense, outside himself as a world that has being, as a metaphysical world, as a 'thing-in-itself,' as a world already in existence. His needs as creator invent the world upon which he works, anticipate it; this anticipation (this 'belief' in truth) is his support" (WP 552). I have already analyzed the problem of positing the source of knowledge inside or outside the metaphorical circle. A similar pattern takes place here. On the one hand, there is the will to power that determines stabilities in a creative manner; on the other hand, by becoming truths, these stabilities support and ground a metaphysical world of things in themselves. The point is that, if this process can be acknowledged, then it is possible to see not only the activity of determining truths within their metaphorical circle as a creative process but also how this creative process is a production of a will that reacts to specific configurations of the world. In describing how the drive to truth tends to expel knowledge outside the metaphorical circle, Nietzsche shows that there is no external authority but only specific determinations of will to truth.

Nietzsche elucidates this double movement in *On the Genealogy of Morality* (2007a, II 12), stating, "everything that occurs in the organic world consists of *overpowering, dominating*, and in their turn, overpowering and dominating consist of re-interpretation, adjustment." This perspective enables seeing the *belief* in truth as a missed opportunity to produce new metaphors. Only by acknowledging this creative process of metaphors can one constantly revaluate truths, which implies that one can keep the metaphorical production alive. Yet, even if one acknowledges this process, how can this will to truth be overcome and how can truth be constantly revaluated?

The reply is to be found in art and, in particular, in art as child's play or, to say it differently, in art as the non-coercive exercise of will. This art can be regarded as a production of a different will to power, a will that overcomes the will to truth and affirms the will to creation. Nietzsche develops this thought in aphorism 585 of the *Will to Power*, which introduces itself as "Tremendous self-examination: becoming conscious of oneself, not as individuals but as mankind." The passage defines the will to truth as "*the impotence of the will to create.*" Nietzsche calls for a different will to power here. The "tremendous self-examination" is the examination that enables becoming conscious of the will to truth. Through this examination one can see the limitation of the will to truth and how it obstructs the will to create. Art, therefore, is the product of this other will in opposition to will to truth. But this will to create is not the final state. The will to will is the next step.

In *The Gay Science* (367), Nietzsche gives an interesting description of self-determination as "a freedom of the will." In this passage, a new important element is introduced: the artistic event of dancing. Here dancing is not the recreational practice of everyday life but the process that allows one to take leave "of all faith and every wish for certainty." This implies a risk. The self-determination that happens in the artistic event of dancing is a process that is not scared of losing ground. This "free spirit" does not renounce itself and dances "even beside abysses." Art, then, cannot be regarded as a simple production of objects. Certainly, in Nietzsche's terms, art is not the financial game that it has become today.[17] Art production can be a dull repetition of objects that has the scope only of preserving the status quo. Therefore, art is neither the "artworld" nor the method of producing art objects. Art is an ethical perspective on the world.

This perspective is the one of the child as expressed in *Zarathustra* (2005, I "On the Three Transformations"): "Innocence the child is and forgetting, a beginning anew, a play, a self-propelling wheel, a first movement, a sacred Yea-saying. Yes, for the play of creating, my brothers, a sacred Yea-saying is needed: the spirit now wills its own will, the one who had lost the world attains its own world." The spirit that wants its will is a will to will that renounces the security of the stable Being in order to will becoming. The will to will is the will that turns on itself as supreme will to power, but this time it does not stop at the creation of a world outside itself: the yes is not toward a single creation but toward a creative becoming. Thus, the will to will creates its own will.

The supreme will to power that wants its will is a will that wants to constantly affirm its power. In this sense, this will to will abandons the secure references of the stable Being to affirm itself as becoming. The supreme will to power that turns on itself as will to will tautologically affirms the movement of its own will. Such a will cannot stop willing; it cannot stop turning on itself saying yes to itself. Thus, the will to will creates itself, constantly.

This idea of art as child's play is present in Nietzsche's thought since *Philosophy in the Tragic Age of the Greeks* (1962, 7) with a connection to Heraclitus's concept of fire. For Nietzsche, "as children and artists play, so plays the ever-living fire." Here, the creative process becomes the "ever self-renewing impulse to play" that produces new worlds. What's more important, however, is that there is no hubris in this process but only "innocent caprice." The child plays, constructing and destroying worlds only to start the play again. The meaning of the play does not reside in the world that comes to be or in the world that ceases to be. The meaning of the play is the play itself and its constant self-renewing impulse. According to Nietzsche, "Only aesthetic man can look thus at the world."

Nietzsche sees aesthetics not from the perspective of the art object but from that of the artist. The art of the child-artist is aimed at the world not as an object but as an action—that is, not as being but as becoming. The action of the child-artist needs to become, despite the danger of losing the world just conceived. To will one more time—no matter the risk of falling into the abyss of the eternal return—is the rejection of the belief in a stable world. Only through this active becoming, "the one who had lost the world attains its own world"—as *Zarathustra* says (2005, I "On the Three Transformations").

But this world is not the subjective and stable world of Being. The world of the child is forgetting of stability, is a play of precarious equilibrium that constantly reshapes its configurations and reference systems. Thus, the aesthetic process does not produce the *recreational* stability but affirms the revaluation of values in which the outcome is not a new value but the process of revaluation itself. In other words, the will that wants its own will creates itself not as truth but as an ever self-renewing re-evaluative value.

Nietzsche was aware that it would not have been easy for people to look at this world in his mirror: not just because the *mise en abyme* that this reflection implies threatens to devour the observer, but also because, paradoxically, in the constant becoming, the subtraction of reference points has a paralyzing effect. Although Nietzsche constantly moves toward the terrible perspective of constant becoming, for him this is not enough. He needs to add one more weight to this paralyzing thought; he needs the eternal recurrence of the same as the "heaviest weight" expressed in *The Gay Science* (341). In a world where the meaning has been completely erased and the value is only a re-evaluative value, the eternal recurrence is the ultimate test that a will needs to prove to itself.

3.3.3 *Amor Fati*

It takes already astonishing strength to say yes and to dance in a world that constantly comes-to-be but never is. Nietzsche does not stop there and asks to say yes to the eternal recurrence of the same, which is, simultaneously, a damnation and a redemption. It is a damnation because no meaning will be gained at the end of the circle, and because nothing will stop this circle from its meaningless recurrence—bringing over and over the instability of becoming (WP 55). It is a redemption because, to say yes to this recurrence means to will backward, for Zarathustra (2005, II "On Redemption") affirms, "To redeem that which has passed away and to re-create all 'It was' into a 'Thus I willed it!'—that alone should I call redemption!" To say yes to the eternal recurrence means to say yes to past and, equally, to future: "All 'It was' is a fragment, a riddle, a cruel coincidence—until the creating will says to it: 'But thus I willed it!' '—Until the creating will says to it: 'But thus do I will it! Thus shall I will it!' "[18]

    In the cyclical repetition of the world, the will that affirms itself does so in the moment which has, simultaneously, already happened infinite times in the past and will happen infinite times in the future. In the cyclical recurrence, the past is the future and vice versa. However, how is it possible that Nietzsche conceives the eternal return as becoming? Are these concepts not in total opposition? How can one say yes to both becoming and eternal recurrence? Moreover, why does Nietzsche affirm in *Ecce Homo* (2007b, III "BT" 3) that Zarathustra's doctrine "is nothing Heraclitus couldn't have said too"? The point is that one should conceive of the doctrines of Zarathustra and Heraclitus not as opposite but as complementary. The hint is in Nietzsche's metaphor *amor fati*: "My formula for human greatness is *amor fati*: that you do not want anything to be different, not forwards, not backwards, not for all eternity. Not just to tolerate necessity, still less to conceal it—all idealism is hypocrisy towards necessity—, but to *love* it" (2007b, II, 10). The strategy that Nietzsche puts in place with *amor fati* is particularly fascinating. In a world that does not have any authority outside the metaphorical circle, fate cannot be known. There is no oracle that can predict one's fate. This means that in loving fate one loves the unpredictable. And yet, unpredictable events are deemed to be resolved not only for one time but for infinite times. Thus, *amor fati* puts one in front of a double challenge: to love the unpredictable and, at the same time, to want these unpredictable events eternally recurrent.

With *amor fati* Nietzsche closes the circle of his ethical and aesthetic vision of the world. A vision that puts together two opposite conceptions: the unpredictable constant becoming and an infinite recurrence of the same in the past and in the future. This is a precise strategy to conceive a world in its manifold possible configurations. *Amor fati* is the love for all these possibilities or, even better, it is the aesthetic *ethos* that affirms all the possible configurations of life.

With *amor fati*, Nietzsche clearly admits the limits of interpretation. After all, even if the supreme will to power wills itself as a constant self-renewing re-evaluative value, this process is just a void self-referential affirmation when detached from the context in which it takes shape. *Amor fati* establishes the drive for the aesthetic *ethos*: not just the blind dominance of the will over the other and over itself but the aesthetic dance that welcomes possibilities and dances with them. The will that wills itself as a constant self-renewing re-evaluative value does so dancing with its fate. And there is no other way to dance with fate than to do it spontaneously—in the sense of *ziran* 自然. Still, Nietzsche did not arrive at conceiving this. It is now time to interpret the *Daodejing* and the *Zhuangzi* and see what they can offer to the conversation on the aesthetic *ethos*.

4

From Ethics to *Ziran* 自然

4.1 Constant Change

In the previous chapter, we saw how Nietzsche overturns the relation between metaphors and concepts. While for the Aristotelian tradition of thought metaphor carries the concept from a "proper" place to a figurative one, for Nietzsche there is no proper place for concepts because they are always metaphorical. Thus, it is possible to reverse the Heideggerian idea that the metaphorical exists only within metaphysics to make the idea that metaphysics exists only within the metaphorical.

Through the analysis of Nietzsche's position on truth and metaphor, I showed how if there is no proper meaning behind or beyond metaphors, then the value of a metaphor is not external to it but inscribed in the metaphor itself. This produces a problem of circularity. Still, this circularity does not only pertain to the metaphoric but to knowledge more generally. As a consequence, one should not confuse what counts as truth—*within the circle*—with the metaphysical truth—*outside the circle*. And this is relevant not only epistemologically but also ethically.

The metaphors that Nietzsche employs in his philosophy highlight the ethical implication of the metaphorical process: by explaining how the drive to truth tends to expel knowledge outside the metaphorical circle, Nietzsche shows that there is no external authority but only specific determinations of will to truth. I have considered, however, that for Nietzsche there are different forms of will and, in the final analysis, the idea of art as child's play affirms its will as becoming. This implies that the will that wants its own will creates itself not as truth but as an ever self-renewing re-evaluative value.

After considering how the Nietzschean metaphors of will to power and eternal return converge into the one of *amor fati*, I suggested the possibility to imagine the aesthetic gesture of dancing with one's own fate as a spontaneous—in the sense of *ziran*—gesture. In this chapter and in the next, my intention is to analyze more attentively the concept of *ziran*, to unpack its ethical implications, and to see the relation between constant change and language in the *Lao-Zhuang*.

I will start my analysis by considering the function of language in the *Daodejing*. I anticipated this topic at the beginning of the previous chapter in relation to Heidegger's idea that language speaks, not humans. This is because, for Heidegger, without Being humans could never be "sayers"—those who say. I mentioned that Daoism has a more critical approach toward language, and this has important ethical repercussions. It is now time to see what this entails in relation to *ziran*.

4.1.1 Reconsidering Chapter 1 of the *Daodejing*

Let me go back to chapter 1 of the *Daodejing* and analyze it in more detail:

Dao ke dao, fei chang dao

道可道，非常道

I have already mentioned how the character *dao* 道 can function as both noun and verb. Regarding the meaning of the second *dao*, Dong Ping (2015, 44) explains that *dao* can be considered as both "to put into words" and "to lead." According to him, *dao* 道 is a cognate of *dao* 導 "to conduct," "lo lead," "to show the way." Therefore, in the *Daodejing* the second *dao* of the first line refers to what leads or what can be followed. Unfortunately, Dong proposes an inconsistent and metaphysical interpretation of this leading process inherent in *dao* that, according to him, proceeds toward the truth. This is contradictory because the second *dao* has a negative meaning insofar as it is negated by the second part of the sentence. Thus, if one were eager to follow Dong in the interpretation of *dao* as leading toward the truth, one would conclude that *this dao* is not the constant *dao* (*fei chang dao* 非常道).

A similar conclusion can be reached in relation to the character *ming* 名 in the second line.

Ming ke ming, fei chang ming

名可名，非常名

The second *ming* has a verbal function. Considering both lines together, they can be translated as

> A way that can be followed is not constant way-making.
> A name that can be named is not constant naming.

Another possible rendering could be the one offered by Chad Hansen (1992, 216), who considers *dao* as "guiding speech" and proposes this translation: "Speaking the speakable is not constant speaking because naming the nameable is not constant naming." Although it is questionable that, as he says, "the second line explains the first," with the consequent addition of a "because" that is not present in the Chinese text, Hansen offers an interesting interpretation.

His major insight is the emphasis put on the verbal function of the last *dao* as well as the last *ming* 名. Contrary to the common opinion that considers these two characters in their nominal function, Hansen interprets them as gerundives. We have seen how Ames and Hall made a similar choice for way-making and how this term needs to be understood in relation to the idea of "inventing"—in the sense of a constant *in-venire*. Therefore, these translations suggest that the last *dao* and the last *ming* need a constant activity.

If one regards the last *dao* and *ming* as gerundives, the function of *chang* 常 as "constant" becomes clearer. Indeed, *chang* and *dao* have a special relation: they define each other. On the one hand, *chang* can assume a metaphysical meaning if *dao* functions as Being or as the substance of the myriad things. I mentioned that some translators even consider *chang* as "Eternal." Yet this reflects the metaphysical interpretation of *dao*. On the other hand, if one considers *dao* not as a substance but as a process, then *chang* also loses the connotation of permanence and acquires the meaning of an ongoing activity.

Zhang Weiyi (2007, 24) explains that the use of *chang* in early Daoism reflects the turbulent political condition of the time (pre-Qin): because of the incessant modifications of the world, change (*bian* 變) becomes constant (*chang*). Wang Bo (1993, 203) deems this the most characteristic element of the *Daodejing*, in which "*chang* and *bian* are unified." According to Wang, because "Laozi considers the process of change constant," *dao*, as *chang dao* 常道, "possesses the character of change."

This is true not only for the *Daodejing* but also for the *Zhuangzi*, which goes one step further in considering *chang* the constant transformation (*hua* 化) of *ziran* (Zhang 2007, 24). Liu Xiaogan (1995, 70) sees the link between *chang* and *ziran* already present in the *Daodejing*. According to him, the condition of *chang* is the condition in which things naturally develop without having any external interference. This is coherent with the idea expressed in chapter 25 that everything follows *ziran*, as I shall discuss soon. Consequently, *chang* is more related to the constant process of what naturally develops by itself than to a static permanence. If one wants to retain the idea of permanence, this is the permanent transformation of *dao* and *ziran*.

Chang dao 常道 and *chang ming* 常名 are, therefore, respectively constant way-making and constant naming. This implies that one ought not to stop this process: the name that can be regarded as a determined name cannot be the process of constant naming. It is important to remember that this critical attitude toward language is not a rejection of it. Quite the opposite. Language—as well as *dao*—needs to be constantly performed. One needs to constantly renew language and renew the process of *dao* to avoid imposing on the world a single order of reference system.

Similarly to what we have seen with Nietzsche, it is fundamental not to forget that language has a metaphorical nature and does not define things in themselves. In its constant relation to the world, language should not determine stable truths because, once fixed, a truth cannot be constantly produced. If a name becomes a stable truth, this name stops being part of the constant naming process. Thus, *chang* helps defining *dao* and *ming* in their constant production and, simultaneously, the processes of way-making and naming help to understand *chang* as a permanent transformation. In these terms, it is clear how far *chang dao* can be from the onto-theological understanding of Being. *You* 有 and *wu* 無 need a similar consideration.

4.1.2 The Movement of *Dao* 道

At the beginning of this study, I discussed some aspects of Chinese grammar and the related issue of how *you* differs from the idea of Being. Now it is time to analyze the meaning of *you* and *wu* in the specific context of the *Daodejing*. In the next chapter, I will also consider the two terms in relation to important passages of the "Qiwulun" in the *Zhuangzi*. For the moment, the starting point is the second chapter of the *Daodejing*.

天下皆知美之為美，斯惡已。皆知善之為善，斯不善已。故有無相生，難易相成，長短相較，高下相傾，音聲相和，前後相隨。是以聖人處無為之事，行不言之教

> As soon as everyone in the world knows that the beautiful are beautiful,
> There is already ugliness.
> As soon as everyone knows the able,
> There is ineptness.
> Determinacy (*you*) and indeterminacy (*wu*) give rise to each other,
> Difficult and easy complement each other,
> Long and short set each other off,
> High and low complete each other,
> Refined notes and raw sounds harmonize (*he*) with each other,
> And before and after lend sequence to each other—
> This is really how it all works.
> It is for this reason that sages keep to service that does not entail coercion (*wuwei*)
> And disseminate teachings that go beyond what can be said.
> (Ames and Hall 2003)

The first consideration here is that *you* and *wu* are regarded in the same way as the other polarities—long–short, high–low, etc. This means that they generate, complement, and harmonize with each other. Here, Ames and Hall translate the two terms as determinacy (*you*) and indeterminacy (*wu*); in other passages, as determinate (*you*) and indeterminate (*wu*).

This choice gets rid of the Western metaphysical concepts of Being and Nonbeing, avoiding any transcendent implication. As seen, *you* refers to what is there and pertains to what is determinate; *wu* refers to what is not there and pertains to what is indeterminate.[1] Thus, what is determinate and what is indeterminate entail and engender each other. Chapter 40 needs to be seen in the same light.

反者道之動；弱者道之用。天下萬物生於有，有生於無。

> Returning (*fan* 反) is the movement of *dao*,
> Weakening is its function.
> The world's myriad things arise from the determinate (*you*),
> And the determinate arises from the indeterminate (*wu*).[2]

Many commentators interpret this passage as giving prominence to *wu*—or, at least, to its weakening aspect.³ Yet *you* and *wu* are mutually engendering. Moreover, the passage on *you* and *wu* is introduced by the important concept of "returning" or "reversing"—*fan* 返 in the Guodian version (A:19).⁴ This is the movement of *dao* and as such it does not allow any final ground to determine the myriad things. If it is true that the myriad things are concretized by *you* (which in turn is the determination of *wu*), the reverse is also true: the myriad things and *you* return to the indeterminate. In this sense, the movement of *dao* is returning and its function is weakening because everything constantly comes to be determinate and returns to be indeterminate in a perpetual cycle.

Although D. C. Lau (1989, xxii) is against this position, he explains that the movement of the *dao* as *fan* can be interpreted "as meaning that the *tao* causes all things to undergo a process of cyclic change. What is weak inevitably develops into something strong, but when this process of development reaches its limit, the opposite process of decline sets in and what is strong once again becomes something weak, and decline reaches its lowest limit only to give way once more to development. Thus there is an endless cycle of development and decline."⁵ Lau opposes this theory and affirms that one can choose to stay weak, thus avoiding the return of the strong. Yet, if only a deliberate decision enables one to stay weak, this indirectly confirms that the general tendency is a cyclical alternation between weak and strong. Consequently, through the constant decision of being weak one can contrast the tendency of returning strong. The problem, however, is to see how it can be possible to remain weak. I believe that the cyclical change itself is a significant strategy that helps to weaken the necessity of having stable reference systems.

Because one cannot live with the absolute absence of references, the process of constant naming becomes necessary. This implies the cyclical alternation of saying and weakening what has been said, which in turn opens the space for other saying. I shall consider how this becomes particularly relevant in the *Zhuangzi* and its concept of "letting both alternatives proceed" (5/2/40) (54).⁶ For now it is worth considering how what has hitherto discussed applies to chapter 42 of the *Daodejing*.

道生一，一生二，二生三，三生萬物。

Literally the passage means

Dao produces one,
One produces two,
Two produces three,
And three produces the myriad things (*wanwu* 萬物).

Generally, interpreters only consider the direction from *dao* to the myriad things, regarding *dao* as the source of the myriad things. Still, one needs to remember that the movement of *dao* is returning. Furthermore, "since the myriad things are constitutive of *dao*, we could run the process back the other way with equal effect" (Hall and Ames 1998, 245). Hall and Ames explain that "The natural cosmology of classical China does not entail a single-ordered cosmos, but invokes an understanding of a 'world' or *dao* constituted by a myriad of unique particulars, 'the ten thousand things.' *Dao* is, thus, the process of the world itself" (1998, 245). Therefore, one needs to contemplate the world not only in its process from *dao* to the myriad things but also in its process of returning from the myriad things to *dao*. In this context, *yi* 一 is not "the One" but the continuity of the myriad things.[7] Ames and Hall (2003) render the passage of chapter 42 thus:

Way-making (*dao*) gives rise to continuity [*yi*],
Continuity gives rise to difference,
Difference gives rise to plurality,
And plurality gives rise to the manifold of everything that is happening (*wanwu*).[8]

In their commentary, Ames and Hall (2003, 144) reaffirm the possibility to read this passage from the particular to the general, that is: "Multiplicity gives rise to plurality / Plurality to difference / Difference to continuity / And continuity to *dao*."[9]

If the process proceeds in both directions, this double movement of *dao* and *wanwu* produces what in the *Zhuangzi* is the transformation of things (*wuhua* 物化). From the point of view of *wuhua* there is no temporal shift between the production of the myriad things and *dao* because everything is simultaneously continuous and plural; that is to say, continuity is a continuous plurality and plurality is a plural continuity. This means that no element can prevail over the other: there is no ultimate *you* or original *wu* that can ground the myriad things. Thus, it is of capital importance not only to think high and low, long and short, *you* and *wu*, and all the myriad things in balance but also to regard them as mutually engendering.

This circulation of *you* and *wu*, this returning movement of *dao*, is the constant renovation of the myriad things and their constant transformation, that is, *wuhua*. I shall come back to this with the analysis of the "Qiwulun." For now, suffice it to say that if the myriad things are never settled, *dao* cannot be static either.

4.1.3 The Unchanging Process of *Dao* 道

Once again, it is fundamental to avoid assimilating *dao* to an essence or a substance. Even with Wang Bi one needs to be careful in considering *wu* the substance of *dao*. Isabelle Robinet (1999, 138) summarizes the issue, stating that sometimes "the term *wu*, which Wang Bi was the first to systematically bring to the fore in speaking of the *Dao*, has been translated as 'substance.'" According to her, however, *wu* "is neither the substance nor the actor behind the world, nor yet its foundation; it does not concern ontology and even less theology." This implies that it is crucial to avoid an understanding of *dao* as static and unchanging.

And yet, in chapter 25, *dao* is described as "standing alone" (*duli* 獨立) and "unchanging" (*bu gai* 不改):

> 有物混成，先天地生。寂兮寥兮，獨立不改，周行而不殆，可以為天下母。吾不知其名，字之曰道

> There was something chaotically (*hun* 混) formed[10]
> Which appeared before the heavens and the earth.
> Silent, empty,
> Standing alone without alteration (*bu gai* 不改),
> Turning around without pause,
> It can be regarded as the mother of the world.
> I do not know its name,
> If I were to style it, I would call it *dao*.

The characterizations of *dao* are apparently contradictory here: how can this process be standing alone without alteration and, at the same time, turning around and with no pause? In commenting on this passage, Chen Guying (2008, 141) explains that some scholars relate Laozi's *dao* to the Parmenidean Being. According to him this is only apparently appropriate because, while it is true that the Parmenidean Being is unique, absolute and permanent, at the same time it is also unchanging and static. Laozi's *dao* is not fixed and unchanging but it is incessantly in motion. Therefore, it is said 'moves in cycles and never ceases [*zhou xing er bu dai* 周行而不殆]' (ch. 25). *Dao* is mutable and moving, incessantly changing; all the myriad things endlessly transform and move along with it. (In this changing movement, each thing will fade away and disappear but *dao* will never vanish and never be extinguished. Thus, Laozi's *dao* 'stands alone without changing'—'without changing' (不改) means that *dao* will never fade away and disappear.) Due to the changing process of *dao*, the myriad things are produced.

Although one may question the idea suggested here that, in the *Daodejing*, *dao* is unique and absolute,[11] Chen is right in his analysis: *dao* is not comparable to the unchanging and static Parmenidean Being. In particular, Chen's interpretation of *bu gai* is coherent with the procedural nature of *dao*. If *dao* is a process in constant movement and in constant transformation, *bu gai* means that the entire process does not change, to wit: does not stop. We can better understand *bu gai* if we relate it to *chang*.

Like the concept of *chang* that describes the constancy of the process of *dao* and not its static immobility, *bu gai* refers to the impossibility of pausing the constant renovation of this changing process. As a consequence, what is constant and unchanging is the returning process of *dao*, which "moves in cycles and never ceases" (*zhou xing er bu dai* 周行而不殆).[12]

Ames (2000, 238) points out that *duli er bu gai* (獨立而不改) has been generally interpreted as "it stands solitary and does not change." For him, this interpretation goes against the "'eventful' world of classical Daoism" in which "change" "is expressed in many different ways, *gai* 改 being only one of them." As a consequence, Ames distinguishes different senses of "change," "some of which are: 1. *bian* 變 (change gradually across time); 2. *yi* 易 (change one thing for an other): 3. *hua* 化 (transform utterly, where A becomes B); 4. *qian* 遷 (change from one place to another); 5. *gai* 改 (correct, reform, improve upon X on the basis of some external and independent standard or model, Y)." Besides the opportunity to reflect on the extreme richness of the concept of change in classical Daoism, the passage clearly explains the idea of reforming *gai* and its relation to an external system of reference. Seen in this way, *bu gai* indicates the impossibility to alter and reform from the outside what has its own course of development.

Ames (2000, 238–239) insists that, although *bu gai* can signify "does not change," this translation is inconsistent with the following line in the received text (*zhou xing er bu dai*) and with "everything else that is said about *dao* in the literature." Ames concludes that the "meaning here is not that *dao* 'does not change,' but being the *sui generis* and autopoietic totality of all that is becoming (*wanwu* 萬物), *dao* is not open to reform by appeal to something other than itself." Going one step further, one can see that this "other than itself" is precisely the static substance that crystallizes the constant process of becoming present in *dao*, *wanwu*, and—even more properly—*wuhua*.

This is coherent with the rest of chapter 25 that reaffirms the cyclical nature of *dao*:

> 吾不知其名，字之曰道，強為之名曰大。大曰逝，逝曰遠，遠曰反。

> I do not know its name,
> If I were to style it, I would call it *dao*.
> Were I forced to assign it a name,
> I would call it grand.
> Being grand, means fading away,
> Fading away, means far-reaching,
> Far-reaching, means returning.

Dao is described as "grand" (*da* 大), which is related to its great cycle more than to an intrinsic quality. Indeed, *da* itself is part of a wider process. The series formed by grand, fading away (*shi* 逝), far-reaching (*yuan* 遠), and returning (*fan* 反) describes a cyclical process that constantly regenerates itself: *dao*, being grand, fades away; this fading away is far-reaching; and this far-reaching is returning. Yet returning is the movement of *dao*. This means that *dao* itself returns, which entails that it returns as *da*. Therefore, the passage describes more precisely the movement of *dao*.[13]

This does not come as a surprise. More importantly, *dao* as *da* fades away, which contradicts the interpretation of Chen Guying, who considers *dao* as never vanishing. *Dao* fades away, even though this fading away will become far-reaching and will return grand again.[14] Thus, the movement of *dao* is not different from the movement of the myriad things (*wanwu* 萬

物) and vice versa: everything participates in this returning process. Still, an important question arises from this analysis, that is: how does this returning movement of *dao* and *wanwu* generate?

4.2 The Ethical Implications of *Ziran* 自然 and *Wuwei* 無為

In the previous section, I started considering the function of language in the *Daodejing* by analyzing the meaning of *chang* in relation to *dao* and *ming*. I suggested that *chang dao* and *chang ming* should be regarded as constant way-making and constant naming, respectively. This is because *chang* refers to the constant change of everything in the world.

We have seen how change is a central concept of the *Daodejing* and how the movement of *dao* is a cyclical returning movement. We have also analyzed how *dao* and *wanwu* are mutually entailing. This implies that, in the constant change, there is no temporal shift between the production of the myriad things and *dao* because everything is simultaneously continuous and plural—in the sense that continuity is a continuous plurality and plurality is a plural continuity.

The problem that I would like to consider in this section is how the returning movement of *dao* and *wanwu* generate. The analysis of the relationship between *dao* and *wanwu* will help to understand more clearly the ethical implications of *ziran* and *wuwei*. I will go back to the question of language in the next section.

4.2.1 The Relationship between *Dao* and *Wanwu* 萬物

In considering the movement of *dao*, it is crucial to analyze the relationship between *dao* and the myriad things. Isabelle Robinet (1999, 134–135) clarifies the issue by stating that "the terms most frequently used by Chinese texts are either *hua* 化 'transform' or *sheng* 生, which signifies at the same time 'to beget' and 'to give life.'" According to Robinet, *sheng* "must be understood in the Chinese context where the notion of filiation is strongly dominated by that of continuity. That the Dao was 'cause' does not imply that the world is its 'effect,' because here it means nothing more than that the world is its unfolding, its manner of appearance. The Dao is 'cause' in the sense of motion, not of creation *ex nihilo*." Robinet is right in her analysis but leaves aside the most important aspect of the problem. Surely *dao* is not the cause of the myriad things and the world is not created *ex nihilo*. Still, what does it mean that *dao* is " 'cause' in the sense of motion"? Is it possible to define more precisely this productive motion?

As previously suggested, to fully understand this issue we need to avoid considering *dao* as an essence: *dao* is not the substance of the myriad things and does not create the myriad things; rather, *dao* describes a process that fades away and returns. Furthermore, in order to produce this process *dao needs* the myriad things. Without *wanwu*, *dao* would be empty: there would be nothing from which it could fade away and there would be nothing to which it could return. Hence, *dao* and *wanwu* entail each other insofar as *dao* describes the general movement of the myriad things and *wanwu* determine the myriad movements of *dao*. In other words, *dao* embraces *wanwu* in its entire process and the myriad things constitute *dao* in their fading away and returning.

This also means that, contrary to the Leibnizian *Monadology* (2014), where the mutual influence of the monads is only "*idéale*"—since the relation between them depends on God (2004, §51)—*dao* is constituted by and simultaneously constitutes the relations of the myriad things. Once again, *dao* cannot be conceived as substance.[15]

Now it is possible to better understand Robinet's assertion that *dao* "is 'cause' in the sense of motion," provided that the myriad things are "causes" in the same sense. That is to say: motion itself produces both *dao* and *wanwu*. Still, one can ask what produces this motion. This is actually the main point that holds the entire process of *dao* in its generality and *wanwu* in their particularities: *dao* and *wanwu*—being grand and fading away, weakening and returning—are all part of a spontaneous process, namely, *ziran*. The conclusion of chapter 25 is particularly clear on the central role of *ziran*:

人法地，地法天，天法道，道法自然

Humans emulate earth,
Earth emulates heavens,
Heavens emulate *dao*,
And *dao* emulates *ziran*.

In this series, everything follows the example of what is spontaneously so (*fa ziran* 法自然): humans, the entire world with the myriad things, and *dao* are all related to *ziran*. This means that there is no priority in their development because they all emerge spontaneously.[16] The " 'cause' in the sense of motion" is the motion in the sense of *ziran*. If everything—*dao* included—emulates *ziran*, the movement that is produced by and produces *wanwu* is spontaneously so. Therefore, fading away and returning are also spontaneously emerging, causes and effects of themselves.

And yet, while *ziran* is the general drive that regulates the movement of *dao* and *wanwu*, this does not mean that its spontaneous process is certain and absolute. People can obstruct the process by interfering with *ziran*. Ames (2000, 239) has a different understanding of this issue, taking for granted the possibility of *ziran*. According to him, "because *dao* is everything, and everything is *dao*, what can it emulate? '*Dao* emulates itself 道法自然.'"[17] Ames identifies *dao* and *ziran* by affirming that if *dao* emulates its own spontaneity, *dao* is *ziran tout court*. Although this seems to be a good understanding of *dao*, it reduces the meaning of *ziran*.

It is true that "*dao* is everything, and everything is *dao*," but this does not mean that, in this reciprocal mirroring, everything proceeds spontaneously without problems. If this were the case, there would be no conflicts, everything would be harmonious, and the authors of the *Lao-Zhuang* would have had no reason to worry about it. Unfortunately, conflicts proliferate because people try to force the spontaneous development of the myriad things. For this reason, the *Daodejing* advocates a return to an unobstructive behavior. Although, in its general meaning, *ziran* eschews all sense of achievement on the part of an agent, people can either inwardly wound their persons by likes and dislikes or go by *ziran*—as we shall see later in relation to the *Zhuangzi* (14/5/55–57). Thus, *ziran* is a state that needs to be sustained or recovered by people, and not something already established or unchanging. In this sense, the end of chapter 25 places a particular emphasis on *ren*, human being.

According to Liu Xiaogan (1995, 69), the intermediate elements of the series "humans—earth—heavens—*dao*—*ziran*" are only concepts that have a rhetorical function.[18] The main focus lies on the relation between the two extremes of the series, namely, the relation between humans and *ziran*. This means that people need to emulate (*xiaofa* 效法) *ziran*. Liu concludes that, for Laozi, society ought to develop spontaneously (*ziran*). This is a legitimate interpretation, but one can object that this is just a consequence of the fact that every single person—and the ruler too in the context of the *Daodejing*—needs to act according to *ziran*. Liu himself asks what this emulation (*fa* 法) of *ziran* is. The reply is that *fa ziran* means "to follow the developing change of the external objects without interfering" (70).

This, however, seems to be a private activity: how could society be able to do this in its entirety? Or should one consider this activity to be only the duty of the ruler who regulates society?

It is true that the *Daodejing* addresses the problem of rulership and its obstructive action (*youwei* 有為). And yet, even if the ruler emulates *ziran* without interfering with the external objects, there is no assurance that the entire society can do the same and everything can proceed spontaneously. On the contrary, if *fa ziran* pertains only to the ruler, every person is completely freed from responsibility even though this responsibility is just to preserve *ziran*.

Obviously, if the ruler acts coercively, this has greater effects than the coercive actions of common people. Still, this does not mean that common people are excluded from this discourse, nor that they are granted the status of spontaneity. Chapter 64 clarifies this point by stating that "people constantly ruin their endeavors just on the verge of their completion" (民之從事，常於幾成而敗之). If *ziran* were an intrinsic essence that regulates everything, there would be no possibility for people to break this quality ruining their own efforts. Rulers and common people undoubtedly act on different levels, but they are all responsible if spontaneity is obstructed.

The interpretation of Liu Xiaogan is not only problematic in relation to society. The other relevant question is: why should *fa ziran* be only related to external objects? Why should one not interfere with the changes of one's own self? Liu presupposes the division between an internal and an external world. However, if *ziran* needs to be followed, one should avoid this differentiation. From the point of view of *ziran* there is no within and without: not only does humanity follow *ziran* but all the myriad things do the same, *dao* included. This entails that, to follow *ziran*, one needs to be attuned to the world and to oneself.

Thus, *fa ziran* not only means that one should act according to *ziran* but also that one ought not to interfere with it; in other words, one needs to follow and not interfere with the spontaneous changes that happen within the world and within one's own self. This implies that *ziran* opens a serious ethical issue: how is it possible to act according to it? How can one act spontaneously? How is it possible to distinguish between a spontaneous conduct and a non-spontaneous one? The answer is *wuwei* 無為.

The analysis of *wuwei* will show how there is an ethical possibility in it that allows the will to be unobstructive toward the other and the world, which in turn helps us to see how the world as will to power can unfold spontaneously—as I suggested at the end of the previous chapter. This different perspective is possible if one partakes in this world not as a will to domination but as a will to renovation. In other words, *wuwei* lets us conceive of a will that is empowered not by the domination of the other but by its self-transformation *through* the other. If one can be "altered and enlarged, 'othered'" (Kearney 2006, xix) by the other, this is allowed by a will that does not obstruct both the self and the other. This will shifts from the metaphysical grounding of the subject to the aesthetic encounter with the world. Yet, to enter this aesthetic dimension, it is paramount to consider the relationship between *ziran* and *wuwei*.

4.2.2 The Relationship between *Ziran* 自然 and *Wuwei* 無為

Ziran and *wuwei* are concepts closely related, to the extent that some scholars consider them interchangeable. Chen Guying (2008, 150), for instance, deems them as a single notion, stating that "'*ziran-wuwei*' is the most important concept of *Laozi*'s philosophy." This is probably excessive and Chen himself differentiates between the two. According to him, *ziran* defines the general course of events in the world and *wuwei* describes how people act. And yet, he believes that the two words "can be combined in one single concept" (152). Although it is true that *wuwei* points in the direction of *ziran*, we need to distinguish the two concepts.

Contrary to Chen's position, *ziran* is not just how things develop in the world. As seen before, human being can get in the way of *ziran* and obstruct the spontaneous development of the world. This means that, although *ziran* is a condition in which everything proceeds without interferences, one needs to allow this process to take its own course. *Wuwei* is instrumental to avoid not only hindering the spontaneous development of events but also hampering one's own spontaneity; that is to say, in helping to proceed spontaneously in one's own behavior, *wuwei* makes possible and preserves *ziran*. Therefore, *wuwei* is the condition that allows *ziran* to be stable.

Karyn Lai (2007, 326) suggests that "*ziran* entails *wuwei*." For her "the two concepts taken in conjunction furnish a philosophically deep and ethically significant notion of spontaneity." Although I agree that the two concepts are "ethically significant," I believe that the main ethical import is provided by *wuwei* insofar as it offers the *ethos* that leads to *ziran*.

I mentioned how people tend to spoil their own deeds, thus interfering with *ziran*. This happens because they do not act according to *wuwei*. Chapter 64 of the *Daodejing* elucidates this aspect.

為者敗之，執者失之。是以聖人無為故無敗；無執故無失。

Those who act (*wei zhe* 為者) ruin their deeds;
Those who want to control things (*zhi zhe* 執者) lose them.
Thus, because the sages act unobstructively (*wuwei*), they do not ruin their deeds;
Because they do not want to control things (*wuzhi* 無執), they do not lose them.

The chapter opposes those who act (*wei zhe*) to the sages who act unobstructively (*wuwei*). It is crucial to read *wei zhe* in relation to *wuwei* (*zhe*) in order to clarify both terms. *Wei zhe* does not designate an agent who simply acts but an agent who acts in a way that obstructs *ziran*. This can be deducted by the double parallel of *wei zhe*–*zhi zhe* and *wuwei*–*wuzhi*.

The second line of the passage helps to clarify the first one: *zhi zhe* specifies the nature of the action criticized. *Zhi* can mean "to control," "to grasp" or "to hold," defining, thus, a specific kind of action: those who act coercively want to stop and control what should be left to its own course. As a result, this kind of act hinders the spontaneous course of events.

The other two lines mirror the first two. In an opposite and parallel direction to *wei zhe*, *wuwei* ought not to be understood as a total absence of action: the sages, as those who act unobstructively—*wuwei* (*zhe*)—do not want to stop and control things—*wuzhi*. In other words, those who act according to *wuwei* do not spoil their deeds and do not obstruct *ziran*. This does not mean that sages do not act. Quite the opposite. *Wuwei* and *wuzhi* define those who have found a balance within the spontaneous course of events which cannot be stopped and cannot be controlled. And yet, one cannot exclude oneself from this course either. Hence, the only solution is to preserve an unobstructive attitude so as to proceed with *ziran*. The conclusion of the passage is clear on this.

聖人欲不欲，不貴難得之貨；學不學，復衆人之所過，以輔萬物之自然而不敢為。

The sages desire not to desire
And do not value rare commodities;
They learn to unlearn (*xue bu xue* 學不學),[19]
And return to what has been missed by the multitude.
Thus, they help the myriad things to proceed spontaneously,
And dare not interfere.[20]

Lau (1989, 164) has a different understanding of the conclusion. He explains that it is natural to take *bu gan wei* 不敢為 "in the general sense of 'not daring to act.'" This is a literal translation but Lau interprets it in the sense of the myriad things and not of the sage. According to him the sage "takes a number of steps in order to help the myriad creatures both to be natural and to refrain from daring to act." For this reason, Lau concludes that "'not daring to act' refers to the myriad creatures." Although it is debatable that *bu gan wei* refers to the myriad things and not to the sage,[21] Lau offers an interesting comparison of the transmitted version with the Mawangdui one (能輔萬物之自然，而弗敢為). He affirms that with *fu* 弗 this interpretation is not possible because, although *fu* and *bu* are both negatives, *fu* implies an object. Therefore, in *fu gan wei* 弗敢為

> 'dare not do it,' the 'it' has to refer to a specific action. The sage can help the myriad creatures to be natural but he can hardly help them not to dare do a specific action. The specific action, in the context, can only refer to the action of helping the myriad creatures to be natural, and the agent of this action can only be the sage. The reading *neng* 能 in place of *yi* 以 also shows this interpretation to be correct. The sage is able to help the myriad creatures to be natural but he dare not do it. The contrast is between 'being able' and 'not daring.' (1989, 164)

If anything, the Mawangdui version seems to confirm the interpretation that the agent of *bu gan wei* is not the myriad things but the one who helps them to spontaneously follow their course. This means that *bu gan wei* reinforces the idea of *wuwei*: in order to facilitate the spontaneous development of the world and its myriad things—human beings included—the best solution is to act unobstructively. Thus, the sages dare not interfere with *ziran*. And yet, if *wuwei* is not the absence of action, how can an action be unobstructive? This question is particularly problematic and needs a careful analysis.

4.2.3 The Problem of *Wuwei* 無為

Scholars have proposed different ideas regarding this issue, often relying on metaphysical assumptions. The clearest example of this approach is represented by Edward Slingerland. Although Slingerland (2003, 6) is right in considering *wuwei* not only "an ideal form of government" but also a personal endeavor, he grounds his understanding in a Cartesian conception of the self. Slingerland employs this theoretical strategy to justify the idea that *wuwei* as "effortless action" is "a state that needs to be achieved." According to him, in the *Daodejing* this means to be "without (*wu* 無) all of the usual possessions of the conventional world: fame, desire, knowledge, activity" (78). Putting on the same plane "fame, desire, knowledge and activity" is already arguable—as if one should and could discard in the same way all knowledge and all activity. Nonetheless, Slingerland goes so far as to affirm that after "the Subject has successfully emptied the Self" of these possessions, "the Essential Self is free to emerge and guide the Subject into a way of being that is 'so-of-itself' (*ziran* 自然) or entirely natural."

This reading is questionable not only because it presupposes a Cartesian self with its classical division subject/object, but also because it equates *ziran* to an "Essential Self."[22] For Slingerland, only after having unlocked the "Essential Self" is one able to be *ziran*. Even though it is crucial to acknowledge the importance of removing obstructions in the world and in one's own behavior, this does not mean that it is possible to presuppose the idea of an "Essential Self" in classical Chinese philosophy.

Slingerland makes what Graham (1990b, 5) believes is a common mistake of Western interpreters: they tend to "fit the mysticism of other civilisations into a Neo-Platonist frame, thinking of a primarily cognitive experience in which the seer rends the veil of illusion and discovers his oneness with the underlying Absolute, Reality, Being." The problem is not confined to just a different approach to mysticism. There is a radical difference that interpreters such as Slingerland fail to acknowledge: for Chinese thinkers "the basic question is not What is the Truth? but Where is the Way? They conceive the ground to which they return in meditation, not as ultimate Reality, but as the Way for which they are searching" (Graham 1990b, 5–6). Thus, supposing there were such a mystical idea in *wuwei*, this would be quite different from the one described by Slingerland.

Furthermore, to be spontaneous one needs precisely to avoid Slingerland's essentialist conception of the self. In other words, avoiding the distinction subject/object one can dismiss the subjectivist perspective and fully participate in the myriad things' transformation. This will become clearer in the next chapter. For now it is worth underlining that *wuwei* has a practical and aesthetic outcome in the world and it is not simply confined "to the state of mind of the actor" or "to the phenomenological state of the doer" as Slingerland (2003, 7) holds. Chris Fraser (2007, 106) points out that the interpretive enterprise of Slingerland is "based on a manifestly Cartesian conception of mind and a confused picture of agency derived from a naively literal interpretation of contemporary American figures of speech.

He imposes these on an ancient Chinese intellectual milieu notable precisely for the absence of anything resembling a Cartesian framework." Although Fraser is precise in his evaluation and rightly stresses the absence of any Cartesian framework in classical Chinese thought, he misses the main issue in Slingerland's understanding of *wuwei*: the Cartesian approach is only a consequence of a deeper metaphysical conception that imposes itself on an extremely wide spectrum of early Chinese thought.

Slingerland (2003, 9) goes so far as to affirm that all the thinkers discussed in his book—Confucius, Laozi, Mencius, Zhuangzi, and Xunzi—"share a religious worldview that has its roots in archaic Chinese religion, in which Heaven, the Way, wu-wei, and Virtue are intimately linked to one another." Slingerland affirms that these authors share not only the same understanding of *wuwei*—this is already a bold statement considering that the *Lunyu* 論語 and the *Mengzi* 孟子 mention this term only twice—but even the same religious worldview.[23]

Slingerland (2003, 10) only partially acknowledges the limits of his interpretation, stating that, "in the absence of a common use of 'wu-wei' as a technical term, one might ask how we are to justify treating the seemingly different ideals in these texts as common expressions of 'the' wu-wei ideal." His justification, however, is not convincing and casts even more shadows on his overall project. According to him, the fact that "wu-wei is not to be understood as literal 'non-doing' but rather refers to the phenomenological state of the actor (who is, in fact, quite active), suggests that we should understand the term metaphorically." As seen in the previous chapter, it is true that one needs to recall the metaphorical nature of concepts. And yet, this cannot become the justification for bundling different predications in different texts under the same label.[24]

Slingerland wants to establish an absolute metaphor—in the sense seen with Blumenberg in the previous chapter—that can justify all the differences present in different times and distinct philosophical thoughts. Regardless of the dissimilarities present even in the *Daodejing* and the *Zhuangzi*—which share a great deal of theoretical elements—Slingerland interprets everything as an undistinguishable amalgam that puts on the same plane not only Confucius, Mencius and Laozi, but also *wuwei* and *tian* 天—understood as "Heaven."[25] It comes as no surprise, therefore, that Slingerland (2003, 8) considers *wuwei* a religious concept:

> whereas spontaneity in the West is typically associated with subjectivity, the opposite may be said of the sort of spontaneity

evinced in wu-wei: it represents the highest degree of objectivity, for it is only in wu-wei that one's embodied mind conforms to the something larger than the individual—the will of Heaven or the order represented by the Way. This is why the state of wu-wei should be seen as a *religious* ideal, for it is only by attaining it that the individual realizes his or her proper place in the cosmos.

At least two considerations are necessary here. On the one hand, Slingerland equates *wuwei* with spontaneity, which means to equate it to *ziran*—as I have already discussed, the two concepts need to be differentiated. On the other hand, *wuwei* becomes the "highest degree of objectivity." This affirmation is particularly problematic considering that *wuwei* is primarily a negation and negates any authoritative and obstructive action. Thus, *wuwei* cannot be seen as objective—let alone as religious—insofar as it formulates the negation of a normative conduct. And yet, Slingerland (2003, 290) regards it as normative and metaphysical. The clarification of his position is revealing:

> I see at least two features of a system of thought to be crucial in marking it [*wuwei*] as 'religious': 1) the postulation of an all-embracing and *normative* order to the cosmos that goes beyond any given particular individual or object (that is, a network of metaphysical claims); and 2) a program for either bringing the individual and society as a whole *back* into their proper place in this order (a soteriological project) or for preserving a realized, but constantly threatened, state of harmony with this order.

Slingerland misses the meaning and the function of *wuwei*, which cannot totally adhere to the concept of *ziran*. The issue with this interpretation is the confusion between the specific quality of an action required to achieve *ziran* and *ziran* itself.

Still, even if one could be indulgent with Slingerland by not considering this confusion, the problem does not change. The point is that *ziran* could not be interpreted as a metaphysical and normative concept even if it had a wider scope than *wuwei*. Indeed, how can spontaneity be something normative? If spontaneity is an imperative, could the action that follows this imperative still be considered spontaneous? Moreover, how can it be possible to know that one's behavior is not detrimental for the spontaneous process? How can one know if a specific conduct does not obstruct *ziran* and the transformation of the myriad things? And even if it could be possible to determine that, in a certain condition, one's action is spontaneous, would this become the standard for future actions? If yes, can a standard be regarded as spontaneous?

4.2.4 Ziran 自然 as a Limit-Concept

It is evident that one can determine neither *ziran* as a standard that guarantees the repeatability of itself nor a system of reference that allows *ziran* to become a standard. If this could be possible, *ziran* would cease to be spontaneously so-of-itself. The function of *wuwei* is to clear the way from the obstructions and to help *ziran* unfold. The outcome, however, is always uncertain because no readymade patter can assure the spontaneous development of the myriad things.

In this sense *ziran* has a counterbalancing role: it functions as a limit-concept that, precisely because it is not normative, leaves to *wuwei* the task of keeping the way clear from obstructions. And yet, the myriad things are in constant transformation. This means that, because conditions constantly change, one constantly needs to try to remove the elements that hinder *ziran*. As will become clearer with the analysis of chapter 37 of the *Daodejing* in the next section, norms are some of the most dangerous obstacles to *ziran*. Thus, spontaneity cannot be a reference for any system because it destabilizes the very idea of reference.

If one cannot establish a unique reference for a spontaneous behavior, *ziran* cannot be a reference for systems of conduct but can only be a limit-concept that asks to constantly adapt to changing conditions. To act spontaneously entails a constant adjustment of the references, not to achieve overarching systems but to constantly configure contextual references. *Wuwei* helps to keep this possibility open.

Therefore, *wuwei*—as well as *ziran*—can be regarded neither as subjective nor as objective. The point is to avoid both subjective and objective determinations, proceeding along with the constant transformation of the myriad things (*wanwu zhi hua* 萬物之化) (*Zhuangzi*, 9/4/33)—as we shall see in more detail in the next chapter. Slingerland, on the other hand, in his attempt to define *wuwei* as "the highest degree of objectivity," reaffirms the Cartesian idea of *subiectum*. As discussed in chapter 2, only through the *subiectum* can objectivity be defined: something is objective because there is a subject that grounds it. In other words, the *subiectum* is the authority which establishes the truth of its objectivity.

To ground his metaphysical framework, Slingerland is not content to just follow Descartes's subject/object dichotomy; he also needs the authority of religion to secure the unconditional objectivity of his interpretation of *wuwei*. Slingerland (2003, 6) needs this kind of authority because he sees in his interpretation a contradiction: since he reads *wuwei* as "effortless action" the possibility to achieve this condition becomes paradoxical. He asks, "How can a program of spiritual striving result in a state that lies beyond striving? It would seem that the very act of striving would inevitably 'contaminate' the end-state." Posed in these terms the conundrum cannot be solved without an external authority.

We have seen how Nietzsche's "will to truth" is the drive to push authorities outside the metaphorical circle. But *wuwei* is the negation of imposing authorities. Even more importantly, there is no paradox for *wuwei* as long as it is understood as unobstructive action—bearing in mind that unobstructive does not mean effortless. *Wuwei* does not entail an action devoid of efforts. It is rather the opposite: one needs to be very careful in the attempt of opening the way to *ziran*.

The problem with interpretations such as "effortless action" is, once again, the confusion between *wuwei* and spontaneity. When one identifies the concept of *wuwei* with the one of *ziran*, it seems coherent to imagine *wuwei* being an action that proceeds without exertion in an "essential *ziran*," as if *ziran* were an intrinsic substance ready to be disclosed in an "Essential Self." Such a disclosure would not be far from what I have analyzed in relation to the Heideggerian ontological difference. This is misleading and allows the infiltration of metaphysical interpretations as Slingerland explicitly shows. I shall argue how this is in total opposition not only with the overall conception of the *Daodejing*, but also with the core concepts of the "Qiwulun" in the *Zhuangzi*. For now, to better understand the function of *wuwei* in the *Daodejing*, it is worth considering one of its most important declinations, namely, *wuming*.

4.3 On the Way to *Ziran* 自然

I started this chapter by analyzing more attentively the first lines of the *Daodejing* and by considering their relation to language. We have seen the function of *ming* and, in particular, the importance of *chang ming* as constant naming. I want to conclude this chapter by returning to the beginning and by discussing the counterpart of *chang ming*: *wuming*.

4.3.1 *Wuming* 無名 and Unassertive Definitions

In the Mawangdui version of chapter 37 we read:

道恆無名，侯王若能守之，萬物將自化。化而欲作，吾將鎮之以無名之樸。 鎮之以無名之樸，夫將不辱。不辱以靜，天地將自正。(61)[26]

Dao constantly lacks names (*wuming* 無名),
If nobles and kings are able to preserve this,
The myriad things will transform on their own (*zihua* 自化).
In this process, if cravings arise,
I will overcome them with the simplicity of *wuming*.
Having overcome them with the simplicity of *wuming*,
There will be no disgrace.
Without disgrace there will be calm,
And the world will be regulated on its own.

The transmitted version has the very well-known opening "dao constantly acts unobstructively and nothing is left undone (*dao chang wuwei er wu bu wei* 道常無為而無不為)."[27] The Guodian (A:7) confirms the version of Wang Bi but has only the first part of the line (*dao heng wuwei ye* 道恆無為也).[28] The Guodian and the Mawangdui stress different aspects of *dao* but they all agree in presenting it as non-assertive. In this sense, *wuming* seems to describe a specific trait of *wuwei*: if *wuwei* is a general concept that defines the unobstructive acting in all its possible manifestations, *wuming* is a specific modality of being unobstructive. Consequently, *wuming* should not be regarded only as "having no name" but also as unnaming, which is the unobstructive action that avoids fixing the world in defined terms.

Wuming has a clear link with the first two lines of the first chapter: there, the name that can be named is not the constant naming; in chapter 37, the constant naming takes shape as constant unnaming. The two aspects are not in contradiction. Rather the reverse: they point in the same direction. If one wants to constantly name the world with its myriad things, one also needs to constantly unname them. Similarly, Wang Bo (1993, 210) considers *youming* 有名 and *wuming* 無名 as mutually engendering and as describing the cyclical movement of *dao*.

Naming and unnaming are, therefore, two sides of the same coin as long as they are constant (*chang* 常 or *heng* 恆). If *dao* is a process, constant naming and unnaming (*chang ming* 常名 and *wuming* 無名) describe a specific and important aspect of it. Hence, *dao heng wuming* 道恆無名 suggests that *dao* not only constantly lacks names but also never produces obstructive definitions.

It is possible to consider the constant process of the naming–unnaming as allowing the myriad things to proceed undisturbed in their metamorphosis: forming names and new ways to replace them is a means to follow the constant transformation of the world. Having new names allows the world to be seen in new ways; simultaneously, the same changing process of the world asks for new ways to replace old names. The naming–unnaming process, therefore, proceeds without imposing fixed systems of reference on the world; it participates in the becoming of the myriad things by constantly transforming itself. Thus, naming–unnaming facilitates *ziran* and does not interfere with it.

The necessity of avoiding fixed systems of references is described in chapter 5:

天地不仁，以萬物為芻狗；聖人不仁，以百姓為芻狗。

The world (*tiandi* 天地) does not impose moral standards (*ren* 仁)[29]
And treats the myriad things as straw dogs (*chu gou* 芻狗).
Sages do not impose moral standards
And treat common people as straw dogs.

The expression *chu gou* "straw dogs" refers to sacrificial objects used with great reverence during ancient ceremony in China. In commenting on this chapter, Chang Chung-Yuan (1975, 49) clarifies that these objects were discarded right afterwards the ceremony, "indicating an attitude of indifference."[30] This means that if there are no abiding moral principles, there is no difference between straw dogs and any other object. Gao Ming (1996, 244) clarifies the entire passage:

> 'The world does not impose moral standards' means that the world does not impose itself on the myriad things but lets them grow by themselves. 'Sages do not impose moral standards' means that sages do not impose themselves on common people but let them develop spontaneously. The myriad things arise and perish, it is inevitable. If there were not this continuous alternation, the myriad things could not proceed continuously. *Laozi* uses 'straw dogs' as a metaphor to let the myriad things take their own course.

It is interesting that Gao Ming mentions the constant progression of life and death (*sheng* 生 and *si* 死) to clarify the meaning of this passage. Indeed, death is not less valuable than life. This will become an important theoretical element in the *Zhuangzi*. Here, however, the point is that the world does not use specific moral values to determine the status of one object. This means that one should refrain from accepting and imposing moral values that obstruct the spontaneous development of the myriad things.

As discussed in relation to chapter 37, nobles and kings should respect and preserve this process by avoiding the imposition of absolute definitions on the world. If giving names is a form of domination imposed on the world and on others, rulers have a particular responsibility not only because they legislate, but also because they educate—or miseducate. In other words, rulers should refrain from imposing hard rules on the world and perpetuating these rules with hard education.

It is interesting that the Guodian *Laozi* (A:6) version of chapter 64 affirms that sages "teach not to teach" *jiao bu jiao* 教不教[31] instead of "learn to unlearn" *xue bu xue* 學不學.[32] To teach not to teach is perfectly in line with naming–unnaming: education should be balanced by un-education. This un-education, however, is not miseducation. Similarly to the unnaming of *wuming*, the un-education undoes the limitations that an education of too strict definitions generates. Thus, *xue bu xue* becomes a natural consequence of *jiao bu jiao*: one learns to unlearn what has been learned from an education that proceeds with hard discriminations. Chapter 48 describes this process of reducing knowledge

為學日益，為道日損。損之又損，以至於無為。

In learning, one increases daily;
In practicing *dao*, one decreases daily.
Decreasing time and again,
One reaches the point of acting unobstructively (*wuwei*).

The issue, therefore, is not to avoid knowledge per se: *xue bu xue* is not merely "learning not to learn" but a process of un-education that can get rid of the obstructive elements imposed by external moral systems.

This process should not be confused with any kind of bracketing or *epoché* in a phenomenological sense. The point here is not to "set aside" one's own assumptions to access a more "authentic" explanation of reality or to reach "the things in themselves." This process is more genealogical—for its enquiring into one's own and other's assumptions—and does not have the scope to delete assumptions—as if it were possible to achieve a state of absence of assumptions. As seen in chapter 2, to believe in the thing-in-itself or in the meaning-in-itself is also an assumption, an interpretation, a worldview and, in the last analysis, a metaphor. Thus, to unlearn means to detect, acknowledge, and disarm the coercive functions of too strict definitions of the world—which in turn allows for a plurality of definitions of the world.

I shall come back to this in relation to the *Zhuangzi* and the idea of sitting and forgetting (*zuowang* 坐忘). For now, it is crucial to consider that people should have the possibility and responsibility to follow the path of learning to unlearn. If rulers respect and protect *wuming*, people—and all the myriad things along with them—can develop on their own, which implies that they can proceed in the naming–unnaming process and learn to unlearn.

It is clear that *wuming*—in the same way as *wuwei*—does not involve only rulers or, at least, it is not confined to the sole problem of rulership.[33] It is not by chance that chapter 37 uses *wu* 吾 "I" as the direct effort of the sage: "if cravings arise, I will overcome them."[34] This is coherent with chapter 33, which stresses the importance of self-understanding and self-control:

知人者智，自知者明。勝人者有力，自勝者強。

Those who know others are wise,
Those who know themselves are bright.
Those who conquer others have power,
Those who conquer themselves are strong.

One of the possibilities of conquering one's own self appears precisely when cravings arise. Cravings are not only external possibilities but also internal ones. In general, scholars interpret these cravings as pertaining to the myriad things, as if human beings were separated from them. Still, humanity is an integral part of the world and cannot be treated independently. Furthermore, the Mawangdui—and the transmitted text—say "I will overcome it," suggesting not only that cravings can arise and upset *ziran* but also that an action is needed to restore the spontaneous development of things. And what else can this craving be if not the desire to impose one's own names and one's own systems of reference upon the world? In this sense, the sages will overcome cravings using the simplicity of unnaming.[35]

Wuming cannot be the absence of names or the absence of naming. *Wuming* is a counteraction that helps undoing the obstructions caused by cravings so as to restore *ziran*. The transmitted text of chapter 37 reinforces this idea by using *yu* 欲 instead of *ru* 辱 "disgrace." Thus, "Having overcome them with the simplicity of *wuming*, there will be no craving (*yu*)" and "without craving there will be calm." *Wuming* can overcome the desire to determine the world in a fixed fashion and can restore the calm of the spontaneous transformation of the myriad things.

Once again, a cyclical process has been described in chapter 37: from the state of spontaneous transformation of things, cravings arise; cravings are overcome with *wuming*; the spontaneous metamorphosis of the world can return to the calm of its own development until new cravings arise; and so on. With the simplicity of *wuming* one can counterbalance the craving for absolute affirmations, which implies that *wuming* is part of a cyclical process that needs to constantly find the balance between naming and unnaming. Chapter 32—very close in content to chapter 37—offers a confirmation of this:

始制有名，名亦既有，夫亦將知止，知止所以不殆。

People have names as soon as they start making restrictions.
As soon as there are names, people should also know how to stop.
Knowing how to stop, people can avoid danger.

4.3.2 The Reversal Process

By now, it should be clear that, in the context of the *Daodejing*, giving names is a dangerous endeavor. Giving names and making restrictions are part of the same intention of controlling the spontaneous development of the world.[36] Still, the text suggests that it is not the naming process per se that is the real problem.

The danger lies in not knowing how to stop making restrictions or assigning restrictive definitions. From another point of view, it is possible to say that the real risk is not knowing how to start learning to unlearn. Insofar as restrictive definitions crystallize the world and obstruct *ziran*, one should know how to stop interfering with *ziran* and start the reversal process. And yet, to know this, one should first know that an interference is in place. In other words, one should acknowledge that restrictive definitions hinder the spontaneous transformation of the myriad things in order to stop interfering with them. This is the meaning of chapter 71, which in the Mawangdui version reads:

知不知，尚矣，不知知，病矣。是以聖人之不也，以其病病也，是以不病。(46)

> Knowing that one does not know is best,
> Not knowing that one knows is a disease.
> Sages are free from this disease:
> Because they recognize it as such
> They are not affected by the disease.

This passage clarifies that the *Daodejing* is not against knowledge *per se*. One should be aware that there is no absolute knowledge, and that knowledge is always limited. In this sense, it is better to recognize this lack of knowledge. On the other side, the passage offers an even deeper consideration: there is no absolute *absence* of knowledge, and one should recognize what is known. This means that one needs to be critical of the acquired knowledge and capable of tracing back the origin, intention, and scope of this knowledge. After all, if it is not possible to recognize the specificity of one's own knowledge, it is not possible to accept its partiality.

This unawareness of knowing is diametrically opposed to the awareness of not knowing and is similar to a disease insofar as it impedes the possibility of discarding obstructive assumptions. Ames and Hall (2003, 189) opportunely comment on this passage, affirming that "In Chinese medicine, disease (*bing* 病) usually entails a blockage of some kind in the healthy circulation of *qi* [氣]. In this case, epistemic disease is the blockage of access to immediate experience." This immediate experience, however, is not a naïve enjoyment of the world. Rather, it is an openness to the possibilities of the world inasmuch as it is the awareness of both knowing and not knowing. In this sense sages are freed from the illness: they regard the unawareness of knowing as the most dangerous aspect of knowledge and for this reason they can open the way to other understandings.

If one reads chapter 32 in light of chapter 37 and 71, it becomes evident that *wuming* proceeds in this direction: removing the block of control that hinders *ziran*, *wuming* removes the risk of narrowing the possible definitions of the world. The transformation of the myriad things implies that things are not determined in an absolute way, which in turn represents the plurality of possible changing meanings. Hence, the central point is not to totally avoid definitions but to avoid stopping the process of formulating unassertive definitions.

Definitions need to allow and follow the transformations of things; if one ceases this process and starts producing assertive definitions, discriminations arise and with them disputations appear. This becomes one of the central theoretical elements in the *Zhuangzi*, but it is also present in the *Daodejing*. The Guodian *Laozi* (A:1) version of chapter 19 affirms,

絕知棄辨，民利百倍

Abandon knowledge and drop discriminations,
Then people will benefit a hundredfold.[37]

If not *wuming*, what else can produce this benefit? Through *wuming* it is possible to abandon obstructive definitions and discriminations, which in turn avoids disputations for establishing a secure knowledge.[38]

Wuming—as part of the general *wuwei*—unnames the named and helps to clear the way from obstructive definitions by replacing them with unobstructive ones—which in turn facilitates *ziran* to proceed undisturbed. *Wuming*, therefore, becomes the symbol of unobstructive and unassertive definitions. All the *wu* terms of the *Daodejing* are consistent in being unobstructive and unassertive: they simultaneously present something and their negation. Chapter 57, which considers more attentively the problem of rulership, is a good opportunity to see three of these:

聖人云：我無為，而民自化；我好靜，而民自正；我無事，而民自富；我無欲，而民自樸。

The sage says:
I act unobstructively (*wuwei*)
And people transform on their own (*zihua* 自化);
I value tranquility
And people are spontaneously regulated;
I do not interfere with the events (*wushi* 無事)
And people spontaneously prosper;
I do not interfere with my cravings (*wuyu* 無欲)
And people spontaneously become simple.

This passage offers a more complete understanding of *wuwei* and the other forms of *wushi* 無事 and *wuyu* 無欲. Yet the most interesting aspect is that of *zihua* 自化: the spontaneous transformation already found in chapter 37 in relation to the myriad things is used here in relation to people. This links and puts on the same plane the myriad things and humanity: when they are not disturbed by obstructive action or names, they can both proceed in their spontaneous metamorphosis. *Wuwei*, as the general idea that includes all the other *wu* terms and their consequences, indicates that unassertive actions not only facilitate *ziran* but also open the space for *zihua*, which in turn gives to everything the same status of ongoing transformation.

Returning for one moment to the end of the previous chapter, I conclude that *wuwei* clarifies how a will does not necessarily result in an imposition on the world. Through *wuwei* one can conceive the will that wills itself as willing to be unobstructive. Thus, in order to dance spontaneously with fate, one needs to open the way to this dance through *wuwei*, which means that one is ready to accept and adapt to different circumstances. This also implies that the world as will to power can unfold spontaneously as long as the self and the other are not in contrast but balance each other in a complementary harmony. This produces important ethical consequences that need careful consideration.

4.3.3 Avoiding Domination

As we have seen so far, the metaphors of *ziran* and *zihua* show a worldview that considers all the myriad things on the same level: in a state in which there are no interferences with *ziran*, everything proceeds in a process of constant metamorphosis and nothing has the desire to rise above the other. In this process everything changes, not only the world and humanity but also definitions. Without a stable world and stable definitions, the possibility itself of ruling and exploiting the world is excluded.

Contrary to the Judeo-Christian tradition, the non-hierarchical structure of the myriad things does not confer any legitimacy on specific entities. This, in turn, excludes the possibility of an external authority that functions as an absolute standard and that grants dominion over the other. Considering *Genesis* 1:26–28, one sees how things are different in this tradition:

> Then God said, "Let us make humankind in our image, according to our likeness; and let them have dominion over the fish of the sea, and over the birds of the air, and over the cattle, and over all the wild animals of the earth, and over every creeping thing that creeps upon the earth."

> So God created humankind in his image,
> in the image of God he created them;
> male and female he created them.
>
> God blessed them, and God said to them, "Be fruitful and multiply, and fill the earth and subdue it; and have dominion over the fish of the sea and over the birds of the air and over every living thing that moves upon the earth."[39]

God is not only the greatest authority but also the guarantor that assigns authority. For this reason, human beings are made in the image of God, which is already a sign of domination over the creation. And yet, this was not enough and God expressly gives humanity the highest position among its creations: the entire world has been made for and given to humankind, which is its ruler. It is evident that in the perspective of the *Daodejing* there is no essence that can provide such a power over the world—and even *dao* needs to emulate *ziran*. Thus, what the *Daodejing* suggests is an alternative to the onto-theological drift of the dominion justification.

Ronald Simkins (2014, 399) criticizes this understanding of the Judeo-Christian tradition, which exemplifies "a post-Cartesian reading of the Bible with the assumption that humankind is separate and distinct from the natural world."[40] For Simkins the Bible proposes not an anthropocentric perspective but a theocentric worldview in which humanity and nature are both the creation of God. Although Simkins is right in warning against too-facile oversimplifications of the biblical texts, it is difficult to neglect that this post-Cartesian reading of the Bible was possible on the ground of the hierarchical structure Creator–creation that is at the base of the biblical texts. This theocentric hierarchical perspective gives to anthropocentrism an unquestionable external authority and justifies the onto-theological drift of domination.

Christoph Cox (1999, 199) offers a synthesis of this drift by affirming that in "the metaphysical tradition, true being serves as origin, aim, essence, and substance for the rest of existence." After considering the Platonic idea of Form that gives an "absolute standard" and "establishes a hierarchy of the more or less real that measures each entity according to its distance from true being," Cox concludes,

> So, too, for the Western tradition, has God been synonymous with Being itself: at once creator, providential director, essence,

substance, and end of all existence. The Christian tradition, too, produces a hierarchy of entities, at the top of which stands 'man,' created 'in the image of God,' and at the bottom of which stands inanimate nature. Moreover, for modern rationalism, God is that which guarantees all knowledge (Descartes), sorts out better from worse and actual from merely possible worlds (Leibniz), exists as the sole substance, of which all else is expression or attribute (Spinoza), and serves as the ultimate unity and ground of all possible experience (Kant).

Here it is possible to see the danger mentioned in chapter 32 of the *Daodejing*. Naming God or Being guarantees the legitimacy of an absolute standard, which in turn allows the legitimacy and standardization of all consequent definitions. This means that an absolute Being provides the ground for truth. The danger is precisely to be trapped in this truth.

As seen in the previous chapter, when one forgets the metaphorical origin of truth, the world solidifies in a stale definition. For this reason, Nietzsche admires Heraclitus. Reading fragment 30 of Heraclitus (in the order of Diels-Kranz), one can see how the idea of becoming avoids any violent and authoritative imposition of creation:

> κόσμον τὸν αὐτὸν ἁπάντων οὔτε τις θεῶν οὔτε ἀνθρώπων ἐποίησεν, ἀλλ' ἦν ἀεὶ καὶ ἔστιν καὶ ἔσται πῦρ ἀείζωον, ἁπτόμενον μέτρα καὶ ἀποσβεννύμενον μέτρα
>
> The ordering, the same for all, no god nor man has made, but it ever was and is and will be: fire everliving, kindled in measures and in measures going out. (Kahn 1979, 44–45)

This calm balance and harmony of the everliving fire that appears and disappears in measure is the spontaneous, cyclical, and ceaseless transformation of everything. What is crucial here, however, is the ethical difference between the Heraclitean becoming and God's dominion mandate: while the appearing and passing away of the former is a balanced and constant process of transformation that treats everything on the same level, the latter entails a power not only over the world but also over the other.

Through God, human beings have the absolute authority to define not only objects but also enemies. As clearly expressed by Carl Schmitt (2005, 36), even when God seems to disappear in the administration of the *res publica*, "all significant concepts of the modern theory of the state are secularized theological concepts." According to Schmitt the state of "exception in jurisprudence is analogous to the miracle in theology."

This is the opposite of the harmonious vision proposed by the *Daodejing*: while the state of exception justifies the violation of the rights of the others and the natural course of the world, *ziran* excludes any sort of exceptions. In the perspective of the *Daodejing*, if an exception arises, it is against the spontaneous transformation of the myriad things; as such, the exception needs to be undone and cannot become the legitimation for oppressing the other and exploiting the environment.

Thus, *wuwei*, *wuming*, and all the *wu* terms describe a conduct that does not simply renounce action but acts to undo the exceptions that upset *ziran*. If it is possible to undo all the cravings and exceptions that arise on one's own path, then one will emulate the spontaneous transformation of the myriad things (*fa ziran*). The end of chapter 5 of the *Zhuangzi* offers an important explanation of *wuqing* 無情 that helps us to better understand what has been said hitherto:

惠子謂莊子曰：「人故無情乎？」莊子曰：「然。……是非吾所謂情也。吾所謂無情者，言人之不以好惡內傷其身，常因自然而不益生也。」(14/5/55–57)

Said Hui Shih to Chuang-tzŭ

'Can people really be without feelings?' [*wuqing* 無情]

'They can.' Chuang-tzŭ replied. . . . 'Judging "That's it, that's not" [*shifei* 是非] is what I mean by "feelings." What I mean by being without feelings is that people do not inwardly wound their persons by likes and dislikes, that they constantly go by the spontaneous and do not add anything to the process of life.' (82)[41]

The *Zhuangzi* offers a clarification of *wuqing* and, indirectly, a confirmation of the meaning of *wuwei* and *wuming*. *Wuqing* is not a mere lack of feelings but the ability of not wounding oneself with differentiations. If *qing* entails *shifei* 是非—the discrimination of "that's it" and "that's not"—then *wuqing* proceeds on the process of life with un-discriminative feelings. To clarify this, let me follow the second chapter of the *Zhuangzi* and analyze the issue of *shifei*.

5

From *Ziran* 自然 to Aesthetics

5.1 Relational Polarities in the *Zhuangzi* 莊子

In the previous chapter, I started considering the ethical implications of *ziran* and *wuwei*. I suggested that *ziran* functions as a limit-concept insofar as one cannot establish a unique reference for a spontaneous behavior. As a result, *ziran* cannot be a reference for systems of conduct but can only be a limit-concept that asks to constantly adapt to changing conditions. In this sense, *ziran* leaves to *wuwei* and *wuming* the task of keeping the way clear from obstructions.

In this chapter, I discuss how the aesthetic awareness proposed by the *Zhuangzi* helps to proceed in the constant adaptation to changing conditions. More precisely, I want to analyze how this adaptation is possible through the aesthetic encounter with the other and the world at large. This encounter, however, is not possible without the implicit acceptance of the continuous plurality inherent in the constant transformation of everything (*wanwu zhi hua* 萬物之化) (9/4/33). The analysis of the cyclical movement of *dao* proposed in the previous chapter was instrumental in this direction.

As seen, *dao* and *wanwu* 萬物 are both part of a spontaneous process (*ziran*). But while *ziran* can be the general drive that regulates the movement of *dao* and *wanwu*, this does not mean that its spontaneous process is certain and absolute. Therefore, *ziran* needs to be sustained through unobstructive actions (*wuwei*) and unassertive definitions (*wuming*). Even more importantly, the analysis of the relation of *ming* and *wuming* showed how one needs to move within the cyclical alternation of saying and weakening what has been said so as to open the space for other saying. Thus, forming names and new ways to replace them is a means to follow the constant transformation of the world.

In the next sections, I will move further in this direction by considering how the aesthetic attunement to the world is linked to *wuming* and to the possibility of unlearning restrictive definitions. Yet, before analyzing the aesthetic awareness proposed by the *Zhuangzi*, it is necessary to consider what the web of relational polarities described in the text has to do with the critique of *shifei*. This will help us to the see why the *Zhuangzi* puts the disputations emerging from affirmations and negations (*shifei*) that inwardly wound people in opposition to the spontaneous process of life—as seen at the end of the previous chapter. And this, in turn, will show how the ability of not wounding oneself with differentiations is a fundamental component of the aesthetic encounter with the world.

5.1.1 Preliminary Remarks on the "Qiwulun" 齊物論

According to Chad Hansen, the "Qiwulun" 齊物論 "is the most profound expression of philosophical Taoism" (1983, 31).[1] This profundity, however, does not explain its content more clearly. Quite the reverse. If philosophical Daoism is already a matter of difficult interpretation,[2] the "Qiwulun" puts the interpreter in an even more difficult position. To begin with, there is the problem of the title.[3]

"Qiwulun" can be read as both *qi* "*wulun*" 齊 "物論" and "*qiwu*" *lun* "齊物" 論. Considering that *qi* means "even" or "equal," the former can be translated as "The Equality of Things and Opinions" as Fung Yu-Lan does (1964); the latter can be rendered as "Discussion on Making All Things Equal" as in the translation of Burton Watson (2013).[4] In his remarkable study, Chen Shaoming (2004, 5) explains that, on the one hand, *qi* "*wulun*" is a philosophical critique against any kind of theory which, in the final analysis, means a critique of what is affirmed and negated (*qi shifei* 齊是非); on the other hand, "*qiwu*" *lun* needs to be regarded as *qi wanwu* 齊萬物, a discourse on the equality of all the myriad things. Given that humanity is part of the myriad things, it is necessary, according to Chen, to consider also the equality of things and self (*qi wu wo* 齊物我).

Looking at this interpretation, it becomes evident that the relations that humans have with themselves, the others, and the world are central, and also that the value of these relations needs to be considered carefully. In a key and especially dense passage, it is possible to find synthesized all the pivotal aspects of the "Qiwulun":

是亦彼也，彼亦是也。彼亦一是非，此亦一是非。果且有彼是乎哉？果且無彼是乎哉？

What is It [*shi* 是] is also Other [*bi* 彼], what is Other is also It. There they say 'That's it, that's not' [*shifei* 是非] from one point of view, here we say 'That's it, that's not' from another point of view. Are there really It and Other [*you bi shi* 有彼是]? Or really no It and Other [*wu bi shi* 無彼是]? (4/2/29–30) (53)[5]

The passage clearly explains that the world is evaluated differently depending on the point of view from which it is seized. As a consequence, reference systems change in relation to their positions. This implies that a good criterion to distinguish between things from one point of view may not be satisfactory from another point of view and vice versa. The values of these positions are, therefore, interchangeable insofar as each of them considers its own perspective to be the right standard for discriminations. Yet the text suggests something more.

In asking if there is an it and an other (*you bi shi*) or if there is not an it and an other (*wu bi shi*), the author introduces a supplementary differentiation, namely *you* 有 and *wu* 無. This does not simply question the possibility of differentiation between "it" and "other" but asks if it is actually possible to have a unique reference system. In other words, the text calls into question the legitimacy itself of any standard that wants to define the world univocally.

Another important passage points directly in this direction:

夫言非吹也。言者有言，其所言者特未定也。果有言邪？其未嘗有言邪？其以為異於鷇音，亦有辯乎，其無辯乎？道惡乎隱而有真偽？

Saying is not blowing breath, saying says something; the only trouble is that what it says is never fixed. Do we really say something? Or have we never said anything? If you think it different from the twitter of fledgelings, is there proof of the distinction? Or isn't there any proof? By what is the Way hidden, that there should be a genuine or a false? (4/2/23–25) (53)

In the previous chapter, I discussed how different the perspective of the *Daodejing* on language is compared to the Heideggerian idea of humans as "*the* sayers." Here, we have a confirmation of this divergence.

The *Zhuangzi* does not merely suggest that saying is never fixed—which implies that saying cannot be determined univocally—but questions the very possibility to know if one says something or not—and that this saying is more meaningful than any other sound of nature. Therefore, how can there be any legitimacy for definitions, any standard to assess controversies, any differentiation between the sayers and the sounds of nature?

Chen Shaoming (2004, 216) is right in considering this the implicit meaning of the *qi "wulun"* as *qi shifei*. Chen, however, also considers this discourse as dissolving differentiations (*min shifei* 泯是非) (220). This can be misleading and needs to be evaluated attentively. It is of great importance to clarify whether the *qi* of the "Qiwulun" is a normative equalization that homogenizes everything and if this has ethical consequences. Let me first consider this aspect from a wider perspective.

5.1.2 Corresponding Pluralities

From a Western epistemological point of view, the discourse about the impossibility of discrimination between alternatives is certainly a cryptic piece of reasoning. As Hall and Ames (1987, 17) have argued, the problem lies in a different approach toward the world that led early Chinese thought to develop a network of complementary oppositions instead of a dialectic of mutual exclusive dichotomies. According to them, this is a reflection of a non-transcendent cosmology.

> The epistemological equivalent of the notion of an immanental cosmos is that of conceptual polarity. Such polarity requires that concepts which are significantly related are in fact symmetrically related, each requiring the other for adequate articulation. This is a truistic assertion about Chinese thinking, of course, and is usually illustrated with regard to the concepts of *yin* 陰 and *yang* 陽. *Yin* does not transcend *yang*, nor vice versa. *Yin* is always "becoming *yang*" and *yang* is always "becoming *yin*," night is always "becoming day" and day is always "becoming night." (1987, 17)

As a result, in early Chinese thought "there is no element or aspect that in the strictest sense transcends the rest. Every element in the world is relative to every other; all elements are *correlative*" (1987, 18). In considering this correlative polarity, Ames and Hall indicate a two-way influence between complementary events each of which requires the other as a necessary condition for being what it is. Each existent is "so of itself" [*ziran* 自然] and does not derive its meaning and order from any transcendent source. The notion of "self" in the locution "so of itself" has a polar relationship with "other." Each particular is a consequence of every other. And there is no contradiction in saying that each particular is both self-determinate and determined by every other particular, since each of the existing particulars is constitutive of every other as well. (1987, 18)

Hence, contrary to the Western dualistic view that tries to define the exact essence of objects and their place in the world, in early Chinese thought there is no transcendent separation between *natura naturans* and *natura naturata* (naturing nature and natured nature). The "Qiwulun" goes one step further in questioning the very possibility of differentiation. This, however, is not a simple negation of the reasoning process leaving everything undistinguished. The text is perfectly clear on this:

彼是莫得其偶，謂之道樞。樞始得其環中，以應無窮。是亦一無窮，非亦一無窮也。故曰「莫若以明」。

Where neither It nor Other finds its opposite is called the axis of the Way [*dao* 道]. When once the axis is found at the centre of the circle there is no limit to responding with either, on the one hand no limit to what is *it*, on the other no limit to what is not. Therefore I say: 'The best means is Illumination.' (4/2/30–31) (53)

It is not by chance that the author uses the metaphors of the circle and light. At the center of the circle everything can be seen and can be reached in every direction. And yet, this does not mean that all directions are the same or that the "other" is totally obliterated in the "it." The issue here is that one cannot use the teleological and idealistic dialectics to solve the polarity of *shifei*, which would result in a synthetic and implicit affirmation of *shi*.[6] Rather, the text suggests that there is no synthesis between dichotomies but they are simultaneously present in the axis of *dao* as non-opposing or as accommodating each other. When one finds this pivot, there is no limit to *shi* as well as no limit to *fei*. The problem, therefore, is to consider the questioning of *shifei* not as a dissolution of polarities but as a boundless possibility of relations.[7] In other words, more than a simple equalization, the *qi* of the "Qiwulun" is a correspondence—*cum-respondere*, literally "to answer together," which implies a mutual response, the rejoining of things to each other—in both its relational and analogical meaning.[8]

5.1.3 The Infinite Regression of Relations

The discourse on corresponding things indicates an ethical stance where opinions are not just equal but are equally corresponding. Therefore, the correspondence of *shifei* does not have the purpose to eliminate them. On the contrary, it aims to eliminate the presupposition that the controversies of *shifei* can be settled once and for all.[9] Looking from the axis of *dao* it is clear that everywhere *shifei* are at play. The difference is that, from this point of view, they are all equally valuable and inseparable insofar as one produces and transforms the other. And yet, even this axis is only metaphoric and cannot be located anywhere because *dao* has no boundaries.

The challenge, therefore, is not dissolving *shifei* by imposing discriminative values. The real challenge is to accept correspondences without deeming and setting permanent boundaries. To appreciate this, it is necessary to step out of the theocentric, anthropocentric, humanistic subject/object dichotomies and see the world from the pluralistic *wanwu*, that is to say, from the myriad things' perspective.[10]

> 夫道未始有封，言未始有常，為是而有畛也。請言其畛：有左，有右，有倫，有義，有分，有辯，有競，有爭，此之謂八德。六合之外，聖人存而不論；六合之內，聖人論而不議。春秋經世，先王之志，聖人議而不辯。

The Way has never had borders, saying has never had norms. It is by a 'That's it' which deems that a boundary is marked. Let me say something about the marking of boundaries. You can locate as there and enclose by a line, sort out and assess, divide up and discriminate between alternatives, compete over and fight over: these I call our Eight Powers. What is outside the cosmos the sage locates as there but does not sort out. What is within the cosmos the sage sorts out but does not assess. The records of the former kings in the successive reigns in the Annals the sage assesses, but he does not argue over alternatives. (5/2/55–57) (57)

All these discriminations and assessments, all the "Eight Powers," are the powers employed by humans in order to make sense of the world. The *Zhuangzi* seems to admit a degree of necessity for these powers. Still, it is meaningful how these necessities are organized in an order of rank. Even if the sage considers the possibilities of something outside the cosmos, he or she does not discuss or theorize about it—thus avoiding what in the Greek tradition was the first step toward metaphysical disputations. Regarding what is within the cosmos, the sage discusses but does not evaluate or criticize—thus avoiding any epistemological standard, so to speak. In the final analysis, even if the sage uses assessments for human affairs, these do not become a means to disputes. Therefore, there is no contention that can divide things because there is no division between them:

> 故分也者，有不分也；辯也者，有不辯也。曰：何也？聖人懷之，眾人辯之以相示也。故曰：辯也者，有不見也。

> To 'divide,' then, is to leave something undivided: to 'discriminate between alternatives' is to leave something which is neither alternative. 'What?' you ask. The sage keeps it in his breast, common men argue over alternatives to show it to each other. Hence I say: 'To "discriminate between alternatives" is to fail to see something.' (5/2/57–58) (57)

It is evident that the "Qiwulun" does not refuse distinctions but, more properly, refuses to turn these into alternatives.[11] In other words, it is necessary to avoid turning distinctions into either-or choices, which means to see distinctions not as excluding each other but as mutually related.

To see the relations between differences is to recognize the polyphony of nature and the polyphonic nature of humanity. To "discriminate between alternatives" is to fail to see this relation and to hear this polyphony. While common people argue over alternatives, the sage keeps everything in his breast. Therefore, "to fail to see something" means to fail to see that everything is continuous.[12] In this sense the "Qiwulun," using its peculiar double rhetorical question, asks if there is an it and an other (*you bi shi*) or if there is not an it and an other (*wu bi shi*) at all.

Someone can argue that there is another kind of discrimination in play here, the discrimination between *you* and *wu*. A reply could ask if there is actually a *youwu* or there is no *youwu* at all. This reply, however, would step in a *regressus ad infinitum*. And yet, this is probably the only way out or, even better, the only way *in*. The "Qiwulun" points precisely in this direction:

> 有始也者，有未始有始也者，有未始有夫未始有始也者。有有也者，有無也者，有未始有無也者，有未始有夫未始有無也者。俄而有無矣，而未知有無之果孰有孰無也。今我則已有謂矣，而未知吾所謂之其果有謂乎，其果無謂乎？

> There is 'beginning,' there is 'not yet having begun having a beginning.'

> —There is 'there not yet having begun to be that "not yet having begun having a beginning."'

> There is 'something,' there is 'nothing.'

> —There is 'not yet having begun being without something.'

> —There is 'there not yet having begun to be that "not yet having begun being without something."'

> All of a sudden '*there is* nothing,' and we do not yet know of something and nothing really which there is and which there is not. Now for my part I have already referred to something, but do not yet know whether my reference really referred to something or really did not refer to anything. (5/2/49–50) (55)

Here the regression is not only toward an origin that cannot be defined but also toward any kind of linguistic determinacy. The text clearly refers to something, but in questioning this reference the author is thematizing the polarity of *you* and *wu* itself. However, this thematization too is put into question by the possibility of not referring to anything. This is a typical strategy of the "Qiwulun" where a polarity is supposed just to be negated. And yet, this polarity needs to be in place in order to be negated.

The constant affirmation and its corresponding negation destabilize any possible ground for univocal standards. Thus, the regression goes in both directions: there is neither a reachable beginning nor a reachable conclusion, neither original meaning nor final determinacy. These infinite regressions are not faults in reasoning, but rather ethical assumptions, provided that one is able to step out of the subject/object dichotomy and step into the myriad things' perspective—which means to see the world from the axis of *dao* and appreciate the infinite relations of *youwu* and *shifei*.

5.1.4 The Self–Other Relationship

Let us consider how these relations are formed.

> 物無非彼，物無非是。自彼則不見，自知則知之。故曰：彼出於是，是亦因彼。彼是，方生之說也。
>
> No thing is not 'other,' no thing is not 'it.' If you treat yourself too as 'other' they do not appear, if you know of yourself [*zi zhi* 自知] you know of them. Hence it is said:
>
> "'Other' comes out from 'it,' 'it' likewise goes by 'other,'"
>
> the opinion that 'it' and 'other' are born simultaneously. (4/2/27–28) (52)[13]

If "no thing is not 'other'" and if "no thing is not 'it,'" one cannot exclude from this relation any single aspect of the world.[14] Whatever emerges in the world does not do so in an autonomous fashion but always in relation to its "other." More precisely, no one is without an other because one gives rise to the other and vice versa, they are mutually engendering. Consequently, it is not possible to single things out hierarchically, and every single new aspect is in reciprocal relation with the rest.

This becomes even clearer in the second part of the passage. Here Graham reaches one of the highest points in his interpretative translation. Since the first commentators, the passage is interpreted as a consideration of subjectivism and the impossibility of knowing from the point of view of the other.[15] Graham, however, overturns the perspective and interprets the sentences in a positive direction giving the reader the result of the critique rather than the critique itself. Therefore, if you conceive yourself as other—that is to say, if you single yourself out—no relation can be seen. If you know yourself—to wit, if you know the other in yourself—then you know the perspective of "it" and "other."[16]

This is directly the result of the preceding discourse. If no thing cannot be conceived as only "it" or only "other," one cannot be "other" from the rest. One not only is "othered" by the other—as we have seen in chapter 2—but is always both "it" and "other."[17] If one is detached from the rest, it is not possible to see the relation between things; that is, to lift oneself above the net of relations is to miss seeing something. The point is precisely to see that the myriad things are mutually engendering, and this clearly includes the self–other relationship.[18]

非彼無我，非我無所取

Without an Other there is no Self, without Self no choosing one thing rather than another. (4/2/14–15) (51)

Going one step further in this direction, it becomes evident how, in the end, all the polarities of the "Qiwulun" are "self–other" (*wo bi* 我彼) polarities. Yet even the self–other polarities need to be conceived in their infinite possibility of relations, without origin or determinacy. Indeed, "since the world and I are born together, the myriad things and I are continuous" (*tiandi yu wo bing sheng, er wanwu yu wo wei yi* 天地與我並生，而萬物與我為一) (5/2/52–53).[19] Hence, from the axis of *dao*, the self corresponds with the world and vice versa. From the myriad things' perspective, self and other are constantly in shifting positions. This opens an extremely broad ethical horizon.

According to Chen Shaoming (2004, Introduction 8), the "Qiwulun" shows how, in facing the world, one not only needs to get rid of the self-centered humanism, but also ought to learn how to respect every single element of the world, "no matter if it is a person, a fish or a bird." He affirms that this is the intimate meaning of "I have lost my-self" (*wu sang wo* 吾喪我). According to him (2004, 11), "the body as dried wood and the heart as dead ashes are precisely the correspondence of things and self."[20] Similarly, Chen Guying (2008, 210) considers the "Qiwulun" not only as a discourse on the equality of things but also as "parting from the self-centered structure." Therefore, in the last analysis, the "Qiwulun" can be considered as *qi wu wo* 齊物我 and, more precisely, as *qi bi wo* 齊彼我, which is only another way of saying *wanwu yu wo wei yi* 萬物與我為一. Still, what does this *yi* 一 entail?

5.2 Walking Both Ways

The discourse on corresponding things has shown how the *Zhuangzi* conceives of the relations of polarities. Through the analysis of *shifei* it became evident that the text calls into question the legitimacy of any standard that wants to define the world univocally. This critical approach toward the discriminative function of language goes so far as to question the differentiation between human saying and the sounds of nature.

As we have seen, however, the point is not to dissolve differentiations but to be aware of them. In this sense, with its critical approach to *shifei*, the *Zhuangzi* proposes not a dissolution of polarities but the boundless possibility of relations. In other words, the text suggests that, rather than turning distinctions into either-or choices, one needs to see them as mutually related possibilities. If this is conceivable, then the sound of language is not in opposition to the sounds of nature but totally inscribed in them. And this, in turn, shows how everything in the world is continuous.

In this section, I would like to expand on this by discussing the aesthetic implications of perceiving the continuity of myriad things in their double movement of assimilation and differentiation. Let me start with a closer analysis of this continuity.

5.2.1 The Continuity of *Yi* 一

Chen Guying (2008, 218) considers *yi* not only as a "comprehensive harmony" that dissolves boundaries, but also as a wholeness in which everything is a constant process of transformation. This means that *yi* is not a static "One," but a comprehensive and harmonious flux in which differentiation always returns on itself. The "Qiwulun" clearly describes this perpetual metamorphosis of things:

其分也，成也；其成也，毀也。凡物無成與毀，復通為一

Their dividing is formation, their formation is dissolution; all things whether forming or dissolving in reverting interchange and are deemed to be one [*fu tong wei yi* 復通為一]. (4/2/35–36) (53)

If a oneness needs to be thought, this is not any kind of substance but a continuity of transformations. Chen Guying (2008, 218) explains that, in its fragmented dissolution, a thing contributes to the formation of a new one and the constitution of this new thing includes the element of the former dissolved one. Thus, fragmentation, formation, and dissolution are all part of a continuous process, namely, *yi*.

The continuity of transformations described by *yi* is the unity of time and space, which implies that not only are the myriad things continuous and without borders but they also proceed continuously. In chapter 22 Zhuangzi says,

物物者與物無際，而物有際者，所謂物際者也；不際之際，際之不際者也。

What makes things things has no border between it and things; it is the borders which are between things which we mean by the borders of things. It is the unbordered borderer, the unbordered which borders. (59/22/50–51) (162)

In commenting on the last part of this passage, Tang Junyi (1988c, 103) affirms that one should not consider the world described here as a Oneness in the Western sense. According to him, this world is an unbounded boundary (*bu ji zhi ji* 不際之際) in which this kind of boundary becomes the no-boundary that bounds (*ji zhi bu ji zhe* 際之不際者). Tang infers that although this is only "one world," it is so because it includes the inexhaustible and boundless change; consequently, it becomes the inexhaustible and boundless world.

The English language, however, cannot fully convey Tang's idea. Aware of this discrepancy of languages and reference systems, Tang (1988c, 103) specifies that "Chinese philosophers say 'our World' and not 'our World is A World'; they also do not say 'it is The World,' they just say, 'World.'" Thus, Tang underlines that the absence of the article before "world" has an important meaning. According to him, while Chinese philosophers consider the world as one, they do not consider it as "The One." That is to say, the unity of Chinese worldview does not rely on the uniqueness but on change: "Chinese philosophers consider 'world' as 'world,' they are indifferent to 'this one' or 'the only one.' Chinese philosophers do not have 'this one' and 'the only one' view" (102). This becomes clearer if one follows Tang's idea of time.

5.2.2 The Shape of Time

In the Chinese perspective, time and space are not distinct: the shape of time is the shape of everything in the world. Since the world is characterized by change, if there were no time in this process, the world could not become what it is (Tang 1988c, 107). Thus, "it can be said that the world is what it is, because it is shaped by time" (1988c, 107–108). Tang concludes that time and the myriad things of the world cannot be divided.[21] To prove this idea, he mentions passages from different sources. Among them, the one from the *Liezi* is particularly interesting: "things that constantly arise and constantly change, there is never a time when they do not arise, there is never a time when they do not change (*chang sheng chang hua zhe, wu shi bu sheng, wu shi bu hua* 常生常化者，無時不生，無時不化)" (1988c, 107).[22] Change is the result of the correspondence between time and space: one produces the other and vice versa in a unity that is also a differentiation.

As a consequence of this unity of time and space, it is essential to understand that *fu tong wei yi* 復通為一 is not a return to a higher status in a teleological fashion but a return to continuity. In the process of transformation, things are constantly arising from each other and dissolving into each other. Simultaneously, the myriad things are constitutive of a wholeness and this wholeness is formed by the transformation of the myriad things, which in turn is produced by and produces time. Therefore, the returning of all things into *yi* means that they return into a continuous wholeness; that is to say, the same continuity returns on itself as transformation. Indeed, *wanwu* and *yi* form a polarity as well, and like all the elements of the other polarities it is crucial to consider them in their reciprocal correspondence: the myriad things form a continuous flux and, simultaneously, a continuous flux produces myriad things.

This, however, must be regarded not as a mere ontological stance but as an ethical one. One needs to think of the world as *yi* in its double aspect of process and wholeness in order to keep all the myriad things in balance: this whole process of becoming allows the myriad things to transform into each other without any of them assuming a higher status. As already seen, the infinite regression proposed by the "Qiwulun" destabilizes any possible ground for univocal standards of judgments. This implies that neither *wu* nor *you* can assume the role of original or final ground.[23] Thus, *yi* as wholeness of transformations is an alternative to the onto-theological structure Being–beings.

Similarly, *dao* cannot be conceived as a Parmenidean Being that grounds the myriad things. If this were the case, it would not be clear how one can damage it. The *Zhuangzi* openly states that *dao* is damaged by the emergence of disputations (5/2/42).[24] This means that *dao* is not a metaphysical essence but the process of the dynamic balance between the myriad things that forms *yi*. From the perspective of *dao*, *shi* and *fei* are in balance and have no limits. As soon as this balance is compromised by the imposition of a univocal standard for judgments that does not consider its correspondence with other values, *dao* starts being harmed.

Thus, *dao* cannot be determined univocally as the essence of the myriad things because, as a dynamic process, it is constantly in the making, that is to say: "*dao* is formed by walking it (*dao xing zhi er cheng* 道行之而成)" (4/2/33). Taking part in this process, one participates in the continuity of the myriad things and their revolving transformation.

5.2.3 Revolving Transformations

In its revolving transformation, everything returns on itself both as part of the myriad things and as a continuity. Hence, in the last analysis, the wholeness is the returning of the myriad things into the continuity of fragmentation, formation, and dissolution, which is produced by and produces time. It is fundamental to understand this double movement of things from differentiation to assimilation and from assimilation to differentiation. Only in this way is it possible to preserve the plurality of values and, at the same time, to keep the correspondence of these same values. This is one of the most important ethical stances of the *Zhuangzi*.

If everything transforms and returns into one continuity, then this same continuity transforms and returns into the myriad things. It is not possible to reduce one to the other: they go both ways—"this is called 'walking both ways'" (*shi zhi wei liang xing* 是之謂兩行) (5/2/40). From the pivot of *dao* these two sides of the polarity are not in contrast but corresponding. Therefore, *wanwu yu wo wei yi* does not reduce everything to one univocal expression. On the contrary, it opens subjectivity to the plurality of the world and, simultaneously, it considers all their corresponding values. Being continuous with the myriad things means to participate in their constant transforming diversification and, concurrently, in their corresponding assimilation.

Therefore, from the perspective of *dao*, inner and outer, subject and object, *wanwu* and *yi*, *shi* and *fei*, and so on and so forth, are constantly revolving—continuously shifting their positions. The intention of the "Qiwulun" is not to obliterate them but to keep them present in a mutual entailing correspondence. As stated by Chen Guying (2008, 222), "abolishing the conflicting relation between the world's myriad things and the self—that is, between the object and the subject—then it is possible to attain a state in which subject/object are organically assimilated. . . . This state is the state of 'being without boundaries.'" Things do not vanish in an indistinguishable homogeneity but they are not in opposition either. This means that, from the perspective of *dao*, the world is not an amorphous and undifferentiated flat plane but an unbounded plurality of relations.[25] Still, it is necessary to recall that this perspective is not provided by a metaphysical essence. Rather, the unbounded plurality seen from the perspective of *dao* is always an understanding and, therefore, an interpretative value, even though this one is not confined to the subject/object dichotomy and entails the ethical possibility of accepting all the other values.

Thus, when Changwuzi 長梧子 says to Ququezi 瞿鵲子 "You and Confucius are both dreams, and I who call you a dream am also a dream" (6/2/83) (60), his rationale overturns the possibility of defining an objective reality—what can be less objective than a dream? Still, not only is the object deprived of its objectivity but the subject is also deprived of its capacity to objectify the other. If subject and object are both dreams, there is no possibility for the subject to ground in itself the objective truth of reality. This entails that the self and the other as dreams can correspond and, simultaneously, can preserve their own diversity.

The butterfly dream reinforces the necessity to step out of the anthropocentric subject/object dichotomy to appreciate the perspective that the "Qiwulun" suggests. If this is possible, it becomes evident how the position proposed in the text is neither subjectivist nor objectivist. Indeed, the critique of *shifei* is intended to undermine any sort of perspectivism. This is not to say that the "Qiwulun" negates the presence of perspectives; rather, by acknowledging the constant opposition of *shifei* in human activities it underlines their intrinsic correspondence. On the other hand, neither does this critique of perspectivism result in any affirmation of objective reality. If *shifei* are at play everywhere, and if they are all corresponding, there is no final ground that allows the formulation of a standard for judgments. Thus, the philosophy proposed by the "Qiwulun" can be defined neither as absolutist nor as relativist or skeptical.[26] The problem is that its philosophy cannot be regarded as merely epistemological. To grasp its content, it is necessary to consider the ethical and aesthetic stances that are naturally implied by its epistemology.

5.3 The Aesthetic Encounter with the World

We have seen so far that the critique offered by the "Qiwulun" through the analysis of *shifei* does not aim to simply affirm any epistemology or ontology. The scope of the discourse on corresponding things is not to define the substance of the myriad things but to consider their values. The myriad things are not simply equal—as if they shared the same substance—but are equally valuable depending on the perspective taken by the observers. This implies a correspondence of values that undermines any affirmation of ontological and metaphysical absolutization. This is not to say that one cannot express absolute stances; it is to say that their values are corresponding to any other one.

For similar reasons some scholars use terms such as "non-metaphysics" (Cheng 1989) or "ametaphysics" (Ames 2015c) to describe early Chinese philosophy. These are authoritative positions and are useful to differentiate the Chinese perspective from the onto-theological nature of Western metaphysics. Cheng Chung-ying (1989, 167–168), however, negates Chinese metaphysics in the sense of a "separation of the sensible from the nonsensible, the practical from the transcendental." According to him, metaphysical thinking in the Chinese context "is a matter of seeking the way, the comprehensive and integrative understanding of reality, with all its changes and transformations. Metaphysics is not to go beyond this reality, but to embrace it" (206).

It is difficult to disagree with this position. And yet, in the context of the *Zhuangzi*, what is this reality that Cheng takes for granted? If there are no standards, it is not clear how one can define reality, let alone embrace it. The butterfly dream at the end of the "Qiwulun" is a clear example of this uncertainty, which undermines any possibility of ontological assurance by dissolving the separation between sensible and nonsensible. If one needs to embrace something, it is precisely this uncertainty—that is, to welcome both reality and dream, affirmation and negation, life and death. Thanks to this, one can accept the world, not just as it is but also as it might be, which entails that one is open to the transformation of things and ready to be part of it.[27]

If it is possible to embrace the unknown and to change through it, if it is possible to dance with one's own fate, then one is open to the other in the widest sense. The possibility to cross boundaries and appreciate values from different perspectives opens an ethical sphere in which a dialogue between the self and the other is not only possible but also facilitated. The self and the other correspond to and welcome each other in a reciprocal hospitality that dissolves limits and, simultaneously, preserves differences.

As seen, contrary to the onto-theological nature of Western metaphysics that imposes a single logic for its hierarchical structure Being–beings, the correspondence of myriad things allows the differentiation and assimilation of values in a comprehensive and harmonious fashion. Thus, the *Zhuangzi* offers an ethical reading of the world in which no single perspective is affirmed, let alone the anthropocentric or theocentric ones. And in so doing the text describes the encounter and correspondence between perspectives along with the revolving transformation of the myriad things and their values. In a historical moment in which the world needs to find a new balance not only among populations but also between humankind and nature, the *Zhuangzi* proposes an ethical stance that should be taken very seriously.

5.3.1 Aesthetic Awareness

While the "Qiwulun," faithful to its nonassertive nature, does not propose a positive moral that indicates a specific code of conduct, it offers a possibility that welcomes other possibilities and thus hints to a wider ethos toward oneself, the other, and the world. Yet, as we have seen at the end of the previous chapter with *wuqing* 無情, the *Zhuangzi* suggests not only that it is possible to assimilate differentiations but also that one can proceed on the process of life with undiscriminative feelings. To do this, one needs to change perspective: on the one hand, this is a shift from anthropocentrism to the perspective of *wanwu*; on the other hand, this shift entails moving from the epistemic to the aesthetic.

It is through the aesthetic encounter with the world that one can know how to deal with it; simultaneously, dealing with the world allows the refinement of an aesthetic awareness in a never-ending process. There can be no pre-set moral norms to guide the encounter with the other at large; one can only act on the basis of contingent aesthetic encounters. This is the intimate meaning of the famous skill stories of the *Zhuangzi*.[28]

In the story of Cook Ding that directly follows the "Qiwulun" in the third chapter of the *Zhuangzi*, the cook affirms,

> 進乎技矣。始臣之解牛之時，所見无非牛者。三年之後，未嘗見全牛也。方今之時，臣以神遇，而不以目視，官知止而神欲行。⋯⋯ 文惠君曰：「善哉！吾聞庖丁之言，得養生焉。」

'I have left skill behind me. When I first began to carve oxen, I saw nothing but oxen wherever I looked. Three years more and I never saw an ox as a whole. Nowadays, I am in touch through the daemonic in me, and do not look with the eye. With the senses I know where to stop, the daemonic I desire to run its course.' . . . 'Excellent!' said Lord Wen-hui. 'Listening to the words of Cook Ting, I have learned from them how to nurture life.' (7/3/5–12) (63–64)

Cook Ding does not practice a pre-established method, he does not act with *ratio*: he proceeds with all his senses.[29] Practicing his art through the years, he becomes able to leave skills behind himself. The story is a clear example of how knowledge can become aesthetic awareness. When this awareness is achieved, the knowledge is no longer needed and can be forgotten giving space to spontaneity (*ziran*). It is not by chance that the lord ends the episode affirming of having learned "how to nurture life."

In other passages, however, the *Zhuangzi* suggests that one needs to actively forget some forms of knowledge in order for the aesthetic to gain priority over the epistemic. But what does it mean to forget knowledge? In the previous chapter, we have seen that the *Daodejing* warns against the risk of assigning restrictive definitions. Yet this kind of definition can be already in place in one's life. And when this is the case, one needs to unlearn what has been learned from an education that proceeds with hard discriminations.

The issue in the *Daodejing* is not to avoid knowledge *per se* but to get rid of the obstructive elements imposed by external systems of reference. In this way, one can stop interfering with *ziran* and start the reversal process. The *Zhuangzi* expresses a similar attitude with concepts such as "I have lost my-self" (*wu sang wo* 吾喪我), "heart fasting" (*xinzhai* 心齋), and "sitting and forgetting" (*zuowang* 坐忘). Let me consider the latter in more detail.

5.3.2 What Is Forgotten in "Sitting and Forgetting" (*Zuowang* 坐忘)?

Zuowang appears in chapter 6 of the *Zhuangzi* in a dialogue between Confucius and his disciple Yan Hui 顏回. Here, however, the main role is played by Yan Hui, who, in describing his gradual progress, makes quite an impression on Confucius, to the extent that he asks to become his disciple:

顏回曰：「回益矣。」仲尼曰：「何謂也？」曰：「回忘仁義矣。」曰：「可矣，猶未也。」他日復見，曰：「回益矣。」曰：「何謂也？」曰：「回忘禮樂矣。」曰：「可矣，猶未也。」他日復見，曰：「回益矣。」曰：「何謂也？」曰：「回坐忘矣。」仲尼蹴然曰：「何謂坐忘？」顏回曰：「墮肢體，黜聰明，離形去知，同於大通，此謂坐忘。」仲尼曰：「同則無好也，化則無常也。而果其賢乎！丘也請從而後也。」

'I make progress,' said Yen Hui.
'Where?' said Confucius.
'I have forgotten about rites and music.'
'Satisfactory. But you still have far to go.'

Another day he saw Confucius again.
'I make progress.'
'Where?'
'I have forgotten about Goodwill and Duty.'
'Satisfactory. But you still have far to go.'

Another day he saw Confucius again.
'I make progress.'
'Where?'
'I just sit and forget [*zuowang*坐忘].'

Confucius was taken aback.
'What do you mean, just sit and forget?'
'I let organs and members drop away, dismiss eyesight and hearing, part from the body [*li xing* 離形] and expel knowledge [*qu zhi* 去知], and go along with the universal thoroughfare [*da tong* 大通]. This is what I mean by "just sit and forget."'
'If you go along with it, you have no preferences; if you let yourself transform, you have no norms. Has it really turned out that you are the better of us? Oblige me by accepting me as your disciple.' (17/6/89–93) (92)

Zuowang entails two main aspects: to part from the body [*li xing* 離形] and to expel knowledge [*qu zhi* 去知]. In commenting on this passage, Chen Guying (1985, 23) explains that to part from the body does not mean to discard it; rather, it means to eliminate the greed that arouses from the physical condition. According to him, the *Zhuangzi* does not negate human desires: since these are part of the human intrinsic nature and since the *Zhuangzi* suggests following one's own nature, it cannot negate them.

To part from the body, therefore, needs to be considered in relation to knowledge. It is necessary to expel all the imposing and coercive limitations—deriving from one's own self-centered perspective—that obstruct the access to the spontaneous continuity with the myriad things. In this sense, Cook Ding does not need to *think* about his art, he can leave behind his skill and *do* what his senses perceive.[30]

Thus, one can go along with *da tong*, the great thoroughfare, without hesitations. This is perfectly in line with what we have seen in the previous chapter in relation to *wuwei* and *wuming*. Regarding *da tong*, Chen Guying (1985, 23) holds that, reaching this kind of state, one can be as the world's myriad things, merging with them without preferential treatments and prejudices: " 'If you go along with it, you have no preferences; if you let yourself transform, you have no norms.' This is precisely the depiction of *da tong*'s state."[31]

As a result, it is not possible to interpret this passage as a rejection of life or as a disruption of the sensible. Keeping Nietzsche in mind, one can also say that *zuowang* does not mean the annihilation of the will. The issue is to understand what needs to be forgotten. If one regards this forgetting as an *absolute* process and considers that everything needs to be discarded, then the sitting and forgetting is equivalent to death. If one were able to forget everything and to keep this state, one would be unable to function—at least in social life—and would not be able to express this state—how can anything be expressed if everything is forgotten?

Talking with Confucius, Yan Hui not only retains the capacity of language but is also perfectly aware of what he has achieved. Similarly to *wuming*, *zuowang* does not erase *everything*, it does not pursue the complete annihilation of one's will; if this were the case, there would be no reason for Yan Hui to express his achievement. And this achievement cannot be questioned since Yan Hui himself refers to it as a progress (*yi* 益). Yan Hui needs to have learned what rites and music, goodwill and duty are in order to forget them. Simultaneously, even when they are forgotten, this process does not result in a total loss. *Zuowang* functions as a removal of obstructions such as the ones represented by rites and duties: when they are put aside, they cannot hinder the way, even if they are still recognizable in the world.

Hence, this removal is not a permanent loss. If this were the case, one would run the risk of not recognizing what has been forgotten and learn it again. Nor is this removal a momentary one. *Zuowang* is not just a meditative practice that allows to temporarily remove obstructions. Confucius himself affirms that "if you go along with it, you have no preferences; if you let yourself transform, you have no norms." This entails that the process of sitting and forgetting is not limited to a meditative moment but is a radical change of perspective.

Yan Hui has a precise notion of what he has achieved and what he has forgotten. To forget does not mean to embrace a vegetative life or to momentarily be absent; it means to undermine the value of one's own systems of reference. In a broader sense, it is possible to follow the indication of Wu Kuang-ming (1982, 31) when he states that

> to come to understand Chuang Tzu involves a revised—indeed, novel—understanding of 'understanding' itself. Such a revision, once started, inevitably ends in a revolution of one's entire life, for one lives according to one's life attitude, which in turn originates in one's *way* of understanding life. To revise understanding is to revise life, and to revise life is to view life anew, that is, a life revolution. . . . All this, however, puts a strain on our *method* of understanding. Since Chuang Tzu seems to insist that a proper understanding of him entails a rejection of usual understandings of understanding, he demands nothing less than a transvaluation in hermeneutics.

And what can this transvaluation be if not a removal of static norms and ossified understandings? If such a transvaluation can be achieved, this will be possible through sitting and forgetting. Yet this "revolution" does not produce new norms. In the *Zhuangzi*, more than a "novel" understanding of understanding, there is a distrust for any stable understanding. Even if a novel understanding of understanding is possible, this cannot become an ultimate understanding. Thus, forgetting is a revision of one's own life attitude insofar as it discards norms in favor of a direct and ever anew aesthetic involvement with the world.

Seen in this way, *zuowang* develops and broadens the possibility of learning to unlearn discussed in the previous chapter.[32] As a consequence, sitting and forgetting does not entail any refusal of the world; quite the reverse: the world is accepted in its plurality without exceptions and norms. Similarly, forgetting the self means not mere oblivion but the most intimate relation to the myriad things and their transformations. Thus, the apprehension of the world becomes an ethic/aesthetic process more than an epistemic one.

Not only is any knowledge relative to its frame of references but also any life experience is relative to the specific configuration of the world in which the experience takes place. Thus, the appraisal of an experience is the result of the relation between reference systems and the configuration of the world in which these systems apply. When one sees this, it becomes evident that knowledge is constantly shifting because the relation to the world cannot be stable and, therefore, systems of reference need to be constantly adjusted to new settings. This makes the appraisal of an experience an active process of adjustments, as the story of Cook Ding suggests when he encounters a difficult cut in a complicated joint. This implies that the *Zhuangzi* proposes an aesthetic ethos that does not rely on normative reference systems and discards stable knowledge.

5.3.3 Aesthetic Ethos

As a consequence of the previous discussion, we can conclude that aesthetic awareness cannot be passed down because it must be learned firsthand. Thus, the epistemological and ethical stances are strictly related to the aesthetic involvement with the world. The resulting value of an experience is the interplay between the self and the other that the aesthetic approach to the world enables. Hence, if values are linked to reference systems and world configurations, and if these systems and configurations are constantly shifting, the values attached to experiences are also unstable. This is intelligible from the story of the wheelwright in the chapter 13 of the *Zhuangzi*:

> 桓公讀書於堂上，輪扁斲輪於堂下，釋椎鑿而上，問桓公曰：「敢問公之所讀者何言邪？」公曰：「聖人之言也。」曰：「聖人在乎？」公曰：「已死矣。」曰：「然則君之所讀者，古人之糟魄已夫！」桓公曰：「寡人讀書，輪人安得議乎！有說則可，無說則死。」輪扁曰：「臣也，以臣之事觀之。斲輪，徐則甘而不固，疾則苦而不入。不徐不疾，得之於手而應於心，口不能言，有數存焉於其間。臣不能以喻臣之子，臣之子亦不能受之於臣，是以行年七十而老斲輪。古之人與其不可傳也死矣，然則君之所讀者，古人之糟魄已夫。」

Duke Huan was reading a book at the top of the hall, wheelwright Pien was chipping a wheel at the bottom of the hall. He put aside his mallet and chisel and went up to ask Duke Huan

> 'May I ask what words my lord is reading?'
> 'The words of a sage.'
> 'Is the sage alive?'
> 'He's dead.'
> 'In that case what my lord is reading is the dregs of the men of old, isn't it?'
> 'What business is it of a wheelwright to criticise what I read? If you can explain yourself, well and good; if not, you die.'

'Speaking for myself, I see it in terms of my own work. If I chip at a wheel too slowly, the chisel slides and does not grip; if too fast, it jams and catches in the wood. Not too slow, not too fast; I feel it in the hand and respond from the heart, the mouth cannot put it into words, there is a knack in it somewhere which I cannot convey to my son and which my son cannot learn from me. This is how through my seventy years I have grown old chipping at wheels. The men of old and their untransmittable message are dead. Then what my lord is reading is the dregs of the men of old, isn't it?' (36/13/68–74) (139–140)

The impossibility to transmit to the son the knowledge acquired avoids any sort of epistemology of absolute truth, which in turn points toward the necessity of a direct aesthetic experience of the world. There is no description of objects and actions that can allow an effective transmission of knowledge which is, *de facto*, impossible in a world of constant transforming things (*wuhua* 物化). Only through an aesthetic experience can one encounter and find a balance with the other at large.

The messages from the past are dead words if they are not actualized and experienced firsthand. Thus, one needs to be constantly ready to perceive the world in new ways, discarding previous knowledge to open the space to new understanding. In this sense, one can only rely on personal aesthetic awareness to be part of the myriad things and their revolving transformation.

It is not by chance that the *Huainanzi* 淮南子, in chapter 12 (110/1–8), connects the story of the wheelwright—which is quoted from the *Zhuangzi* almost exactly—with the first lines of the *Daodejing*.[33] The link between these two passages indicates, on the one hand, the impossibility of transmitting knowledge and, on the other hand, the importance of personally and aesthetically engaging with the world. The wheelwright, whose work method is "not too slow, not too fast," perfectly describes a *dao* that cannot be followed—not even by his own son—but needs to be constantly found and put into practice through the personal encounter with the world.

The tale of the wheelwright does not give a unique solution for all conducts but, rather, affirms that, in every new circumstance, a new conduct needs to be found. Moreover, conducts cannot be taught and cannot be learned; they must be directly experienced. This aesthetic ethos suggests that, in dealing with the world and with the other at large, one needs to constantly find new balances. "Not too slow, not too fast" helps to understand how only through the attunement to the other one can understand and find a direction of conduct. The *Zhuangzi* suggests this asystematic reasoning that requires a more general awareness of the world and the other along with a more direct engagement with them.

We can now see how *wuqing* 無情 clears the way from the impediments of preconceived structures of approaching the world. The undesiring process—similarly to the sitting and forgetting—helps to regain the spontaneous engagement with oneself, the other, and the world. *Wuqing* opens the possibility for an experience of the other that is nondiscriminative in its feelings. In acknowledging *wuqing*—as well as *wuwei, wuming,* and *zuowang*—one undoes norms and their restrictions so as to avoid inwardly wounding one's own self. Without wounds and with nondiscriminative feelings, one opens the self to the other, to the world, and to the revolving transformation of things. With this unwounded and nondiscriminative self, one is aesthetically involved with the world inasmuch as one is touched by and touches others spontaneously: not too slow, not too fast, the encounter with the world proceeds as a harmonious dance.

Returning to the Beginning
(by Way of Conclusion)

This book ought to conclude by returning to the beginning. I started this journey toward a philosophy of comparisons and toward the encounter with the other. The aim was to produce what Allinson (1989b, 3) defines as "a shift in our fundamental way of understanding, which is, in the end, the only way to understand across cultures." It is time now to define this shift as the passage from metaphysical representations to aesthetic life.

To begin with, this shift cannot be performed without some intermediate steps. We have seen in chapter 2—in relation to the discussion on the *Weltbild*—that the possibility to determine an internal and an external world is the foundation of the subject/object dichotomy. Along with this dichotomy, the possibility of representing a truthful and objective world grounded on the subjective self arises. I have analyzed how the Cartesian *cogito* defines not only what a *subiectum* is but also what objects are, thus grounding the distinctions between an internal and an external world. On the other side, I have discussed how the *Zhuangzi* proceeds in the opposite direction.

According to the *Zhuangzi* one should avoid making categorical distinctions and, even more importantly, one should avoid wounding oneself with likes and dislikes. With the analysis of the "Qiwulun" and with the discussion on *shifei* 是非 we have seen the importance of considering the self and the other as corresponding and not as distinct. In this respect, the most serious wound is the one that divides the continuity of things, determining "what is" and "what is not." The analysis of the *Zhuangzi* led me to conclude that in stepping out of the anthropocentric perspective one can preserve the continuity of self and other as well as humanity and cosmos.

I can now consider how the perspectives proposed by *cogito* and *qiwulun* derive from and produce two different aesthetic configurations: more precisely, the former can be regarded as an-aesthetic and the latter as aesthetic. The vision of the world proposed by the onto-theology is a sealed vision of the self that determines the world in an absolute and categorical fashion. Conversely, the vision proposed by a correspondence of relations implies the impossibility of separation between elements of the world. On the one side, the world as truthful world loses any aesthetic value and acquires pure conceptual and numerical values. On the other side, the world of correspondences is a world based on the maximum of aesthetic value. The truthful world is a measurable word that is tested and ordered to prove the theories of a detached self that re-presents it as objective.[1] The world of correspondences is an unmeasurable and unquantifiable world that needs to be aesthetically experienced firsthand in its continuity of self and other.

From the Western standpoint, the condemnation of the senses can be traced back to Plato. His allegory of the cave is a case in point: the senses are misleading because they interpret the shadows as real, which implies that only the intellect can see the reality of the outside world. This metaphysical approach has profound consequences for Plato's aesthetic theory. In the *Ion*, Plato puts Socrates in dialogue with Ion, a professional reciter specializing in poetry. Through Socrates, Plato questions the value of both rhapsody and poetry, expanding the critique of poets already present in the *Apology* (22 a–b).

The crucial critique that Socrates moves to Ion is that he has no art because the real power comes from a god. Similarly, "it is not by art that poets compose and say many beautiful things about their subjects . . . but by divine apportionment." This means that "the god takes the mind out of them and uses them as his servants, as he uses oracles and divine prophets: so that we their hearers may know it is not they, in whom mind is not present, who tell things of such great value, but the god himself who speaks, making utterance to us through them" (*Ion* 533d–534c).[2] In this passage, it is patent that art is something deriving from outside human beings, something that can only exist insofar as there is a god that allows it. This perspective implies a radical separation between art and artist that undermines the role of the artist.

In his comment on the text, Reginald Allen (Plato 1996, 7) underlines that the "*Ion* does not present a theory of poetry, or of rhapsody, and to describe rhapsody or poetry as a matter of divine apportionment without intelligence is not to praise it but to dismiss it." The main element here, similarly to the one of the cave allegory, is that the knowledge of the world cannot derive from the senses because the senses are far from the realm of *ideas*. This becomes even clearer in relation to visual arts. In Plato's philosophy, "the function of imitating sensory reality is so base that it not only depresses the visual arts and imitative poetry to the level of technique but even places these accomplishments at the lowest rung of technique, lower even than the work of an honest handicraft" (Tatarkiewicz 1980, 101). In this view, if art wants to abandon the function of imitating sensory reality, it ought to be an-aesthetic.

Here, the roles of mimesis (μίμησις, mainly translated as "imitation" but also meaning "representation" and "emulation") and form (*eîdos* εἶδος) are central. In the well-known passage of *Republic* 596–601, Plato suggests that there are forms that are references for categories of objects such as tables and couches made by carpenters. Although these objects only resemble the pure forms, they are real. The same cannot be said for paintings.

The passage explains that there are forms created by a god as unique and, for this reason, they are the truthful references for any other production. In other words, the carpenter who produces a couch resembles the truth of that form. This, however, does not mean that the product of the carpenter has anything special. Quite the reverse: in being only one particular imitation of the general form, the carpenter's creation is far removed from the truthful form created by the god. The product of the painter has even less dignity: while the objects of the craftsman are shaped taking the unique forms as models, the products of the painter imitate not the forms but the objects already present in the world. For this reason, Plato says that the painter

> 'is an imitator of what those craftsmen make.'
> 'Very well' I said. 'So you call "imitator" the maker of the product which is two removes from nature, do you?'
> 'I do indeed,' he said. (597e)[3]

If the painter is twice removed from nature, then the question for Plato becomes, "What is the object of painting? Does it aim to imitate what is, as it is? Or imitate what appears, as it appears? Is it imitation of appearance, or of truth?" (598a) It is not difficult to imagine the reply: the painting is imitation of appearance and, therefore, "the art of imitation is a far cry from truth" (598b). The main reason for this is that "the creator of images, the imitator, has no knowledge of what is, but only of what appears to be" (601b). We are back to the allegory of the cave.

The crucial element in Plato's view is that, in the production of an artwork, there is no knowledge because the reference is not the truthful form but the appearance. The appearance is such because the senses are deceiving. Hence, in the last instance, the condemnation of art is the condemnation of the senses in a progressive anaesthetization of the aesthetic and idealization of the metaphysical world as the *real* world. The senses are incapable of seeing what knowledge requires: that is, the *real* light of the sun, the truth, the absolute forms, the eternal ideas.

This vision had a profound influence on the Western philosophical tradition, to the extent that, not long ago, Pierre Hadot (1995, 94) claimed that the separation of the soul from the body is "nothing other than *the* fundamental philosophical choice." According to him, "the goal of this philosophical separation is for the soul to liberate itself, shedding the passions linked to the corporeal senses, so as to attain to the autonomy of thought." In quoting a similar passage in which Hadot affirms that "the theoretical philosophical discourse is completely different from the lived exercises by which the soul purifies itself of its passions and spiritually separates itself from the body," Arnold Davidson (1995, 28) concludes that "philosophy consists of a lived concrete exercise and not of a theory or a conceptual edifice." This is quite contradictory: if the soul separates itself from the body, would this not leave space only to the conceptual edifice without possibility for any aesthetic experience?

Although one can agree with Hadot that the act of philosophizing is not confined to the philosophical discourse and is embedded in the lived experience, it is difficult to accept that such an experience is restricted to the separation of the soul from the body. Otherwise, this "philosophy as way of life" would only be a *Platonic-Cartesian* philosophy: the "pathway to the withdrawal of our mind from the senses" (Descartes 2008, 10, AT VII, 12).[4] One can argue that, for Hadot, this is the only "fundamental philosophical choice" and there is no other philosophy outside this tradition. He himself suggests this in saying that

> the word 'philosophy' corresponds first of all to an historical phenomenon. It was the Greeks who created the word, probably in the sixth or fifth century BC, and it was Plato who gave it its strongest meaning: *philo-sophia*, 'love of wisdom,' the wisdom which one lacks. Since that time there has been an intellectual, spiritual, and social phenomenon, which has taken on a variety of forms, and which has been called philosophy. From this point

of view, it is legitimate to ask whether there exists a 'philosophy' outside of the Western tradition. (1995, 281)

This only restates the opinion of Heidegger that we encountered in chapters 1 and 3, which makes the position of Hadot not only derivative but also heavily biased in the context of a philosophy of comparisons.

As we have seen, one of the main scopes of Western philosophy is to inquire what *is*. Because the truth is an absolute idea, it is necessary to divide the realm of truth from the realm of appearances, the *kosmos noetos* from the *kosmos aisthetos*, the outside world where the sun shines and the inside world of the cave where there are only shadows. The natural consequence of this logic is the subordination of the perceptual to the conceptual with the metaphysical distinctions of sensible and supersensible, aesthetic and an-aesthetic. This implies that even the *appreciation* of beauty is subordinated to the *knowledge* of beauty as an absolute idea. David Sedley (2007, 259) synthesizes this metaphysical aspect in relation to the form of beauty, stating that when

> you come to know the essence or definition of beauty, you acquire understanding of an unchangeable truth that no more invites later revision than (Plato might say) your understanding of the properties of the number 2 could ever become out of date or inapplicable. What beauty itself is, it simply and unequivocally *is*. It is precisely by their detachment from the here and now, and their intellectual gravitation to the realm occupied by the changeless Forms, that philosophers gain cognitive access to Being, thus exercising the only faculty that can correctly be called 'knowledge.'

This rationale has profound repercussions on the Western aesthetic experience of the world because it sets what Ferraris (2012, 11) defines the *défaillances* of the senses. These *défaillances* have the function of excluding the perception from the epistemic realm since they cause faults in reasoning. Thus, the superiority of the conceptual over the perceptual is established and, along with it, the opposition of senses and reason. For Ferraris (2012, 12), the problem is "*to ascribe to the senses a primarily epistemological function*, as if they were first and foremost means of knowledge. After it has been established that the sensible knowledge cannot guarantee any certainty, the interest in the perception is revoked. From the random doubt, the general doubt is reached and this means an excessive load of science." This is what happens with skepticism. In his analysis of perception, Ferraris continues, affirming that "the Kantian philosophy has become the philosophical mainstream of the last two centuries because it was able to solve the skeptic impasse defined in the Humean critique of induction."

For Kant, knowledge starts with the senses but is really knowledge only when is fixed by conceptual schemes independent from experience and *a priori* to it. This affirms once more the priority of the conceptual over the perceptual, which implies the primacy of the epistemic. And yet, why one should give priority to the epistemic in relation to the aesthetic?

Ferraris (2012, 13) is right when he affirms that "it is easy to undermine the perception from the epistemological standpoint because it is not regarded as perception but as representation." The point is that, as we have seen with the story of the wheelwright in the *Zhuangzi*, the aesthetic understanding of the world cannot be transferable. Subjective reason, on the contrary, in defining and re-presenting an objective world, can establish a reliable knowledge that can be reified and passed on. The representation, therefore, is the re-presentation of what the reason has certified as reliable. In other words, the re-presentation becomes the validation of the objective world by the representative subject—as discussed in chapter 2. The knowledge represented in this way is the mirror of the certified stable and reliable world: a knowledge that can be transmitted.

In the *Lao-Zhuang*'s approach, the parts are reversed and the transferability of knowledge itself is questioned. As we have seen, in the skill stories of the *Zhuangzi* there is a correspondence between aesthetic and epistemic. Zhu Rui (2002, 59) rightly holds that "*wu-wei-wu-bu-wei* [無為無不為] finds its root, not in the intellectual exercise of mind, but in a person's aesthetic experience of nature."[5] Zhu's desire to compare Zhuangzi to Kant, however, leads him toward a common misinterpretation. In the *Zhuangzi* there is nothing that can resemble an aesthetic judgment. Quite the reverse. As seen in relation to the "Qiwulun," the main point is to avoid univocal judgments, including aesthetic judgments. The well-known example of the beautiful women Maoqiang and Liji is worth mentioning.

庸詎知吾所謂知之非不知邪？庸詎知吾所謂不知之非知邪？……民食芻豢，麋鹿食薦，蝍且甘帶，鴟鴉耆鼠，四者孰知正味？猨，猵狙以為雌，麋與鹿交，鰌與魚游。毛嬙、麗姬，人之所美也，魚見之深入，鳥見之高飛，麋鹿見之決驟。四者孰知天下之正色哉？

How do I know that what I call knowing is not ignorance? How do I know that what I call ignorance is not knowing? . . . Humans eat the flesh of hay-fed and grain-fed beasts, deer eat the grass, centipedes relish snakes, owls and crows crave mice; which of the four has a proper sense of taste? Gibbons are sought by baboons as mates, elaphures like the company of deer, loaches play with fish. Mao-ch'iang and Lady Li were beautiful in the eyes of men; but when the fish saw them they plunged deep, when the birds saw them they flew high, when the deer saw them they broke into a run. Which of these four knows what is truly beautiful in the world? (6/2/66–70) (58)

The point is that there is no beauty in itself because the references for judging something beautiful are always culturally determined. Therefore, in the *Zhuangzi*, the aesthetic is not a judgment and is not aimed toward beauty. The aesthetic is an ethical stance, an ethos aimed at the world. This, however, does not mean that, in perceiving the world aesthetically, one sees it as beautiful; it only means to perceive it as corresponding with and to oneself.

Hence, it is not possible to agree with Zhu (2002, 62) when he says that "from the Daoist perspective, beauty is truth. That is all." This Platonic statement is far removed from the perspective of the *Zhuangzi* in which there is no standard for beauty and no standard for truth. As many skill stories exemplify, there is no absolute reference system and the only possibility to be efficacious is to find the right balance in the specific circumstances. Therefore, there is nothing beautiful in itself and nothing truthful in itself. To say that "from the Daoist perspective, beauty is truth" is to misinterpret Daoism twice. It is not by chance that the aforementioned passage of the *Zhuangzi* concludes

自我觀之，仁義之端，是非之塗，樊然殽亂，吾惡能知其辯！

In my judgement [*guan* 觀] the principles of Goodwill and Duty, the paths of 'That's it, that's not' [*shifei*], are inextricably confused; how could I know how to discriminate between them? (6/2/70) (58)

The text is clear: *shifei* does not help to formulate a judgment (*guan* 觀, literally "to look," "viewpoint"). The perspective of *guan*, therefore, does not produce a discrimination. Wu Kuang-ming (1982, 19) is particularly accurate in saying that Zhuangzi "wants us to adopt a flexible 'attitude' that best fits our disposition *and* the disposition of the situation in which we are at the moment. Since both the subjective and the objective dispositions are constantly changing, our positions should accordingly shift. This is what it means to be *alive*. It entails a vivacious playing with any position and a meandering among many situations." For this same reason, the skill stories are so important to understand how the aesthetic involvement with the world does not offer a reference system for judgments. Rather, they suggest a fluid *ethos* that favors a constant process of adjustments. As Steve Coutinho (2014, 168) puts it, "we live wisely when we are able to cope skillfully with circumstances."

Coutinho (2014, 173), however, misses an important element of Daoism when he affirms that "the success of science and technology is based on the very techniques criticized by the Daoists—explicit verbal description, and technological manipulation in accordance with human desires." Daoism does not question the possibility of handing down a verbal or numerical knowledge. Daoism questions the actual relevance of this knowledge in one's own life. Indeed, technological manipulation, objectifying the world, makes it an object present at hand. We have seen how this is particularly problematic when it comes to separate the observer from the observed. This is what Daoism tries to avoid.

It is not a problem of being able to measure the weight of an ox or an atom. It is not even a problem of being able to verbally explain theories that describe the behavior of subatomic particles, as Coutinho holds. The problem is that the world cannot only be a numeric equation; it cannot be confined to a description. The world cannot be reduced to an object of research and inquiry. Or should one think that emotions are only chemical reactions? Should one believe that to be happy it is sufficient to alter the amount of these chemical reactions? And who can define the right amount of these reactions? Is there a perfect amount of happiness? It is clear that calculations and verbal communications of knowledge are not the real problem. The issue is the danger that a mere cognitive knowledge separates human being from its environment. For this reason, the *Zhuangzi* says that one fails to see something in discriminating between alternatives. And to avoid this failure one needs to be aesthetically alert.

This is a perspective very close to the one expressed by John Dewey in his important book *Art as Experience*. For Dewey (1934, 19) the "complete interpenetration of self and the world of objects and events" allows an aesthetic configuration in which there is an "active and alert commerce with the world." This implies that, when one is active and alert, it is possible to activate the aesthetic configuration that sees the world and the self as mutually entailing.

It is relevant that Dewey (1934, 44) considers the thinker's interaction with ideas as an experience, affirming that also this experience concludes in "a felt harmony." This means that the thinking process cannot be disjointed from the senses. The "mutual adaptation of the self and the object" produces harmony and harmony can only be achieved with a full engagement of the senses. The perceptual helps this process without introducing categorical divisions between the self and the world. The consequence is that the conceptual itself is not distinct from the perceptual: along with the dissolution of the self/world distinction, the mind/body opposition vanishes as well. This means that one needs to keep a close aesthetic contact with the world in order to be optimally reactive as a whole. When one is reactive, it is possible to find the balance and to *feel* the harmony.

Similarly, the aesthetic configuration of early Daoism derives from and produces a dynamic adaptation to the other at large: in a world that is not divided into internal and external parts, there is no outside that does not correspond to an inside. This means that one knows the other insofar as one knows oneself—which in turn implies that, in order to be efficacious, this correspondence needs to be kept as tight as possible.

If we consider chapter 12 of the *Daodejing*, it becomes evident how the perceptual assumes a different meaning compared to the one suggested by the tradition of Plato:

五色令人目盲；五音令人耳聾；五味令人口爽

The five colors make the eyes of people blind;
The five notes make the hears of people deaf;
The five flavors make the palate of people spoiled[6]

Here, there is no condemnation of the senses. The passage is not concerned with knowledge and does not consider the senses as deceiving. Rather, the passage warns against the anaesthetization of the senses in order to preserve their efficacy. The five colors, the five notes, and the five flavors refer to the overabundance that results in a loss of perception. This relates to chapter 46:

罪莫厚於甚欲，咎莫憯於欲得，禍莫大乎不知足。知足之為足，
此恆足矣。

There is no crime graver than greed,
There is no misfortune more dangerous than the desire to attain,
There is no disaster greater than not knowing satiety.
Knowing when enough is enough
Will always be satisfying.

We have already seen how, in chapter 37, the *Daodejing* expresses the idea that "knowing how to stop, people can avoid danger." Chapters 12 and 46 refer to a similar idea: one needs to find a balance between desires and attainments, between pleasure and contentment. The problem, therefore, is not to distrust the senses because they are not capable of knowing an external world, but to preserve their efficacy so as to keep balancing the equilibrium of one's own *ethos*.

Senses are an important part of being in contact with the world and one needs to avoid obstructing this contact. This implies an ethical stance toward the self and the world more than an epistemological problem. One needs to avoid the intoxication of the senses from the five colors, the five notes, and the five flavors; that is, one needs to know how to stop desiring and to *feel* when enough is enough. This knowledge is an aesthetic knowledge, so to speak: in keeping one's senses clear, one is able to be attuned to oneself and to the world. Thus, in the Daoist perspective, the aesthetic experience of the world becomes the path through which one can acquire an ethical posture in relation to the myriad things.

It is clear that, contrary to the Western condemnation of the senses, the Daoist aesthetic configuration needs to trust sensations in order to know when to stop. To better understand the difference between these two aesthetic approaches, it is useful to consider more closely the dream argument. This helps to clarify how different aesthetic configurations derive from and produce different experiences of the world.

Both Descartes and Zhuangzi consider the dream issue. Zhuangzi, however, doubts about it in a specific and not general way: waking up from a dream, Zhuangzi does not know whether it was him dreaming he was a butterfly or a butterfly dreaming it was him.[7] Here, the dream is not really questioned. Rather, the dream is affirmed in its experience. What is questioned is the possibility to define from which standpoint one can determine the dreamer and the dreamed.

It is crucial to stress that the possibility for the butterfly of dreaming to be Zhuangzi does not undermine Zhuangzi. The dream does not have a negative connotation and the impossibility of determining whether the dream is dreamed by Zhuangzi or by the butterfly posits the two dreamers on the same level.[8] In other words, the dream is not the symbol of the *défaillances* of the senses, but it considers the perspective from inside the dream itself. Zhuangzi does not doubt about the reality of the dream because for him it is not a problem of senses but a problem of recognizing the correlation between reality and dream. Zhuangzi opens the possibility of this correlation by mirroring dreamer and dreamed and by making them corresponding.

The two, however are not the same: "between Zhuangzi and the butterfly there must be a difference. This is what is called the transformations of things."[9] With these words, Zhuangzi suggests that the transformation of things itself can produce a difference such as the one between dreamer and dreamed. Therefore, the difference is not between what is real and what is not, what is true and what is not, but between two different aspects of the same transformation of things. It is not a matter of dissecting the world into categories that can establish a secure dominion of calculation. Rather, it is a matter of participating in the continuous transformation of the myriad things by corresponding with and to their multiple perspectives. This means that the dream does not hinder the experience of the world; on the contrary, it helps it by showing how things correspond and change.

The position of Descartes is different from the outset to the outcome. His question in *Meditations on First Philosophy* (II, 19) is:

> am I not a human being, and therefore in the habit of sleeping at night, when in my dreams I have all the same experiences as these madmen do when they are awake—or sometimes even stranger ones? How often my sleep at night has convinced me of all these familiar things—that I was here, wrapped in my gown, sitting by the fire—when in fact I was lying naked under the bedclothes.—All the same, I am now perceiving this paper with eyes that are certainly awake; the head I am nodding is not drowsy; I stretch out my hand and feel it knowingly and deliberately; a sleeper would not have these experiences so distinctly.—But have I then forgotten those other occasions on which I have been deceived by similar thoughts in my dreams? When I think this over more carefully I see so clearly that waking can never be distinguished from sleep by any conclusive indications that I am stupefied; and this very stupor comes close to persuading me that I am asleep after all.

Here, the dream immediately acquires a negative connotation. The first parallel is between the dream and the experiences of madmen when they are awake—the experience of the dream can actually be "stranger" than those.¹⁰ This, however, is not the main point. The sleep *convinces* Descartes of something that is not real; this is the central problem. The dream, being so convincing in the sleep, casts doubt on the reality itself. The question, therefore, becomes: how can people know that they are not dreaming when they are awake? The senses in the dream are deceiving and so they can be in the awake life.

Descartes equates the sensory deception of dreams with the sensory deception of the waking life. The clear consequence is that there is a separation between the real external world that can be known only with the reason—which depends on that of God—and a misleading internal world of senses. The conclusion that Descartes draws from his idea of *cogito* is that he is a thinking thing, a Soul (*Âme*) entirely distinct from the body (AT VI, 33). This implies that

> the experience of doubt is an experience of imperfection: but this presupposes the idea of a being more perfect than oneself. Such an idea, Descartes argues, can only come from outside ourselves—from an actually existing perfect being, God. In fact, as an imperfect being, he himself cannot be independent; he could not even exist, were there not a perfect being on which he, and indeed all other finite beings, depended. . . . From the concept itself, we can thus infer God's actual existence. Descartes goes on to argue that all knowledge depends on that of God. (Moriarty 2008, xii)

We have seen in chapter 3 the implications of putting the source of knowledge outside the metaphorical circle. Here it is worth noticing that, similarly to what happens in Plato's philosophy, with the distinction between an internal and an external world one more important separation is affirmed: the one between the sensible and the non-sensible. In this context, however, metaphysics defines the value of the aesthetic experience of the world insofar as it subordinates it to the absolute knowledge of God.¹¹ Thus, the aesthetic distinction between an internal and an external world becomes not only the metaphysical separations of *res cogitans* and *res extensa*, mind and body, but also the distinction between the dependent humanity and the independent God.

It is possible to conclude that if one wants to perform the shift from metaphysical representations to aesthetic life, the first step in this direction is to abandon the division of the world into sensible and non-sensible. As seen in chapter 3, the metaphysical representations of sensible and supersensible are not the only conceivable. Through metaphors one can formulate alternatives to the re-presentations of a divided world. We have discussed how for Nietzsche art itself becomes a metaphor that can describe the aesthetic approach to the world in a more direct and immediate fashion. In the *Zhuangzi*, something similar happens.

Graham Parkes (1983, 237) explains how both Nietzsche and Zhuangzi oppose anthropocentrism and "seek to foster an appreciation of alternative perspectives by weighting the imagery on the side of the nonhuman cosmos." Clarifying that the motivations of the two are "somewhat different," Parkes defines their specificity:

> Chuang Tzu is reacting against the tendency of many of the Hundred Schools which preceded him, and of Confucianism and Mohism in particular, to place man at the center of the cosmos, though still acknowledging his participation in it. Nietzsche has a more serious imbalance to redress, the result of two millennia of Platonic/Christian denial of the body and man's animal nature: the tendency, encouraged by Cartesianism, for man to identify himself as being essentially mind, or spirit, and to ignore or devalue his participation in the physical world.

Despite these differences, both Zhuangzi and Nietzsche advocate for an aesthetic attunement to the world with important ethical consequences.[12]

In his analysis, Zhuo Dawei (2010, 113) suggests precisely this. In commenting on the passage of "Zarathustra's Prologue" (1)—"Behold! This cup wants to become empty again, and Zarathustra wants to become human again"—Zhuo interprets the attempt of the cup to be empty as Zarathustra's desire of forgetting himself (*wangque ziwo* 忘卻自我). According to Zhuo, this process of forgetting the self is similar to the one present in the *Zhuangzi*.

Zhuo too acknowledges that there are differences, the most important being the painful process that Zarathustra needs to undertake to achieve his aim (the reference is to the story of the snake). This conflictual relation between humankind and nature—a characteristic aspect of romanticism—is absent in the Daoist conception. And yet, the result is similar. According to Zhuo (and other scholars as I discussed in chapter 5), the purpose of the Daoist sage (in particular in the *Zhuangzi*) is to abandon the anthropocentric perspective and to be attuned to the world.

When Zarathustra says that the "Overhuman is the sense of the earth" or beseeches "my brothers, stay true to the earth and do not believe those who talk of over-earthly hopes" (2005, "Zarathustra's Prologue" 3), he does not just oppose the Platonic denial of the perceptual, he also asks to abandon the illusion of simplistic anthropocentric and theocentric perspectives, returning thus to an earthly vision. To say it with the words of *Beyond Good and Evil* (2002, 230), it is necessary to "translate humanity back into nature; to gain control of the many vain and fanciful interpretations and incidental meanings that have been scribbled and drawn over that eternal basic text of *homo natura* so far." The shift from metaphysics to aesthetics is, therefore, the attempt to translate "humanity back into nature." Let me consider this possibility in detail.

Gu Feng and Dai Wenjing (2017, 126) state that "in the traditional Chinese literature and art, the relationship between man and nature was the main theme and many natural images became the main carriers and media to express the feelings and wishes of Chinese." For this reason, in "opposition to the aesthetics in the West which is set up on the basis of the relationship between human beings, the aesthetics in China is established on the foundation of the relationship between man and nature." This implies that the artistic production in China derives from a different experience of the world. The centrality of the relationship between humanity and nature is emblematic of a different sensibility toward the world.[13]

In this sense, one can affirm that an aesthetic configuration derives from and produces a different approach to the world. Similarly to what we have seen in chapter 2 regarding the fact that one always uses and, at the same time, produces worldviews through language, it can be said that, in the experience of the world, one always uses and produces aesthetic configurations. I can now conclude that worldviews describe aesthetic configurations—even when they try to undermine themselves as an-aesthetic.

If one considers the aesthetic configuration proposed by the *Lao-Zhuang*, the attempt to eliminate all the cultural determinations for a direct access to the experience of the world is evident. The *wu* terms point in this direction: there is no need to hinder the spontaneous experience of the world with actions that do not correspond with the myriad things. Therefore, when Johann Wolfgang von Goethe (1883, 211) says that Chinese people and Chinese aesthetics "differ from us, inasmuch as with them external nature is always associated with the human figures," there is a Western distortion to the overall right consideration. The difference is that there is no external nature in the Chinese perspective: the human figures are associated with nature because there is no separation between humanity and the rest of the myriad things.

One of the most important terms of Chinese aesthetics is *yixiang* 意象 "image," "imagery." This word is interesting because is composed of *yi* 意, which means "idea," "intention," "desire," and *xiang* 象, which means "image." The implication of *yixiang* "is 'mingling emotion with scenes,' in which 'emotion' relates to '*yi*,' meaning 'coming from man,' while "scenes" relates to '*xiang*,' that indicates something coming from nature" (Gu and Dai 2017, 127). Thus, *yixiang* not only describes "a precise summary of the aesthetic relationship between man and nature" but also defines the "aesthetic integration of 'the man and the nature'" (Gu and Dai 2017, 127). This echoes Tang Junyi's (1988b, 128) assertion that the idea of continuity between humanity and cosmos (*tianrenheyi* 天人合一) is a central concept in Chinese philosophy.

Tang acknowledges that one can feel detached from the rest of the myriad things because desires, ambitions, sentiments, likes, and dislikes can be seen as opposed to the external world. When one sees the world as frustrating one's desires and sensations, then one also determines an internal and external world. When these two realms are distinct, it becomes impossible to perceive their continuity (1988b, 136). Tang holds that this is not the case for early Chinese thought. This does not mean that Chinese philosophers did not consider an internal realm of feelings and sensations. It only means that they saw these in mutual relation and not in opposition to the world: feelings and sensations permeate the world and merge together with it (1988b, 136). Tang offers many examples from different classics to demonstrate his thesis, including the passage of the "Qiwulun" (5/2/52) considered in the last chapter—"the myriad things and I are continuous" (*wanwu yu wo wei yi* 萬物與我為一).

For Tang (1988b, 133), because of its epistemology, Western thought divides the world in internal and external parts. This dualism separates humanity and cosmos, thus hindering the idea of unity. We have seen how Western epistemology not only separates humanity from the world but, in undermining the perceptual in favor of the conceptual, it also separates mind and body. Tang explains that "since Chinese philosophers do not distinguish between life and matter, then life and matter are not in opposition. Since they do not distinguish between mind and body, then mind and body are not in opposition" (1988c, 126). Tang goes on analyzing other dichotomies in order to reach the final conclusion that people and cosmos are one.

As seen in the last chapter, this oneness needs to be considered in the wider process of the myriad things' revolving transformation. Here I shall only add that, to understand the perspective proposed by the *Lao-Zhuang*, one needs to put aside the metaphysical standpoint that separates the real world from the apparent one and conceive of oneself and the world as continuous. This implies that one needs to shift from the representations of the world divided into sensible and supersensible to the aesthetic and undivided experience of the world. Still, in order to move from metaphysical representations to aesthetic life toward the encounter with the other in the perspective of Daoism, one needs to move *together* with the other, which implies a non-dualistic experience of the other. Let me try to make this last attempt before concluding.

In criticizing the still very present Platonic separation between the authentic world of ideas and the inauthentic world of appearances, Gianni Vattimo (1981, 11) affirms that "there is no liberation beyond appearances in a supposed dominion of authentic Being; rather, there is freedom as mobility between the appearances." Following Nietzsche, Vattimo specifies that these appearances are no longer called such: "now that 'the real world has become fable' there is no true Being that can degrade them to lie and falsehood." These appearances, therefore, are "liberated from that Platonic condemnation which, in making them copies of a transcendent original, immediately creates hierarchies and ascesis" (Vattimo 1993, 2). Along this line of thought, Vattimo (1981, 12) defines the "Platonic fallacy" as the prevalent mystification of ideology: "according to this mystification, knowledge would have the task of identifying the truth, a first principle, a final and secure reference point toward which the entire existence is directed and from which it takes its 'guidelines.'" In this way, Vattimo summarizes all the steps needed to reconsider the metaphysical standpoint.

First and foremost, it is necessary to rehabilitate the function of senses, not as a means of knowledge and even less as a means of achieving a superior realm of truth—thus excluding any mystical and metaphysical teleology. Rather, senses are a means of communication with oneself, the other, and the world at large. The "freedom as mobility" between what appears in the world is the perceptual exchange that happens as a correspondence among the myriad things.[14] If there is no original or final truth to be discovered beyond or underneath what appears, there is no grounding knowledge that can be achieved or established. Thus, it becomes clear how the efficacy of Cook Ding, the wheelwright, etc., is based not on the truth of knowledge but on the communication with the world in its specific configuration of the moment.

Without the "Platonic fallacy" one can undertake a communication even with the dream in which there is no differentiation between dreamer and dreamed. For the *Zhuangzi* what really matters in the dream is dreaming itself. Nietzsche offers a crucial help to shift more in this direction. In aphorism 45 of *The Gay Science* (2001)—significantly entitled "The consciousness of appearance"—after having specified that "appearance is the active and living itself" and not "the opposite of some essence," Nietzsche states,

> the one who comes to know is a means of prolonging the earthly dance and thus is one of the masters of ceremony of existence . . . the sublime consistency and interrelatedness of all knowledge may be and will be the highest means to sustain the universality of dreaming, the mutual comprehension of all dreamers, and thereby also the *duration of the dream*.

Two elements are crucial in this fragment. On the one hand, there is a significant shift in the meaning of "knowledge": knowledge is no longer an end but a means and, even more importantly, it is a means that does not concern the subject but concerns the entire existence by prolonging the "earthly dance." Knowing, therefore, becomes an artistic gesture: the one who comes to know dances the earthly dance. On the other hand, this knowledge is not aimed at any stable and final truth, but it is a means for the "*duration of the dream*"; that is to say, it is a means for the continuation of the experience of the dream. Nietzsche uses this as a stronger example of the artistic gesture: knowledge as dancing and dreaming is the means through which the world is not just an object for a subject but a flux of correspondences. The "mutual comprehension of all dreamers" is this correspondence as aesthetic gesture that does not impose a single structure of truth but puts in contact all the possible interpretations of the world.

The dream in *The Gay Science* offers an interesting alternative to the will to power. Although in both cases there is a critique of the essentialist tradition and the affirmation of a world of relations and interpretations, the dream seems to dispel the possibility of a self-centered and preconceived purpose. In other words, the metaphor of the dream suggests a spontaneity that is difficult to identify only with the self. A dream is certainly personal and yet there is no possibility of regarding it as an object for a subject because there is no possibility of control. The inherent creative character of the dream is spontaneous insofar as it is not something that one can possess in the sense of an object ready to hand. Thus, the experience of the dream shows in a clearer way how there is no separation between the world and the self. That is to say: the creative aspect of the dream is a metaphor for the spontaneous creativity of the world.

It comes as no surprise, therefore, that Nietzsche juxtaposes the earthly dance and the dream. In both cases the spontaneity of the artistic gesture is central. As a result, this shift from the metaphysical representation of the world divided in sensible and non-sensible to the aesthetic and undivided experience of the world entails the shift from the separation of subject/object to the correspondence between the producer and the production of the artistic gesture.

This becomes evident in the fragment 796 of *The Will to Power*, in which Nietzsche affirms, "The work of art where it appears without an artist. . . . The world as a work of art that gives birth to itself." In such a world, not only is the artwork as an object undermined, but also the artist as producer becomes superfluous. What is central is the spontaneous aesthetic gesture of the world that produces itself. This does not mean that the human being is excluded from this process. Quite the reverse. Similarly to what we have seen in relation to *dao*, the humanity is an integral part of this production as long as it does not obstruct its spontaneous development.[15] What is excluded in this context is the idea of a subjective or external creator that shapes objects. What is highlighted, on the contrary, is the acting: the aesthetic gesture in its production.[16]

In this sense, Heidegger (2002a, 22) is right to affirm that the work of art could open a world and that, in its being a work, the artwork is "something that sets up. What is it that the work, as work, sets up? Rising-up-within-itself the work opens up a *world* and keeps it abidingly in force. To be a work means: to set up a world." Yet the world that the artwork sets up is not stable because the artwork itself is susceptible of interpretations. This means that the artwork not only sets up a world but is also set up by a world. Hence, the artwork does not belong "uniquely within the region it itself opens up," as supposed by Heidegger (2002a, 20), but it also belongs to the world that opens it up as a work of art.[17] This implies that the shift from a dualistic representation of the world to a non-dualistic experience of the world brings the relation of self and other back inside the metaphorical circle with a spontaneous aesthetic gesture.

David Loy (1985, 77) explains that this non-dualistic experience is "nondual in the sense that there is no differentiation between subject and object, between self and world," adding that the "implication of this for action is that there is no longer any bifurcation between an agent, the self that is believed to do the action, and the objective action that is done." Loy identifies the possibility of this nondual experience in the concept of *weiwuwei* 為無為 (literally, the action of non-action or, more properly, acting unobstructive actions): "As usually understood, 'action' requires an agent that is active; 'nonaction' implies a subject that is passive, which does nothing and/or yields. The 'action of nonaction' occurs when there is no 'I' to be either active or passive, which is an experience that can be expressed only paradoxically" (1985, 77). Loy is aware that the paradox of a non-dual agent-act does not help the understanding of *weiwuwei*. His solution of the problem, however, is particularly interesting. He explains that "one may accept the negation of a subject, in which case the action cannot be something 'objective,' yet there is still an action." In other words, "when one completely *becomes* an action, one loses the sense that it is an action" (1985, 79). This implies that if "each particular is not isolated but contains and manifests that whole, then whenever 'I' act it is not 'I' but the whole universe that 'does' the action or rather is the action. If we accept that the universe is self-caused, then it acts freely whenever anything is done" (1985, 84). This idea of an action that is acted by the entire universe is not far from the Nietzschean perspective of the "world as a work of art that gives birth to itself" (1967, 796) and can be compared to the Heideggerian expression "the world worlds" (*die Welt weltet*) (2002a, 23; 1977, 33), provided that one considers this *worlding* process not as the unconcealment of Being into beings but as spontaneous transformation of things or, to say it better, self-transformation (*zihua* 自化). To conclude, let me try to push this idea a bit further.

If *weiwuwei* describes a non-dualistic experience of the world in which the action that is acted is the action of the world, then *ziran* describes the aesthetic attunement of the world to itself made possible by non-obstructive actions. That is to say: *wuwei* does not obstruct but facilitates *ziran*—conceived as the movement of a world that worlds insofar as it wants this same movement. There is no outside to which the intention can be aimed. The intention of the action is the action itself.

And yet, even if there is no outside, this does not mean that there is no plurality. The act that acts does so being attuned to itself, which implies the attunement of all the myriad things. Thus, the self and the other act in a reciprocal balance. The action wants itself not as a defined action that aims at one specific thing; it aims at itself as the possibility of change. At this point it is possible to say that *ziran* is the way the world worlds and also the way time times. The act that wants itself unobstructively allows *ziran* to produce change and time. In this sense, everything—humans, earth, heavens, and *dao*—emulates *ziran* (*fa ziran* 法自然).

We have seen that change and time are the same thing. The clear consequence is that the change of the other is also one's own change. The time of the other is also one's own time. Thus, the revolving transformation of the myriad things returns as change and time of both self and other. The aesthetic experience of the unity of self and other—as well as of change and time—allows an *ethos* that regards action as attuned to itself: the action that wants itself does so in the revolving transformation of the myriad things.

This means not only that every action is perceived as having effect over every other, but also that the action returns on itself as action that is produced by and produces itself. The movement of *dao* is returning in the sense that the action returns on itself by means of itself. As a consequence, the balance of the action is not determined by a gain or a loss. The balance is the simple adjustment that the action effects on itself. The attunement that the action performs is the constant feedback of the revolving transformation of the myriad things. Thus, the other is not only the other and the self is not only the self.

In this perspective, the dance and the dancer cannot be separated, they are one thing. In the same way, the action that is aesthetically attuned to itself does not distinguish between the actor and the acted, there is only acting; and it does not distinguish between the sayer and the said, there is only saying. Therefore, the act of the other is not separated from one's own act. The act of the other is one's own act. Similarly, the saying of the other is one's own saying. The differences of the said and the sayer are absorbed and preserved in the act of saying itself.

A conversation, therefore, is the spontaneous balance of the saying. The world's saying unfolds in an infinite variety of sayings and only if one is attuned to oneself is it possible to perceive the uniqueness of this infinite variety. The separation of this saying results in failing to see something—namely, that one is always synchronically in conversation with oneself, the other, and the world at large. To recognize this, it is only a matter of listening attentively.

If everything is in a mutually entailing correspondence and returns in the revolving transformation of the myriad things, then the world not only worlds but is also *worlded*. Similarly, the other *others* and is *othered*. The movement of *dao* is a stream that *streams* and is *streamed*. One way leads to the other and vice versa; "this is called 'walking both ways'" (*Zhuangzi*,

5/2/40). In this sense, there is neither transcendence nor immanence: the mutually entailing *natura naturans* and *natura naturata* are part of a revolving process that goes both ways without presupposing any origin or univocal substance and without dividing subject and object. Thus, in shifting from metaphysical representations to aesthetic life—toward the encounter with the other in the perspective of Daoism—one encounters not just the other but the other as self, the self as world, and the world as aesthetic gesture.

Notes

Introduction

1. For a comprehensive account of moral philosophy in both metaethics and normative ethics, see Copp (2006). For an introduction to environmental ethics, see Jamieson (2008).

2. For the definition of Kant's "transcendental aesthetic" in relation to Baumgarten's idea of aesthetics, see Kant's *Critique of Pure Reason* (A21n).

3. On the different interpretations in relation to the problem of the harmony of the faculties in Kant's *Critique of Judgement*, see Guyer (2006). For an in-depth study of Kant's critique of aesthetic judgment, see Allison (2001).

4. For a detailed exposition of Western aesthetics, see Beardsley (1966), Tatarkiewicz (1980), and Cazeaux (2000). For an account of Chinese aesthetics, see Ye (1985), Li (1994), and Li (2010).

5. Regarding the new documents found in Guodian 郭店 in 1993 and the relative problems of authorship and periodisation, see Henricks (2000). For a detailed analysis of the Mawangdui 马王堆 version, see Xu (1985) and Henricks (1989). For a general account of Daoism and the *Daodejing*, see Liu (2015) and Lau (1989).

6. The *Zhuangzi* was edited by Guo Xiang 郭象 (died 312 CE). On this and on the division of the text in inner, outer, and miscellaneous chapters, see Graham (1979), Liu (1987; 1994), and Klein (2010). Notwithstanding the important issue of authorship for both the *Daodejing* and the *Zhuangzi*, I believe that the *intentio operis* and its philosophical relevance has priority over the historical determination of the *intentio auctoris*.

7. For the edition of the *Huainanzi*, see Liu and Chen (1992).

8. For a definition and analysis of philosophical Daoism *daojia* 道家 and religious Daoism *daojiao* 道教, see Sivin (1978), Robinet (2008), and Barrett (2008).

9. See, for instance, the seminal work of Parkes (1987a). See also the detailed analysis of May (1996).

10. It is quite surprising that none of the authors (Parkes 1987a, May 1996, Froese 2006, Ma 2008, Burik 2009) who analyze Heidegger's philosophy in relation to Asian thought critically discusses the concept of worldview.

11. On *Verwindung*, see how Gianni Vattimo (1987, 12), in quoting Heidegger from *Vorträge und Aufsätze* who affirms that "metaphysics is not something 'which one can brush aside like an opinion. Nor can one leave it behind oneself as though it were a doctrine that no one believes in anymore,' " and concludes that metaphysics "is something one retains in oneself, like the traces of an illness or a sorrow to which one is resigned."

12. Pierre Bourdieu (1991, 62) goes so far as to assert that Heidegger produces a " 'conservative revolution' in philosophy" by means of a strategy that wants "to change everything without changing anything." Probably Bourdieu's assessment is excessive, but I agree with John Caputo (1993, 280) when he affirms that "it is clear to everyone but Heidegger's most fanatic disciples that he [Heidegger] is clearly Hellenizing and secularizing a fundamentally biblical conception of the history of salvation" despite the fact that he "went on to say that his deeply historical conception of being, which included even an 'eschatological' conception of the 'history of Being,' was fundamentally Greek in inspiration." For an account of how Heidegger's thought dissimulates its Jewish influences, see Zarader (2006), who analyzes the tension between what Heidegger "*says*" and "*does*" in relation to the "antagonistic couple God/Being" (124). For the equivocal nature of Heidegger's philosophy in relation to Judaism and Nazism, see Nancy (2017).

13. I take as a significant definition of the Other in Levinas's philosophy the one given in *Totality and Infinity* (1979, 78–79): "The Other [*Autrui*] is the very locus of metaphysical truth, and is indispensable for my relation with God. He does not play the role of mediator. The Other [*Autrui*] is not the incarnation of God, but precisely by his face, in which he is disincarnate, is the manifestation of the height in which God is revealed." Although I generally agree with Levinas's ethical project that, through the relational "face-to-face," opposes the reduction to the Same in the thinking of Being, I do not believe that the ethical relation with the other should be limited to the face of the other human being without considering the world at large. Moreover, I do not find necessary to link the other to God, even if this is an immanent God. In this sense, the "otherwise than Being" can be found in the Chinese tradition more than in the Hebraic one.

14. For a general overview of the different dimensions of comparison in philosophy—that is, the interpretative, the constructive and the reflective dimensions—see Connolly (2015, 28–45).

15. *Weltanschauung* is a combination of *Welt* "world" and *Anschauung* "view." It is commonly translated as "worldview" or "vision of the world."

16. "Anarchy" in the sense of "absence of origin"—from the Greek *anarkhía* (ἀναρχία), which derives from the composition of *an* (ἀν) "without" and *arkhḗ* (ἀρχή) "origin," "beginning."

17. Although there is an increasing number of studies that advocates for a non-metaphysical understanding of *dao*, a vast part of scholarship holds on to the idea that *dao* is a metaphysical substance, to the extent that, in the 2002 edition of

the *Journal of Chinese Philosophy* dedicated to "Tao and God," the article of Masato Mitsuda offers a "discussion on Chuang Tzu and a feminist Catholic poet-philosopher, Sor Juana Ines de la Cruz, in the interest of relating Dao to belief in God" (Cheng 2002, 1).

18. These terms can be literally translated as, respectively, "no action," "no name," and "no desire." These translations, however, are misleading and I shall discuss in detail how they can be understood.

19. This is another complex concept that can be only provisionally translated as "no feeling."

20. *Shifei* refers to the affirmation (*shi*) and negation (*fei*) and, therefore, refers to the act of distinguishing between elements of the world. For this reason, according to the *Zhuangzi*, *shifei* leads to disputations.

Chapter 1

1. For a detailed analysis of translation's problem in comparative studies and how it has always been overcome, see Scharfstein (1978). For a philosophical investigation of this problem, see Derrida (1987).

2. In this context "system" means not a static and unchangeable order but a dynamic flux of interdependent concepts. For a further analysis of the notion of concept clusters, see Ames and Rosemont (2013).

3. It is worth mentioning that the first attempts to translate religious and philosophical concepts in Chinese were made by Jesuits. In revising Chinese books and documents from the Jesuit archives in Rome, Albert Chan (2015, 216) asserts that "the Catholic terms are often rendered by transliteration." Among these terms, we find the transliterations of *philósophía* as *feiluosuofeiya* 費絡瑣費亞 (2015, 216) and *feilusuofeiya* 斐錄所費亞 (362). For an account of the Japanese formulation of *zhe xue* 哲學 (*tetsugaku* in Japanese) as a translation of *philósophía* and its acquisition in China, see Cua (2009, 44–45) and Tang (2007). For a definition of the "sage" in the Chinese tradition, see Shankman (2002). See also the Defoort-Raud debate on Chinese philosophy in *Philosophy East and West* (Defoort 2001, 2006; Raud 2006).

4. As mentioned, the work of Heidegger is useful in the philosophical comparative analysis for its critique of the Western metaphysical tradition. It is not my intention to consider Heidegger's various connections with Asian thought in this context. However, I agree with Ma Lin (2008, 208), who is suspicious that there is a genuine East–West dialogue in Heidegger's philosophy. In the next chapter, I will discuss how this has roots in Heidegger's conception of worldview philosophy (*Weltanschauungsphilosophie*). For a more positive account of Heidegger's interest in the *Lao-Zhuang*, see Parkes (1987b), Froese (2006), and Burik (2009).

5. See Sheehan (1978, 288) for an account of Heidegger's intentions regarding this translation.

6. For a grammatical analysis of *Sein* and *seiend* and their relation to the Heideggerian ontological difference, see Inwood (1999, 26–27). Almost as a remark on the importance of these terms, in the first note of *Being and Time* (1962) Macquarrie and Robinson specifically discuss them (19). Commenting on a passage of *Being and Time*, Barbara Cassin (2014, 1209) explains that "one of the main difficulties in standard English is that *Sein* (infinitive) is normally translated as 'Being,'—that is to say, already a present participle. How then shall we distinguish between *Seiend* (*étant*, 'being') and *Sein* (*être*, 'Being')? The solution adopted by Macquarrie and Robinson is to translate the present participle *seiend* using 'entity'/'entities' (the difference between singular and plural in the English translation seems arbitrary), and to maintain Being for *Sein*. Two problems then arise: 1. The so-called ontological difference *Sein/seiend*, *être/étant* is no longer recognizable in the word pair 'Being'/'entity.' 2. It is difficult to maintain the translation 'entity' when Heidegger underlines the present participle and the presence of the present in it." In this context, I translate *Sein* and *seiend* as "Being" and "being" respectively.

7. Heidegger himself considers Heraclitus pre-metaphysical. Cf. Heidegger and Fink (1979, 64–76).

8. For an analysis of the relation between Daoism and metaphysics, see Cheng (1989). For a radical questioning of the metaphysical nature of Daoism, see Burik (2010).

9. In his more recent translation of the *Daodejing* (2008), Ryden translates *tian xia* as "world" but leaves unchanged "being" and "beingless" for *you* and *wu*. Similarly, Chang Chung-yuan (1975, 112) translates *tian xia* as "universe." Yet the problem of being remains the same in his version, which goes, "Ten thousand things in the universe are created from being. Being is created from non-being." More interestingly, Philip Ivanhoe (2001, 43) translates *you* and *wu* as "what is there" and "what is not there," but he capitalizes *dao*, reducing thus the consistency of the passage: "Turning back is how the Way moves. / Weakness is how the Way operates. / The world and all its creatures arise from what is there; / What is there arises from what is not there." D. C. Lau (1989, 61), on the contrary, does not capitalize *dao* but translates *you* and *wu* as "Something" and "Nothing," which, being capitalized, again suggest metaphysical concepts. His translation is "Turning back is how the way moves; / Weakness is the means the way employs. / The myriad creatures in the world are born from Something, and Something from Nothing." Besides Arthur Waley (2005), who translates *you* and *wu* as "Being" and "Not-being," Chan Wing-tsit (1963) translates them as "being" and "non-being," Robert Henricks (1989) as "being" and "nonbeing," Lin Yutang (1958) as "Being" and "Non-being." Many others follow the same path. Only Roger Ames and David Hall (2003) offer a real alternative to *you* and *wu*, translating them as "determinate" and "indeterminate." I shall come back to this in chapter 4.

10. Among others, Zhang openly criticizes the position of Roger Ames and David Hall. For a reply to these critiques, see Ames and Rosemont (2013).

11. Common interpretations consider the first *dao* as a noun; the second *dao* as a verb attached to the modal verb *ke* 可, which implies possibility (can, may); and the third *dao* as a noun again. The other two characters, *fei* 非 and *chang* 常, have the function of defining *dao*: *fei* negates the sentence and *chang* means "constant" or, more rarely, "common" or "everyday." The second line of the *Daodejing* mirrors the structure of the first one, with the only difference being the substitution of *dao* with *ming* 名 'name': *ming ke ming, fei chang ming* (名可名，非常名).

12. The reference is to chapter 42 of the *Daodejing*. A related problem is the reception of Daoism as a religion by the first Jesuits of the seventeenth century, who regarded it in a negative light. Matteo Ricci (1985, 99), for instance, in referring to the concept of *wu* 無, regarded it as "at variance with the doctrine concerning the Lord of Heaven [*tianzhu* 天主]."

13. For a specific account of Couplet's positions on Laozi—regarded as "philosopher"—and later Daoism—regarded as heresy—see Huang (2014).

14. On the work of Legge, see Girardot (1999).

15. The reference text for the translation of Ames and Hall is not the transmitted version of Wang Bi but the Mawangdui version, which reads 道，可道也，非恆道也. For a detailed analysis of the Mawangdui, see Xu (1985) and Henricks (1989). For a comparison and an appraisal of the different versions of the *Daodejing*, see Liu (2006). For the transcript of the Mawangdui Laozi A and B, see Mawangdui Han mu boshu zhengli xiaozu 馬王堆漢墓帛書整理小組 (1976). A useful tool is Han (2002), a translation in Chinese of the two books of Henricks (1989; 2000), which offers both the Mawangdui and Guodian *Laozi*.

16. Ames (2015b, 264) asserts that "*dao* references the human sojourn through the life experience and might alternatively be translated as 'world-making' with the understanding that the etymology of the term 'world' is literally 'the age of man.'"

17. Chen Guying (2008, 46) affirms that this thought has its origin precisely in the *Daodejing*. On this passage, see also Lynn (1994a, 53), Cheng (1991, 363), Graham (1990b, 58), and Chan (1963, 266). Unfortunately, it is not possible to analyze the complexity of the *Yijing* in this context. For further analysis, see Lynn (1994b), Wang (2012), and Ames (2015a).

18. "Dieses transitiv gebrauchte Zeitwort besagt: einen Weg bilden, bildend ihn bereit halten. Be-wëgen (Be-wëgung) heißt, so gedacht, nicht mehr: etwas nur auf einem schon vorhandenen Weg hin- und herschaffen, sondern: den Weg zu . . . allererst erbringen und so der Weg »sein«" (Heidegger 1985, 229)

19. "das »es«, was hier »gibt«, ist das Sein selbst" (Heidegger 1976, 334).

20. In commenting on "es gibt das Sein," Herman Philipse (1998, 191) goes so far as to state that "this reminds us of the metaphysical notion of God as *causa sui*" even though Heidegger's *Sein* is not the *Summum Ens*. For Philipse (1998, 187), Heidegger's later thought is "postmonotheist" in the sense that it attempts "*to replace the Christian religion by a different variety of religious discourse*, the meaning of which is parasitic upon the monotheist Christian discourse that it intends to destroy."

21. "könnte der Tao der alles be-wëgende Weg sein" (Heidegger 1985, 187).

22. This seems to be in line with Froese's interpretation which, sometimes, tends toward a metaphysical representation of Daoism. She affirms, for instance, that "Daoist thinkers use the term '*Dao*' (道) to refer to a cosmic first principle" (45), and she suggests that it is possible "to liken the Dao to the center of a rotating circle, which itself does not move but that makes movement possible by drawing all things towards it" (48). This is quite surprising, not only because Froese proposes a nonmetaphysical understanding of Daoism, but also because the idea of a *dao* that "does not move" is totally foreign to the *Lao-Zhuang*. In fact, "returning" is the movement of *dao*, as we shall see in chapter 4.

23. Cheng Chung-Ying also affirms that "Heidegger himself tried to understand the *tao* in terms of Being or vice versa in his later years" (1991, 368).

24. For the *Zhuangzi* I refer to Hung (1947).

Chapter 2

1. The scope of Benjamin's essay is, however, far more complex than this as it is possible to see in Derrida (1987). For an anthropological reading of this passage, see Talal Asad (1989), who makes clear that translations always involve "cultural translations."

2. The position of Humboldt influenced the so-called Sapir-Whorf hypothesis. On this, see Sapir (1929), Whorf (1940), and Kay and Kempton (1984). On the developments of linguistic relativism, see Brown (1976) and Pütz and Verspoor (2000). See also the position of Graham (1989a, 389–428; 2018) on linguistic relativism in relation to Chinese.

3. For an interesting analysis of language objectification, see Trabant (2000).

4. This course was given by Heidegger when he was preparing the publication of *Being and Time*. *The Basic Problems of Phenomenology* was intended to be division 3 of part 1 of *Being and Time*. This, however, was never published and Heidegger allowed the publication of *Basic Problems* only in 1975. For an introduction of the story of the two books, see Hofstadter (1988).

5. The critique to the philosophy of worldview presented in *The Basic Problems* is a development of what is synthetically defined in the lecture course *The Idea of Philosophy and the Problem of Worldview* that Heidegger gave in 1919 at Freiburg and published in 1987 as the first part of *Towards the Definition of Philosophy*. In 1919, however, Heidegger is far from the depths of the ontological difference and still totally inscribed in phenomenology, which he defines as "the philosophy without standpoints!" (162).

6. Although Heidegger is more on the trajectory of Husserl's phenomenology, essential distinctions are expressly stated by Heidegger himself, in particular with regard to the "phenomenological reduction" (BPP 21).

7. For a critique of the Heidegger's philosophical relationship with Husserl, see Moran (2007). For a more positive account, see Crowell (2005). For an analysis of Heidegger's phenomenology as "hermeneutical phenomenology," see Palmer (1969, 124 ff.).

8. I agree with Ma Lin (2008, 208) when she affirms that "the general drift of Heidegger's thinking tends toward a picture of East-West dialogue in which the East is invited to join in, or to be of aid to, the central task of leaping into the other beginning of the Western metaphysical tradition."

9. On the withdrawal and unconcealment of Being, see Heidegger (2002c, 253; 1991b, 213–214).

10. Philipse (1998, 98) aptly asks what justifies Heidegger's critical view "that Greek philosophy did not succeed in acknowledging the ontological difference between being and beings, although acknowledging this difference would have been its internal *telos*? Should we not rather conclude that Heidegger projected the notion of an ontological difference onto the Greeks?"

11. For a detailed account of philosophy as the "eternal aspiration toward self-foundation," see Gasché (1986).

Chapter 3

1. "Eine wesentliche Übersetzung entspricht jeweils in einer Epoche des Seinsgeschickes der Weise, wie im Geschick des Seins eine Sprache spricht" (Heidegger 1997, 145). Heidegger warns us that we "usually understand Geschick [destiny] as being that which has been determined and imposed through fate: a sorrowful, an evil, a fortunate Geschick. This meaning is a derivative one. For schicken ['sending'] originally denotes: 'preparing,' 'ordering,' 'bringing each thing to that place where it belongs'; consequently it also means to 'furnish' [*einräumen*] and 'admit'; 'to appoint' [*beschicken*] a house, a room, means: 'to keep in good order,' 'straightened up and tidied' " (PR 61).

2. In *Identity and Difference* (1969, 36), Heidegger mentions the concept of *Ereignis* along with *lógos* λόγος and *dao*. Some scholars interpret *Ereignis* as event, other as appropriation. Joan Stambaugh translates it as "event of appropriation." Heidegger (1971c, 127) explains that *Ereignis*, "seen as it is shown by Saying, cannot be represented either as an occurrence or a happening—it can only be experienced as the abiding gift yielded by Saying."

3. For the concept of *Ereignis* and its connections with those of *es gibt* and *Geschick*, see Llewelyn (1985, 18 ff.).

4. "Seinsgeschichte ist das Geschick des Seins, das sich uns zuschickt, indem es sein Wesen entzieht" (Heidegger 1997, 90).

5. "die Er-gebnis, deren reichendes Geben erst dergleichen wie ein »Es gibt« gewährt, dessen auch noch »das Sein« bedarf, um als Anwesen in sein Eigenes zu gelangen" (Heidegger 1985, 247).

6. "Das in der Sage Waltende, das Ereignis, können wir nur so nennen, daß wir sagen: Es—das Ereignis—eignet. Sagen wir dies, dann sprechen wir in unserer eigenen schon gesprochenen Sprache" (Heidegger 1985, 247).

7. Frederick Olafson highlights the tension between the independence of language and its need for human utterance. Olafson (1993, 109) links this tension to the one that Heidegger was facing in "reorienting his conception of being in such a way as to assert as complete an independence of being from entities as possible." Yet, for Olafson (1993, 120) it is not altogether clear how one needs to understand this independence within dependence of language. Marlène Zarader (2006, 51–57), however, shows how there is no tension here insofar as Heidegger resembles the relationship that connects the word of God to the biblical prophet.

8. This is also the problem of Heidegger's "first beginning" and "other beginning" or, to use the words of Jean-Luc Nancy (2017, 62), the motif of *commencement*, "that is, of an initial and self-sufficient form of what is—or even of what must be . . . the logical, political, veritative, and destinal auto-foundation."

9. For a more critical analysis of this controversial Heideggerian position on language, see Wu (1998, 430).

10. For an extensive analysis of the development of the metaphor in modern Western philosophy, see Cazeaux (2007).

11. For a general analysis of the problem of circularity, see Bontekoe (1996).

12. For a reply to the Ricoeurian criticism and for a reaffirmation of the debt Derrida pays to Heidegger, see Derrida (2007).

13. Translation modified.

14. It is not possible in this context to further discuss this aspect of metaphysics, which would entail a painstaking consideration of Derrida's "The *Retrait* of Metaphor" (2007).

15. For a detailed analysis of different positions regarding Nietzsche's metaphysics, see Meyer (2014).

16. It is necessary to stress that "war" ought not to be interpreted as physical fight and violence. For Nietzsche war is an ideological and noble opposition. In *Ecce Homo* (2007b, I 7), he makes clear this meaning of war, stating that "My practice of war can be summed up in four propositions. First: I attack only causes that are victorious—on occasion, I wait till they are victorious. Second: I attack causes only when there are no allies to be found, when I am standing alone—when I am compromising myself alone. . . . I have never made a move in public that was not compromising: this is *my* criterion for right action. Third: I never attack people—I make use of a person only as a kind of strong magnifying glass with which one can make visible some general but insidious and quite intangible exigency." It is clear that war is not violence against people but a dialogic attack against causes or "general but insidious and quite intangible exigency." In this attack there is no resentment: "attacking is for me a proof of benevolence, even of gratitude. By linking my name with that of a cause or a person—whether for or against is indifferent to me—I honour them, I set them apart." This is Nietzsche's fourth position.

17. For an account of Nietzsche relation to aesthetics, see Came (2014).

18. This means that the eternal recurrence is not an ontological statement. It should be regarded as a limit metaphor and not as a metaphysical truth. On this, see Nehamas (1985, 151) and Richardson (2006, 209).

Chapter 4

1. Ames and Hall (2003, 215) specify that *you* and *wu* "might be translated as 'something' and 'nothing' respectively. They refer to the more determinate and indeterminate aspects of the ongoing process of experience. Importantly, rather than ontological terms, these are explanatory categories necessary to make sense of the process of experience."

2. I retain the indication of Ames and Hall for *you* and *wu* here. Translations from Chinese are by the author unless otherwise indicated.

3. D. C. Lau (1989, xxiii) is one of them.

4. For the Guodian text I follow the transcription offered by Henricks (2000).

5. An example of this interpretation is offered by Fung Yu-lan (2016, 78).

6. For the *Zhuangzi* I follow the translation of Graham (1989b), which offers a good balance between a meaningful interpretation and a poetical rendering. In the absence of Graham's reference (given after the original), the translation is my own. For a critique of Graham's translation see Lin (2003).

7. More on *yi* in the next chapter.

8. When I quote from other sources, insertions in square brackets are my own whereas the ones in parentheses are in the original. In my own translations, my insertions are in parentheses.

9. On this, see also the discussion in Ames (1998b, 15–17).

10. Regarding *hun* 混, Ames and Hall explain that it is "sometimes translated as 'chaos,' but this puts a negative twist on an idea that is basically positive in classical Chinese. 'Spontaneity' might be a more appropriate rendering" (2003, 209). This is a good indication and needs consideration. Certainly, spontaneity is part of the chaotic formation described here. Still, it is important to keep the idea of chaos insofar as it shows more clearly the absence of a scope or of a cause. Although it is true that chaos ought not to be regarded negatively, it is also necessary to distinguish it from *ziran*, which can be considered more properly as spontaneous.

11. Chen's position on the production of the myriad things is also questionable. As discussed, *dao* produces the myriad things but the myriad things are constitutive of *dao*, thus excluding the priority of one element over the other. It is also worth considering that, in this same chapter, *dao* is described as grand (*da* 大), which in turn is described as passing away (*shi* 逝). More on this soon.

12. Tang Junyi (1988a, 9) quotes this sentence to explain that the Chinese worldview does not have a fixed component because everything in the world is a process and outside of this process there is no fixed "substratum." This line is not

present in the Guodian and in Mawangdui versions. The passage *duli er bu gai* is also slightly different in the Guodian version, which has *duli bu hai* 獨立不亥. On this, see Ames (2000, 239).

13. Tang Junyi (1988a, 11) uses this passage to underline another important component of the Chinese worldview, namely, the cyclical arising and change of everything. According to him, however, this is not a specificity of the *Daodejing* and all Daoist philosophers will follow this same idea. As it will become clearer in the next chapter, this component is particularly relevant in the *Zhuangzi*.

14. This also contradicts the theory of Lau discussed above: it is undeniable that the process does not stop at the weak point of *shi* and returns to *da*.

15. For an analysis of *Monadology* §51, see the comment of Lloyd Strickland in Leibniz (2014, 113–115).

16. If one considers chapter 25 in its entirety, it is possible to see that it describes a perpetual cycle. Thus, the beginning and the end are connected. The process that is described at the beginning is a spontaneous one, which has been generated before the world. However, the author names this process *dao* and *dao* emulates *ziran*, which entails that the process at the beginning was not generated but developed spontaneously.

17. Chen Guying (2008, 150) gives a similar interpretation.

18. Lai Shen-chon (2010, 74) follows the same path in considering *ren* the grammatical subject of the four levels. According to him, the passage should be read as "people emulate earth, heavens, *dao* and *ziran*." Lai also offers an interesting comparison between these four levels and Heidegger's concept of *Geviert* (fourfold).

19. *Xue bu xue* literally means "to learn not to learn." Yet, in other chapters—as in chapter 48—there is a clear definition of reducing knowledge and not just refusing knowledge. For this line, the Guodian *Laozi* (A:6) has "to teach not to teach" (*jiao bu jiao* 教不教) instead of *xue bu xue*. More on this later.

20. Both the Mawangdui and Guodian versions have *neng fu wanwu* 能輔萬物 instead of *yi fu wanwu* 以輔萬物. The Mawangdui version ends with *er fu gan wei* 而弗敢為. The Guodian *Laozi* A version has a different conclusion: *er fu neng wei* 而弗能為 (they cannot do so) instead of *er bu gan wei* 而不敢為. The *Laozi* A version is, therefore, contradictory, having both *neng fu* and *fu neng*. According to Ames and Hall (2003, 226), the passage appears corrupt in this version.

21. Many translations in modern Chinese consider the sage to be the subject of *bu gan wei*. See, for instance, Chen Guying (1984, 310).

22. It is indicative that Slingerland (2013, 8) wants to "move beyond culturally essentialistic stereotypes of China" believing in "mind–body dualism being a human universal." As if this were not an essentialistic position.

23. For the *Lunyu* and the *Mengzi*, see respectively Liu D. (1995) and Liu and Chen (1995).

24. Once again, Fraser (2007, 103) rightly considers that, applied as Slingerland does, "the conceptual metaphor approach can hardly even be taken seriously."

25. In the *Daodejing*, chapters 18, 19, and 38 are directly against Confucian principles. On this see Henricks (2000, 12–15), who explains how chapter 19 in the Guodian version is "still very 'anti-Confucian,' but it is not yet 'anti-Mencian.'" According to him, the tone becomes more explicitly anti-Mencian with the changes of later editors. In any case, it is evident that Slingerland's position is highly questionable.

26. For the Mawangdui version, I follow the transcription present in Mawangdui Han mu boshu zhengli xiaozu 馬王堆漢墓帛書整理小組 (1976). The numbers after quotations indicate the pages.

27. This concept is presented in the *Zhuangzi* (57/22/9–10) as well. See also the translation of Graham (1989b, 159).

28. For an analysis and a comparison of the characters used in the Guodian *Laozi* and in the other versions, see Liao (2003). For a specific comparison of this passage, see Gao (1996, 414–416).

29. *Ren* is a clear reference to Confucian morality. Vincent Shen (2003b, 643) explains that in Confucian philosophy "*ren* can be construed as an ethical virtue, as the summation of all ethical virtues." Therefore, *buren* 不仁 is a negation of this summation. Ames and Hall (2003, 206) point out that in the *Daodejing ren* functions "as a suspect Confucian value that emerges only when genuine moral feeling has been overwritten by conventionalized rules for living." I shall discuss in more detail how this is relevant in relation to *wuming*. Regarding *tiandi* (literally "heavens and earth"), Wang Keping (1998, 29) clarifies that this expression "is usually employed in Chinese to mean either nature or the universe as a whole."

30. See also the description of the straw dogs given by the *Zhuangzi* (37/14/30–35).

31. The Guodian *Laozi* C has *xue bu xue* 學不學 (C:4).

32. This is not only in opposition with the Confucian educational idea but also against what has been developed in the Judeo-Christian tradition.

33. If rulership needs to be considered, it has to be in the most general sense: to some extent, everyone is a ruler, even if this means to rule one's own self. The *Zhuangzi* (4/2/16–20) pushes the problem of rulership to the organs of the body. See on this Graham's comment (1989b, 51).

34. The Guodian *Laozi* (A:7) does not have *wu*.

35. Chinese commentators such as Chen Guying (1984, 210) and Xu Kangsheng (1985, 130) consider that *wuming* refers directly to *dao*. This is true if *dao* is regarded as a process and, therefore, the unnaming becomes part of it. However, *wuming* and *dao* cannot be synonyms as Chen Guying implies. I have mentioned that *dao* describes an indeterminate continuous process. Thanks to *wuwei* and *wuming* this process can spontaneously arise. Hence, the distinction between *dao* and *wuming* is similar to the distinction between *ziran* and *wuwei*.

36. Hall and Ames (1987, 210) remind us the close link between the homophones *ming* 名 "to name" and *ming* 命 "to command." According to them "*ming*

[命] is nothing less than one's *created world*. This explains the apparent relationship between 'naming' (*ming* [名]) and *ming* [命]: to *ming* is to 'articulate' the world." Thus also the reversal is true: "'To name (*ming* 名)' is 'to command (*ming* 命).' If you have something's name, you not only know it, but can contain it and hold it subject to your will. To invoke a name brings power and mastery with it" (Ames and Hall 2003, 134–135).

37. The received text has a different opening: 絕聖棄智 "Abandon sageliness and drop knowledge."

38. Chad Hansen (2003a, 694) recognizes the link that "abandon knowledge" has with names and distinguishes the notion of "antiknowledge" in the *Daodejing* from the one of Shen Dao (c. 350–275 BCE). According to Hansen (2003b, 785), in the *Daodejing* the "core idea is that ordinary (guiding) knowledge is based on names and thus relies on social conventions. Daoism is suspicious of social conventions (favored by Confucianism). Allowing conventions to control us amounts to losing our natural spontaneity."

39. I follow the version of Brettler, Newsom, and Perkins (2010, 12–13).

40. Simkins's main argument is directed against the famous essay "The Historical Roots of Our Ecologic Crisis" in which Lynn White (1967) criticizes the anthropocentrism of the Judeo-Christian tradition.

41. Graham's translation has been slightly modified here. Graham uses "the essentials of man" to translate *qing* 情, which obscures the link between *qing* and *haowu* 好惡 (likes and dislikes). For a detailed analysis of *qing*, see Puett (2004) and Bruya (2004).

Chapter 5

1. Angus Graham (1969–70, 137) also believes there is a wide consensus that the "Qiwulun" is the most important chapter of the *Zhuangzi* 莊子, "which amounts to saying that it is the most important document of early Taoism outside the *Tao te ching* itself."

2. According to Graham (1983, 3), "even among the philosophies commonly called 'mystical,' there can hardly be one more resistant to an analytic approach than Taoism." Although it is true that the analytic approach does not offer enough instruments to interpret texts such as the *Daodejing* or the *Zhuangzi*, it is also necessary not to consider them as inscrutable and mystical. Lin Yutang (1958, 31) affirms that when "Laotse and Chuangtse spoke in mystic phraseology of the 'elusiveness' of Tao, it must be remembered that they were not being mystic, but merely good observers of life."

3. It is well known that the *Zhuangzi* is not the work of a single author—on this see Liu Xiaogan (1987; 1994)—and that it was edited by Guo Xiang 郭象 (died 312 CE). Regarding the headings of the chapters, Graham (1989b, 29) holds that,

most probably, an editor of the second century BCE devised them. These titles, therefore, can be considered as early synthetic interpretations of the chapters' contents.

4. *Wu* 物 is generally translated as "thing" but it is not limited to inanimate objects. In this context, the word is meant as an integral part of the *wanwu* 萬物 "myriad things" and must not be regarded as an objectifying concept. *Lun* 論 means "discourse" or "to discuss" but also "to arrange," "to sort." Graham (1989b) understands it in this last sense and translates "Qiwulun" as "The sorting which evens things out." For further analysis on the title, see Huang (2005). For an account of the title's interpretations in Chinese history, see Wang (1988, 39–40).

5. To understand the quality of Graham's translation we can consider how he deals with one of the most difficult terminological problems of the "Qiwulun." In this text "there is some difficulty in finding English equivalents of the key terms *shih* [是] and *fei* [非] which will not obscure this part of the argument. Ordinarily we translate them by 'right' and 'wrong,' and are not worried by the fact that *shih* is basically a demonstrative ('this, it, the one in question') used verbally ('is the one in question'). . . . Disputation therefore assumes agreement as to what is *shih*, 'this, the one in question,' in contrast to what is *pi* [彼], 'that, other.' For Chuang-tzu it is highly significant that judgments are made with demonstratives, which are obviously relative to the speaker's standpoint; just as if you and I stand at different places my 'here' will be your 'there,' so if we start from different systems of naming (for example the different moral terminologies of Confucians and Mohists) what is *shih* for me will be *fei* for you. Previous translators have generally abandoned all hope of making this part of the argument intelligible in English by such inconsistencies as translating *shih* and *pi* by 'this' and 'that' but *shih* and *fei* by 'right' and 'wrong.' It is admittedly difficult to achieve a consistent set of equivalents without resorting to very forced English. I have used 'it' and 'other' for *shih* and *pi*, and such phrases as 'that's it, that's not' for *shih* and *fei* (in their transitive uses 'accept' and 'reject'), always avoiding 'right' and 'wrong' even when they would allow much smoother English" (Graham 1969–70, 142–143).

6. In his acute interpretation of the "Qiwulun," Liu Xiaogan (1986, 122) proceeds in an opposite direction using the Hegelian dialectics as the main tool of his reading. According to him, dialectics can lead people to properly understand the antitheses of the objective world and to see the truth that sophistry twists. Considering these premises, it is evident that, from Liu's perspective, although the "Qiwulun" uses a dialectical approach toward the world, it constantly falls into sophistry. Still, even if dialectics were a proper and scientific method of disclosing an objective world, this method would affirm precisely the subject/object opposition, activating the *shifei* process that the "Qiwulun" tries to neutralize. As a consequence, although the "Qiwulun" uses oppositions, these are meant to show the corresponding value of conflicting argumentations. Thus, supposing that one could use this terminology in this context, from the point of view of the "Qiwulun," the primary sophistry is dialectics itself if this is believed to solve the oppositions in a synthesis.

For a detailed analysis of the discursive strategy in the *Zhuangzi* and its relation to the other traditional Chinese schools of thought, see Hansen (1992, 269–292).

7. According to Hansen (1992, 284), the point is precisely "to appreciate that many languages, many ways of *shi-fei*ing are possible. The useful advice is that we should be flexible, tolerant, aware of the infinite range of possible ways to respond to life."

8. Although controversial and metaphysically indebted, Wu Kuang-ming's idea of *qi* as a "spontaneous system of ontological reciprocity" (1990, 171) is an interesting interpretation.

9. Hall and Ames (1995, 237) underline that there are no "hierarchies built upon implicit ontological claims. No 'Great Chain of Being' or 'Ladder of Perfection' exists in the Daoist thinking." We shall come back to the problem of ontology.

10. For the anti-anthropocentric view, see Chen Guying (1985, 20), Moeller (2006, 55, 133; 2009, 37), and Parkes (2013).

11. Graham (1989, 190) explains that "It is all right to make fluid distinctions varying with circumstances, it is when we make rigid distinctions misleading us into judging that something is permanently what it is temporarily convenient to name it that thinking goes wrong." Indeed, to say something means to distinguish something from something else. However, this saying is never fixed, which implies that distinctions are also never fixed. It is not possible, therefore, to agree with Bryan Van Norden (1996, 259), who proposes that the sage "does *not* make evaluative judgments at all."

12. We shall see how this continuity is crucial to understand the transformation of the myriad things. For now it is worth emphasising how Ames (1998a, 3) states that "A recognition of the mutuality one shares with one's environments leads to a reconciliation of opposites: a transcending of self/other distinction and freedom from the desires, attachments, and dichotomous values that are generated from the notion of a discrete self (that is, a reconciliation of 'this/that,' 'good/bad,' 'right/wrong,' 'life/death,' and so on)." By the same token Graham (1989, 193) affirms that "The Taoist sage is unselfish, neither by acting out his nature nor by obeying moral principle, but by seeing through all dichotomies including self and other."

13. We have seen how in the *Daodejing* it is possible to find a similar concept when it is said that *you* and *wu* are mutually generating (*youwu xiangsheng* 有無相生).

14. In his commentary, Guo Xiang interprets this passage underlining its negative aspect. Nevertheless, the centrality of reciprocity between polarities remains untouched: "Since each and every thing considers itself 'it,' no one cannot be considered 'it.' All things consider one another 'other,' hence no one cannot be considered 'other.' For no thing is not 'other,' there is no 'it' in the world. No thing is not 'it,' thus there is no 'other' in the world. Since there is no 'other' and no 'it,' then they profoundly correspond" (Guo 1961, 66).

15. Regarding this passage and the issue of considering *zi shi* 自是 instead of *zi zhi* 自知, see Chen Guying (2007, 68). Ziporyn (2003, 46) explains that this

line "constitutes an essential turning point in the discussion, but it is very hard to construe." He interprets the line as critical toward the possibility of seeing from the other point of view. This, however, is only one aspect of the passage—indeed, Ziporyn needs to "assume an intersubjective concept of 'thing'" to justify the inconsistency of this reading. Only by acknowledging that the other point of view also has awareness of both perspectives is it possible to have a correspondence between one's own standpoint and the other. Chen Guying (1985, 22) points in this direction by explaining how the *yi ming* 以明—which precedes and concludes this passage—suggests a mutual illumination: "'that' is enlightened by 'this' and 'this' is enlightened by 'that.'"

16. Graham holds that "ceasing to choose and simply 'being about to' the sage thinks of other people as 'I'" (1989, 193).

17. In his commentary on this passage, Cheng Xuanying 成玄英 (608–669 CE) concludes by saying that "if one can really perceive the other and the self, then there is no *shi* and no *fei*" (Guo 1961, 65). However, as we have seen, in the "Qiwulun" the scope is not to dissolve oppositions but to assimilate them. More on this below.

18. For a history of the self's conceptions in China, see Elvin (1985). For a detailed analysis of the concept of the self in the Daoist thought, see Hall and Ames (1998, 45 ff.). For a discussion of the self in the "Qiwulun," see Chen Guying (2008, 212–213).

19. I have already considered *yi* as "continuity" in relation to the *Daodejing* in the previous chapter. Coutinho (2014, 64) explains that *yi* 一 cannot be regarded as "the One" because in early Chinese philosophy *yi* as "one" has a "different set of connotations from those of Western philosophy: it often has a temporalized sense, referring to the continuity between past and present." According to him concepts such as integration and continuity are more consistent with the early Daoist understanding of *yi*. The "Qiwulun" (5/2/53) itself reminds us of the impossibility of naming the "one" as "unity," because the saying itself constitutes an addition to it. Therefore, as clarified by Hansen (1992, 291), it is of paramount importance not to think of the "Qiwulun" as a monistic assertion. For an analysis and distinction between this passage and the similar one of Hui Shi 惠施, see Fung Yu-lan (2016, 82–84). Although the overall analysis of Fung is fascinating, it is compromised by its transcendent perspective.

20. For a different reading on this and on the *Zhuangzi* ethics, see Huang (2010).

21. Tang (1988c, 112) reaffirms this concept in more detail by analyzing the term "cosmos" (*yuzhou* 宇宙; literally "space-time").

22. For the *Liezi*, see Liu (1996). This passage is at the beginning of the first chapter. The *Zhuangzi* expresses more vehemently a similar idea in chapter 17: "The life of things is like a galloping rush, there is no movement without a change, there is no moment without a shift. What is to be done? What is not to be done?

Everything will certainly transform by itself" (物之生也若驟若馳，無動而不變，無時而不移。何為乎？何不為乎？夫固將自化) (44/17/46–47). Here, it is interesting to see how change assumes the spontaneous character of self-transformation *zihua* 自化.

23. On this, it is not possible to accept the position of Tang Junyi (1988d, 263–264), who interprets the *Zhuangzi* as giving priority to *wu* over *you*. In his analysis Tang wants to find an exact counterpart of the Hegelian priority of Being. As we have seen, however, *you* and Being have different meanings. Hence, the metaphysical comparison between Hegel and the *Zhuangzi* proposed by Tang is self-defeating from the outset. Nevertheless, the analysis of change (*bianhua* 變化) proposed by Tang is remarkable.

24. On this, see Chen Yinchi (2016, 236–237).

25. Ziporyn (2003, 35) proposes the interesting concept of "*omnicentric holism.*" This seems to resemble the concept of focus/field develop by Hall and Ames (1987, 239), which in turn refers back to Fazang's 法藏 Hall of Mirrors. On a different note but with similar conclusions, Graham (1969–70, 145) states, "Chuang-tzu's position is that we should cease to distinguish between one thing and another, but this does not entitle us to affirm that 'everything is one,' a proposition which immediately distinguishes itself from the world which is other than it."

26. On the problematic characterization of the *Zhuangzi*'s philosophy as relativist or sceptical, see Kjellberg and Ivanhoe (1996). For a critique of the position that interprets the *Zhuangzi* as neither absolutist nor relativist, see Allinson (1989a, 117–120).

27. Chen Guying states that "we must understand our own transformation, that is *zihua* 自化" (1985, 25).

28. Graham (1989b, 5) explains that "stories about special knacks were popular in the school of Chuang-tzǔ; only one of them, the tale of Cook Ting carving the ox, belongs to the *Inner chapters* which can be confidently ascribed to Chuang-tzǔ himself, but as concrete illustrations of the Taoist approach they are as instructive to the modern reader as they evidently were to ancient apprentices of the school."

29. For Froese (2006, 61) Cook Ding "is able carve an ox with grace because he ignores 'sense' and follows his 'spirit.'" I disagree with the general mystical interpretation that holds this position. For a more detailed analysis of this passage and of its mystical interpretation, see Lacertosa (2022).

30. Hansen (2003c, 917) reminds us that we should avoid considering the advancement of Ding's skill as a mystical achievement.

31. I keep Graham's translation to render the passage of the *Zhuangzi* (同則無好也，化則無常也, 17/6/93) quoted by Chen.

32. Fung Yu-lan (2016, 91) makes an important distinction between having no knowledge as ignorance and having achieved no knowledge. He calls the latter "post gained absence of knowledge" (*hou de di wuzhi* 後得底無知).

33. For the edition of the *Huainanzi*, see Liu and Chen (1992).

Returning to the Beginning
(by Way of Conclusion)

1. I have already discussed the problem of representation in chapter 2. Here, it is worth recalling that to represent means "of oneself, to set something before one and to make what has been set in place [*das Gestellte*] secure as thus set in place. This placing-in-securedness must be a calculating, since only calculation guarantees being certain, in advance and always, of that which is to be presented. . . . Representation, setting-before, is a making everything stand over and against as object [*Ver-gegen-ständlichung*] which masters and proceeds against. In this way, representation drives everything into the unity of the thus-objectified. Representation is *coagitatio*" (Heidegger 2002b, 82; 1977, 108).

2. Translations of the *Ion* are from Allen (1996).

3. Translations of the *Republic* are from Griffith (2000).

4. It is worth recalling that, in his first objection to the Cartesian first meditation, Thomas Hobbes links Descartes's position on senses to the one of Plato (Descartes 2008, 107, AT VII, 171). AT refers to the standard edition *Œuvres de Descartes* edited by Charles Adam and Paul Tannery (1964–76). For an extensive account of Descartes's historical references, see Menn (1998).

5. Zhu refers to chapter 37 of the *Daodejing*, which I have analyzed in chapter 4.

6. This and the following translations from Chinese are by the author.

7. "不知周之夢為胡蝶與，胡蝶之夢為周與" (7/2/95–96).

8. Another important aspect of the butterfly dream is considered by Graham Parkes, one of the few who have detected this crucial element. According to Parkes (1983, 242–243), the butterfly dream not only establishes "the universality of dreaming for Chuang Tzu," but also "points up an important feature of his perspectivism and its further congruence with Nietzsche's. Like Nietzsche, who emphasizes that experience is always necessarily perspectival, Chuang Tzu does not believe that we could ever attain a kind of 'perspectiveless seeing.' What we wake up to is the realization that we are always bound by some perspective: this awakening is itself a perspective—but one that acknowledges and embraces the multiplicity of all possible perspectives, and is thus 'open in every direction.'" I shall discuss soon how Nietzsche interprets the act of dreaming.

9. "周與胡蝶，則必有分矣。此之謂物化" (7/2/96).

10. For a critique of this passage, see the exchange of Derrida and Foucault in part collected in the appendices of Foucault (2006).

11. Vincent Shen (2003a, 358) emphasizes how the divinity has a complete different role in the *Daodejing*: "in all versions of *Laozi*, divinities came on the scene much later. In the Guodian texts, divine intellects come to be after the formation of heaven and earth and before that of *yin* and *yang* [he is referring to the text *The*

Great One Gave Birth to Water, Taiyi Shengshui 太一生水]. And in Wang Bi's version and the Mawangdui version, the *dao* 'seems to have preceded the supreme deity,' *di* (ch. 4). The supreme deity was produced by the ever-creative self-manifesting *dao*, which is nonsubstantial in itself." Shen concludes that "in this way, Laozi seems to avoid the ontological, theological metaphysics that we find in western philosophy."

12. For a general account of the relation between Nietzsche and Asian thought, see Parkes (1991). For a more critical position, see Ma and van Brakel (2016, 23), who affirm that "in spite of his compliments for Asiatic civilizations, Nietzsche always emphasizes the uniqueness and supreme importance of Greek culture."

13. Li Zehou (2010, 97) specifies that "nature—whether actual nature or that found in poetry and paintings—is always in intimate communication and relationship with human life and emotion. For this reason, the Chinese painter's or poet's interest in nature is seldom in the depiction of the details of an individual natural object—its color, fragrance, sound, or smell—but rather in capturing the landscape or scene as a whole. Thus, whether it be an awesome peak or a swollen river, a fish's scale or the claw of a bird, the natural object will always be treated in the context of the close relationship between people and the whole of nature. This explains how nature in Chinese landscape painting can be both untouched and full of human presence."

14. In relation to this correspondence, it is worth recalling how, in *Phenomenology of Perception*, Merleau-Ponty (2012, xxv) describes *la chose*, the thing: "the thing is the correlate of my body and, more generally, of my existence of which my body is merely the stabilized structure. . . . The thing can never be separated from someone who perceives it. . . . To this extent, every perception is a communication or a communion" (334). Commenting on this passage, Claude Lefort (2012, xxv) synthesizes its main idea as "reversibility of sensing and sensed."

15. Ames (1998a, 4) affirms that one of "the *Zhuangzi*'s central concerns is maximizing human creativity. Creativity can be compromised, however, where one attempts to express one's unique particularity in a 'dis-integrative' way that fails to accommodate the mutuality and interdependence of other things. This diminution in creativity can be brought about either by interpreting one's environment reductionistically through one's own fixed conceptual structures and values, thereby impoverishing context in service to oneself, or by allowing oneself to be shaped wholly by context without contributing one's own uniqueness, thereby abnegating oneself in service to context. To be fully integrative, individuals must overcome the sense of discreteness and discontinuity with their environment, and they must contribute personally and creatively to the emerging pattern and regularity of existence called *dao*." We have seen in the previous chapters how this can be done through the unobstructive actions of *wuwei* and through the unassertive definitions of *wuming*.

16. Burton Watson (2013, xi–xii) asserts that to "describe this mindless, purposeless mode of life, Zhuangzi turns most often to the analogy of the artist or craftsman. The skilled woodcarver, the skilled butcher, the skilled swimmer does not

ponder or ratiocinate on the course of action he should take; his skill has become so much a part of him that he merely acts instinctively and spontaneously and, without knowing why, achieves success." In these stories, the focus is on the action in a way that helps to describe how the artist is attuned to the world. Watson, however, seems to miss the main point when he states that "Zhuangzi employs the metaphor of a totally free and purposeless journey, using the word *you* [遊] (to wander, or a wandering) to designate the way in which the enlightened man wanders through all of creation, enjoying its delights without ever becoming attached to any one part of it" (2013, xii). But here *you* is not a mere wandering without purpose, it is the actual merging in the flow of the world. Indeed, *you* is homophone of 游 (to swim, to float). It is not by chance, therefore, that, in the well-known story of Zhuangzi and Huizi discussing on the bridge over the river Hao, Zhuangzi uses *you* 遊 to describe the swimming of the fish (45/17/88).

17. Caravaggio, for instance, was completely ignored before the reinterpretation of his work by Roberto Longhi (1890–1970). Before being ignored, Caravaggio's work was despised by many. Philip Sohm (2002, 455) offers a good synthesis of these positions: "Poussin thought that Caravaggio had betrayed art, accusing him of having 'destroyed painting,' and according to Baglione, he was not alone in this view. Francesco Albani blamed Caravaggio for 'the decline and total ruin' of painting. Federico Borromeo thought that Caravaggio's 'taverns and debauchery' lacked beauty and that this made him the 'opposite' of Raphael. Vincenzo Carducho called Caravaggio the 'anti-Christ' and the 'anti-Michelangelo' because he led followers away from the truth." The problem with all these comments was the sensuous and carnal realism of Caravaggio. Judging from a perspective perfectly in line with the Platonic tradition, Caravaggio's style was too base and far removed from the truth of absolute ideas. Different times and different generations interpret the work of art differently. In relation to Caravaggio, Maurizio Calvesi (1986, 4) affirms that the history of a painter, as well as the history of a painter's work, is constantly rewritten by the interpreters, "since every interpretation modifies that interior image from which stems the work of an artist."

References

Allinson, Robert E. 1989a. *Chuang-Tzu for Spiritual Transformation: An Analysis of the Inner Chapters*. Albany: State University of New York Press.
Allinson, Robert E. 1989b. "An Overview of the Chinese Mind." In *Understanding the Chinese Mind: The Philosophical Roots*, edited by Robert E. Allinson, 1–25. Oxford: Oxford University Press.
Allison, Henry E. 2001. *Kant's Theory of Taste: A Reading of the Critique of Aesthetic Judgment*. Cambridge: Cambridge University Press.
Ames, Roger T. 1998a. "Introduction." In *Wandering at Ease in the Zhuangzi*, edited by Roger T. Ames, 1–14. Albany: State University of New York Press.
Ames, Roger T. 1998b. "Introduction." In D. C. Lau and Roger T. Ames, *Yuan Dao: Tracing Dao to Its Source*, 3–59. New York: Ballantine Books.
Ames, Roger T. 2000. "Reinterpreting Chapter 25 (A 21:1 to 23:12)." In *The Guodian Laozi: Proceedings of the International Conference, Dartmouth College, May 1998*, edited by Sarah Allan and Crispin Williams, 238–239. Berkeley: Society for the Study of Early China and Institute of East Asian Studies, University of California.
Ames, Roger T. 2015a. "The *Great Commentary* (*Dazhuan* 大傳) and Chinese natural cosmology." *International Communication of Chinese Culture* 2, no. 1: 1–18.
Ames, Roger T. 2015b. " 'Knowing' as the 'Realizing of Happiness' Here, on the Bridge, over the River Hao." In *Zhuangzi and the Happy Fish*, edited by Roger T. Ames and Takahiro Nakajima, 261–290. Honolulu: University of Hawai'i Press.
Ames, Roger T. 2015c. "Reading the *Zhongyong* 'metaphysically.' " In *Chinese Metaphysics and its Problems*, edited by Chenyang Li and Franklin Perkins, 85–105. Cambridge: Cambridge University Press.
Ames, Roger T., and David L. Hall, trans. 2003. *Daodejing: "Making This Life Significant": A Philosophical Translation*. New York: Ballantine Books.
Ames, Roger T., and Henry Rosemont Jr. 2013. "On Translation and Interpretation in Comparative Studies—With Special Reference to Classical Chinese." *Comparative Studies of China and the West* 1: 25–32.

Aquinas, Thomas. 1688. *Summa totius theologiae*. Lugduni (Lyon): Sumptibus Joannis Baptistae Barbier, in vico Mercatorio, sub signo Angeli Custodis.

Aquinas, Thomas. 1915–1925. *The Summa Theologica of St. Thomas Aquinas. Literally Translated by the Fathers of the English Dominican Province*. 22 vols. London: Burns Oates & Washbourne Ltd.

Aristotle. 2000. *Nicomachean Ethics*. Translated by Roger Crisp. Cambridge: Cambridge University Press.

Asad, Talal. 1989. "The Concept of Cultural Translation." In *Writing Culture: The Poetics and Politics of Ethnography*, edited by James Clifford and George E. Marcus, 141–164. Berkeley: University of California Press.

Barrett, T. H. 2008. "*daojiao*" 道教. In *The Encyclopedia of Taoism*, edited by Fabrizio Pregadio, 8–10. New York: Routledge.

Baumgarten, Alexander Gottlieb. 1961. *Aesthetica*. Hildesheim: G. Olms.

Beardsley, Monroe C. 1966. *Aesthetics from Classical Greece to the Present*. New York: Macmillan.

Benjamin, Walter. 1968. "The Task of the Translator." In *Illuminations*, edited by Hannah Arendt. Translated by Harry Zohn, 69–82. New York: Schocken Books.

Blumenberg, Hans. 2010. *Paradigms for a Metaphorology*. Translated by Robert Savage. Ithaca, NY: Cornell University Press and Cornell University Library.

Bontekoe, Ronald. 1996. *Dimensions of the Hermeneutic Circle*. Atlantic Highlands, NJ: Humanities Press International.

Bourdieu, Pierre. 1991. *The Political Ontology of Martin Heidegger*. Translated by Peter Collier. Stanford, CA: Stanford University Press.

Brettler, Marc Z., Carol A. Newsom, and Pheme Perkins. 2010. *The New Oxford Annotated Bible: New Revised Standard Version with the Apocrypha*. Fully revised 4th ed. Oxford: Oxford University Press.

Brown, Roger. 1976. "Reference: In Memorial Tribute to Eric Lenneberg." *Cognition* 4: 125–153.

Bruya, Brian James. 2004. "Aesthetic Spontaneity: A Theory of Action Based on Affective Responsiveness." PhD Thesis, University of Hawaii at Manoa. http://hdl.handle.net/10125/11793

Burik, Steven. 2009. *The End of Comparative Philosophy and the Task of Comparative Thinking: Heidegger, Derrida, and Daoism*. Albany: State University of New York Press.

Burik, Steven. 2010. "Thinking on the Edge: Heidegger, Derrida, and the Daoist Gateway (Men 門)." *Philosophy East and West* 60, no. 4: 499–516.

Calvesi, Maurizio. 1986. *Caravaggio*. Firenze: Giunti.

Came, Daniel. 2014. "Introduction." In *Nietzsche on Art and Life*, edited by Daniel Came, 1–13. Oxford: Oxford University Press.

Caputo, John D. 1993. "Heidegger and theology." In *The Cambridge Companion to Heidegger*, edited by Charles B. Guignon, 270–288. Cambridge: Cambridge University Press.

Cassin, Barbara, ed. 2014. *Dictionary of Untranslatables: A Philosophical Lexicon*. Princeton, NJ: Princeton University Press.
Cazeaux, Clive. 2000. *The Continental Aesthetics Reader*. New York: Routledge.
Cazeaux, Clive. 2007. *Metaphor and Continental Philosophy: From Kant to Derrida*. New York: Routledge.
Chan, Albert. 2015. *Chinese Books and Documents from the Jesuit Archives in Rome: A Descriptive Catalogue*. New York: Routledge.
Chan, Wing-tsit. 1963. *A Source Book in Chinese Philosophy*. Princeton, NJ: Princeton University Press.
Chang, Chung-Yuan, ed. 1975. *Tao, a New Way of Thinking: A Translation of the Tao Te Ching, with an Introduction and Commentaries*. Taipei: Dun Huang.
Chen, Guying 陈鼓应. 1984. *Laozi zhu yi ji pingjie* 老子注譯及評介. Beijing 北京: Zhonghua Shuju 中華書局.
Chen, Guying 陳鼓應. 1985. "Zhuangzi renshi xitong de tese" 莊子認識系統的特色. *Anhui Shifan Daxue Xuebao* 安徽師範大學學報 no. 2: 19–26.
Chen, Guying 陳鼓應. 2007. *Zhuangzi jin zhu jinyi* 莊子今注今譯. Beijing 北京: Shangwu Yinshuguan 商務印書館.
Chen, Guying 陳鼓應. 2008. *Laozhuang xin lun* 老莊新論. Beijing 北京: Shangwu Yinshuguan 商務印書館.
Chen, Shaoming 陳少明. 2004. 〈*Qiwulun*〉*ji qi yingxiang* 〈齊物論〉及其影響. Beijing 北京: Beijing Daxue Chubanshe 北京大學出版社.
Chen, Yinchi 陳引馳. 2016. *Wuwei yu xiaoyao: Zhuangzi liu zhang* 無為與逍遙：莊子六章. Beijing 北京: Zhonghua Shuju 中華書局.
Cheng, Chung-ying. 1989. "Chinese Metaphysics as Non-metaphysics: Confucian and Taoist Insights into the Nature of Reality." In *Understanding the Chinese Mind: The Philosophical Roots*, edited by Robert E. Allinson, 167–208. Oxford: Oxford University Press.
Cheng, Chung-ying. 1991. *New Dimensions of Confucian and Neo-Confucian Philosophy*. Albany: State University of New York Press.
Cheng, Chung-ying. 2002. "Preface." *Journal of Chinese Philosophy* 29, no. 1: 1.
Clarke, J. J. 2000. *The Tao of the West: Western Transformations of Taoist Thought*. New York: Routledge.
Collani, Claudia von, Harald Holz, and Konrad Wegmann. 2008. *Uroffenbarung und Daoismus: Jesuitische Missionshermeneutik des Daoismus*. Berlin: European University Press.
Connolly, Tim. 2015. *Doing Philosophy Comparatively*. London: Bloomsbury.
Copp, David. 2006. *The Oxford Handbook of Ethical Theory*. New York: Oxford University Press.
Couplet, Philippe. 1687. *Confucius Sinarum Philosophus*. Parisiis (Paris): Ex Typographia Andreae Cramoisy.
Coutinho, Steve. 2014. *An Introduction to Daoist Philosophies*. New York: Columbia University Press.

Cox, Christoph. 1999. *Nietzsche: Naturalism and Interpretation*. Berkeley: University of California Press.
Crowell, S. Galt. 2005. "Heidegger and Husserl: The Matter and Method of Philosophy." In *A Companion to Heidegger*, edited by Hubert L. Dreyfus and Mark A. Wrathall, 49–64. Oxford: Blackwell.
Crystal, David. 2009. "Introduction." In H. W. Fowler, *A Dictionary of Modern English Usage*, vii–xxv. Oxford: Oxford University Press.
Cua, Antonio S. 柯雄文. 2009. "The emergence of the history of Chinese philosophy." In *History of Chinese Philosophy*, edited by Bo Mou, 43–68. New York: Routledge.
Davidson, Arnold I. 1995. "Introduction." In Pierre Hadot, *Philosophy as a Way of Life: Spiritual Exercises from Socrates to Foucault*, 1–45. Malden, MA: Blackwell.
Defoort, Carine. 2001. "Is There Such a Thing as Chinese Philosophy? Arguments of an Implicit Debate." *Philosophy East and West* 51, no. 3: 393–413.
Defoort, Carine. 2006. "Is 'Chinese Philosophy' a Proper Name? A Response to Rein Raud." *Philosophy East and West* 56, no. 4: 625–660.
Deleuze, Gilles. 1983. *Nietzsche and Philosophy*. Translated by Hugh Tomlinson. London: Athlone Press.
Derrida, Jacques. 1982a. *Margins of Philosophy*. Brighton: Harvester Press.
Derrida, Jacques. 1982b. "Sending: On Representation." *Social Research* 49, no. 2: 294–326.
Derrida, Jacques. 1987. "Des Tours de Babel." In *Psyche: Inventions of the Other, Volume I*, edited by Peggy Kamuf and Elizabeth Rottenberg, 191–225. Stanford, CA: Stanford University Press. 2007.
Derrida, Jacques. 2007. "The *Retrait* of Metaphor." In *Psyche: Inventions of the Other, Volume I*, edited by Peggy Kamuf and Elizabeth Rottenberg, 48–80. Stanford, CA: Stanford University Press.
Descartes, René. 1964–76. *Œuvres de Descartes*. Rev ed. Edited by Charles Adam and Paul Tannery. 12 vols. Paris: Vrin/C.N.R.S.
Descartes, René. 2008. *Meditations on First Philosophy: With Selections from the Objections and Replies*. Translated by Michael Moriarty. New York: Oxford University Press.
Dewey, John. 1934. *Art as Experience*. New York: Perigee.
Dong, Ping 董平. 2015. *Laozi yandu* 老子研讀. Beijing 北京: Zhonghua Shuju 中華書局.
Elvin, Mark. 1985. "Between the Earth and Heaven: Conceptions of the Self in China." In *The Category of the Person: Anthropology, Philosophy, History*, edited by Michael Carrithers, Steven Collins and Steven Lukes, 156–189. Cambridge: Cambridge University Press.
Ferraris, Maurizio. 2012. "Percezione." *Aisthesis. Pratiche, linguaggi e saperi dell'estetico* 5: 9–20.

Fornero, Giovanni, and Salvatore Tassinari. 2002. *Le filosofie del novecento*. Milano: Bruno Mondadori.
Foucault, Michel. 1987. "The Ethic of the Care for the Self as a Practice of Freedom: An Interview with Michael Foucault on 20th January 1984 Conducted by Raúl Fornet-Betancourt, Helmut Becker, Alfredo Gomez-Müller translated by J. D. Gauthier, S. J." *Philosophy & Social Criticism* 12, no. 2–3: 112–131.
Foucault, Michel. 2006. *History of Madness*. Translated by Jean Khalfa. New York: Routledge.
Fraser, Chris. 2007. "On Wu-Wei as a Unifying Metaphor." Review of *Effortless Action: Wu-Wei as Conceptual Metaphor and Spiritual Ideal in Early China* by Edward Slingerland. *Philosophy East and West* 57, no. 1: 97–106.
Fried, Gregory. 2001. "What's in a Word? Heidegger's Grammar and Etymology of 'Being.'" In *A Companion to Heidegger's Introduction to Metaphysics*, edited by Richard Polt and Gregory Fried, 125–142. New Haven: Yale University Press.
Froese, Katrin. 2006. *Nietzsche, Heidegger, and Daoist Thought: Crossing Paths In-Between*. Albany: State University of New York Press.
Fung, Yu-lan, trans. (1933) 1964. *Chuang-tzŭ: A New Selected Translation with an Exposition of the Philosophy of Kuo Hsiang*. 2nd ed. New York: Paragon Book Reprint Corp.
Fung, Yu-lan 馮友蘭. (1945) 2016. *Xin yuan dao: Zhongguo zhexue zhi jingshen* 新原道: 中國哲學之精神. Beijing 北京: Xinshijie Chubanshe 新世界出版社.
Gadamer, Hans-Georg. 1989. "Letter to Dallmayr." In *Dialogue and Deconstruction: The Gadamer-Derrida Encounter*, edited by Diane P. Michelfelder and Richard E. Palmer, 93–101. Albany: State University of New York Press.
Gadamer, Hans-Georg. 2004. *Truth and Method*. Translated by Joel Weinsheimer and Donald G. Marshall. 2nd rev. ed. London: Continuum.
Gao, Ming 高明. 1996. *Boshu Laozi jiaozhu* 帛書老子校注. Beijing 北京: Zhonghua Shuju 中華書局.
Gasché, Rodolphe. 1986. *The Tain of the Mirror: Derrida and the Philosophy of Reflection*. Cambridge, MA: Harvard University Press.
Girardot, N. J. 1999. "'Finding the Way': James Legge and the Victorian Invention of Taoism." *Religion* 29, no. 2: 107–121.
Goethe, Johann Wolfgang von. 1883. *Conversations of Goethe with Eckermann and Soret*. Translated by John Oxenford. Rev. ed. London: G. Bell & Sons.
Goodman, Nelson. 1976. *Languages of Art: An Approach to a Theory of Symbols*. 2nd ed. Indianapolis: Hackett.
Goodman, Nelson. 1978. *Ways of Worldmaking*. Indianapolis: Hackett.
Graham, A. C. 1969–70. "Chuang-tzu's Essay on Seeing Things as Equal." *History of Religions* 9, no. 2/3: 137–159.
Graham, A. C. 1979. "How Much of *Chuang Tzu* Did Chuang Tzu Write?" *Journal of the American Academy of Religion*, 47, no. 3: 459–501.

Graham, A. C. 1983. "Taoist Spontaneity and the Dichotomy of 'Is' and 'Ought.'" In *Experimental Essays on Chuang-tzu*, edited by Victor H. Mair, 3–23. Honolulu: University of Hawai'i Press.

Graham, A. C. (1960) 1986. "'Being' in Western Philosophy Compared with shih/fei and yu/wu in Chinese Philosophy." In *Studies in Chinese Philosophy and Philosophical Literature*, 322–359. Singapore: Institute of East Asian Philosophies, National University of Singapore.

Graham, A. C. 1989a. *Disputers of the Tao: Philosophical Argument in Ancient China*. La Salle, IL: Open Court.

Graham, A. C., trans. 1989b. *Chuang-tzŭ: The Seven Inner Chapters and Other Writings. From the Book Chuang-tzŭ*. London: Unwin Paperbacks.

Graham, A. C. 1990a. *Studies in Chinese Philosophy and Philosophical Literature*. Albany: State University of New York Press.

Graham, A. C., trans. 1990b. *The Book of Lieh-tzŭ: A Classic of the Tao*. New York: Columbia University Press.

Graham, A. C. 2018. "Conceptual Schemes and Linguistic Relativism in Relation to Chinese." In *Philosophy of Language, Chinese Language, Chinese Philosophy: Constructive Engagement*, edited by Bo Mou, 247–268. Leiden: Brill.

Gu, Feng, and Dai Wenjing. 2017. "What Is the Aesthetics in China?" *Aisthesis. Pratiche, linguaggi e saperi dell'estetico* 10, no. 2: 125–134.

Guldin, Rainer. 2016. *Translation as Metaphor*. New York: Routledge.

Guo, Qingfan 郭慶藩. 1961. *Zhuangzi jishi* 莊子集釋. Beijing 北京: Zhonghua Shuju 中華書局.

Guyer, Paul. 2006. "The Harmony of the Faculties Revisited." In *Aesthetics and Cognition in Kant's Critical Philosophy*, edited by Rebecca Kukla, 162–193. Cambridge: Cambridge University Press.

Hadot, Pierre. 1995. *Philosophy as a Way of Life: Spiritual Exercises from Socrates to Foucault*. Translated by Michael Chase. Malden, MA: Blackwell.

Hall, David L. 2002. "What Has Athens to Do with Alexandria? or Why Sinologists Can't Get Along with(out) Philosophers." In *Early China/Ancient Greece: Thinking through Comparisons*, edited by Steven Shankman and Stephen W. Durrant, 15–34. Albany: State University of New York Press.

Hall, David L., and Roger T. Ames. 1987. *Thinking through Confucius*. Albany: State University of New York Press.

Hall, David L., and Roger T. Ames. 1995. *Anticipating China: Thinking through the Narratives of Chinese and Western Culture*. Albany: State University of New York Press.

Hall, David L., and Roger T. Ames. 1998. *Thinking from the Han: Self, Truth, and Transcendence in Chinese and Western Culture*. Albany: State University of New York Press.

Han, Lubo 韓祿伯. 2002. *Jian Bo Laozi yanjiu* 簡帛老子研究. Translated by Yu Jin 余瑾. Beijing 北京: Xueyuan Chubanshe 學苑出版社.

Hansen, Chad. 1983. "A Tao of Tao in Chuang-tzu." In *Experimental Essays on Chuang-tzu*, edited by Victor H. Mair, 24–55. Honolulu: University of Hawai'i Press.
Hansen, Chad. 1992. *A Daoist Theory of Chinese Thought: A Philosophical Interpretation*. Oxford: Oxford University Press.
Hansen, Chad. 2003a. "*Shen Dao (Shen Tao)*." In *Encyclopedia of Chinese Philosophy*, edited by Antonio S. Cua, 692–695. New York: Routledge.
Hansen, Chad. 2003b. "*Wuwei (Wu-wei)*: Taking No Action." In *Encyclopedia of Chinese Philosophy*, edited by Antonio S. Cua, 784–786. New York: Routledge.
Hansen, Chad. 2003c. "Zhuangzi (Chuang Tzu)." In *Encyclopedia of Chinese Philosophy*, edited by Antonio S. Cua, 918–911. New York: Routledge.
Heidegger, Martin. (1956) 1958. *What is Philosophy?* Translated by William Kluback and Jean T. Wilde. London: Vision Press.
Heidegger, Martin. (1927) 1962. *Being and Time*. Translated by John Macquarrie and Edward Robinson. Oxford: Blackwell.
Heidegger, Martin. (1956) 1966. *Was Ist Das—Die Philosophie?* 4th ed. Tübingen: Verlag Gunther Neske Pfullingen.
Heidegger, Martin. (1957) 1969. *Identity and Difference*. Translated by Joan Stambaugh. New York: Harper & Row.
Heidegger, Martin. (1959) 1971a. "A Dialogue on Language." Translated by Peter D. Hertz. In *On the Way to Language*, 1–54. New York: Harper & Row.
Heidegger, Martin. (1959) 1971b. "The Nature of Language." Translated by Peter D. Hertz. In *On the Way to Language*, 57–108. New York: Harper & Row.
Heidegger, Martin. (1959) 1971c. "The Way to Language." Translated by Peter D. Hertz. In *On the Way to Language*, 111–138. New York: Harper & Row.
Heidegger, Martin. 1976. *Wegmarken*. Frankfurt am Main: Klostermann.
Heidegger, Martin. 1977. *Holzwege*. Frankfurt am Main: Klostermann.
Heidegger, Martin. (1975) 1982. *The Basic Problems of Phenomenology*. Translated by Albert Hofstadter. Bloomington: Indiana University Press.
Heidegger, Martin. 1985. *Unterwegs zur Sprache*. Frankfurt am Main: Klostermann.
Heidegger, Martin. (1957) 1991a. *The Principle of Reason*. Translated by Reginald Lilly. Bloomington: Indiana University Press.
Heidegger, Martin. (1961) 1991b. *Nietzsche*. Translated by David Farrell Krell. 2 vols. San Francisco: HarperSanFrancisco.
Heidegger, Martin. (1983) 1995. *The Fundamental Concepts of Metaphysics: World, Finitude, Solitude*. Translated by William McNeill. Bloomington: Indiana University Press.
Heidegger, Martin. 1997. *Der Satz vom Grund*. Frankfurt am Main: Klostermann.
Heidegger, Martin. (1919–21) 1998a. "Comments on Karl Jaspers's *Psychology of Worldviews*." Translated by John Van Buren. In *Pathmarks*, 1–38. Cambridge: Cambridge University Press.

Heidegger, Martin. (1929) 1998b. "What is Metaphysics?" Translated by David Farrell Krell. In *Pathmarks*, 82–96. Cambridge: Cambridge University Press.

Heidegger, Martin. (1943) 1998c. "Postscript to 'What is Metaphysics?'" Translated by William McNeill. In *Pathmarks*, 231–238. Cambridge: Cambridge University Press.

Heidegger, Martin. (1946) 1998d. "Letter on 'Humanism.'" Translated by Frank A. Capuzzi. In *Pathmarks*, 239–276. Cambridge: Cambridge University Press.

Heidegger, Martin. (1949) 1998e. "Introduction to 'What is Metaphysics?'" Translated by Walter Kaufmann. In *Pathmarks*, 277–290. Cambridge: Cambridge University Press.

Heidegger, Martin. (1953) 2000. *Introduction to Metaphysics*. Translated by Gregory Fried and Richard Polt. New Haven, CT: Yale University Press.

Heidegger, Martin. (1935–36) 2002a. "The Origin of the Work of Art." Translated by Julian Young and Kenneth Haynes. In *Off the Beaten Track*, 1–56. Cambridge: Cambridge University Press.

Heidegger, Martin. (1938) 2002b. "The Age of World Picture." Translated by Julian Young and Kenneth Haynes. In *Off the Beaten Track*, 57–85. Cambridge: Cambridge University Press.

Heidegger, Martin. (1946) 2002c. "Anaximander's Saying." Translated by Julian Young and Kenneth Haynes. In *Off the Beaten Track*, 242–281. Cambridge: Cambridge University Press.

Heidegger, Martin. (1987) 2008. *Towards the Definition of Philosophy*. Translated by Ted Sadler. London: Continuum.

Heidegger, Martin. (1989) 2012. *Contributions to Philosophy (of the Event)*. Translated by Richard Rojcewicz and Daniela Vallega-Neu. Bloomington: Indiana University Press.

Heidegger, Martin, and Eugen Fink. (1970) 1979. *Heraclitus Seminar, 1966/67*. Translated by Charles H. Seibert. Tuscaloosa: University of Alabama Press.

Henricks, Robert G. 1989. *Lao Tzu: Te-Tao Ching: A New Translation Based on the Recently Discovered Ma-wang-tui Texts*. New York: Ballantine Books.

Henricks, Robert G. 2000. *Lao Tzu's Tao Te Ching: A Translation of the Startling New Documents Found at Guodian*. New York: Columbia University Press.

Hofstadter, Albert. 1988. "Translator's Introduction." In Martin Heidegger, *The Basic Problems of Phenomenology*, xv–xxxi. Bloomington: Indiana University Press.

Huang, Mei Tin. 2014. "The Encounter of Christianity and Daoism in Philippe Couplet's *Confucius Sinarum Philosophus*." *Frontiers of Philosophy in China* 9, no. 4: 615–624.

Huang, Yong. 2005. "What Does 'Qi wu lun' Mean?—A Thought Prompted by Vincent Shen's Article." *Journal of Chinese Philosophy and Culture* 3: 362–370.

Huang, Yong. 2010. "The Ethics of Difference in the *Zhuangzi*." *Journal of the American Academy of Religion* 78, no. 1: 65–99.

Humboldt, Wilhelm von. (1827) 1907. "Ueber den Dualis." In Wilhelm von Humboldt, *Gesammelte Schriften* vol. 6.1. Berlin: B. Behr's Verlag.

Humboldt, Wilhelm von. (1820) 1997. "On the Comparative Study of Languages and Its Relation to the Different Periods of Language Development." In *Essays on Language*, 1–22. Frankfurt am Main: P. Lang, 1997.
Hung, William (Hong Ye 洪業) et al., ed. 1947. *A Concordance to Chuang Tzu* 莊子引得. Harvard-Yenching Institute Sinological Index Series, Supplement No. 20. Beijing: Harvard-Yenching Institute.
Inwood, Michael J. 1999. *A Heidegger Dictionary*. Malden: Blackwell.
Iser, Wolfgang. 1996. "Coda to the Discussion." In *The Translatability of Cultures: Figurations of the Space Between*, edited by Sanford Budick and Wolfgang Iser, 294–302. Stanford, CA: Stanford University Press.
Ivanhoe, Philip. J., trans. 2001. *The Daodejing of Laozi*. New York: Seven Bridges Press.
Jamieson, Dale. 2008. *Ethics and the Environment: An Introduction*. Cambridge: Cambridge University Press.
Jaspers, Karl. 1919. *Psychologie der Weltanschauungen*. Berlin: Springer.
Kahn, Charles H. 1979. *The Art and Thought of Heraclitus: An Edition of the Fragments with Translation and Commentary*. Cambridge: Cambridge University Press.
Kant, Immanuel. (1781) 1998. *The Critique of Pure Reason*. Translated by Paul Guyer and Allen W. Wood. Cambridge: Cambridge University Press.
Kant, Immanuel. (1790) 2000. *Critique of the Power of Judgment*. Translated by Paul Guyer and Eric Matthews. Cambridge: Cambridge University Press.
Kay, Paul, and Willett Kempton. 1984. "What Is the Sapir-Whorf Hypothesis?" *American Anthropologist* 86, no. 1: 65–79.
Kearney, Richard. 2006. "Introduction: Ricoeur's philosophy of translation." In Paul Ricoeur, *On Translation*, vii–xx. New York: Routledge.
Kjellberg, Paul, and P. J. Ivanhoe, eds. 1996. *Essays on Skepticism, Relativism, and Ethics in the Zhuangzi*. New York: State University of New York Press.
Klein, Esther. 2010. "Were there 'Inner Chapters' in the Warring States? A New Examination of Evidence about the *Zhuangzi*." *T'oung Pao* 96, no. 4/5: 299–369.
Kofman, Sarah. 1993. *Nietzsche and Metaphor*. Translated by Duncan Large. London: Athlone Press.
Lacertosa, Massimiliano. 2022. "Sense Perception in the *Zhuangzi* 莊子." *Philosophy Compass* 17, no. 1: e12798.
Lai, Karyn. 2007. "*Ziran* and *Wuwei* in the *Daodejing*: An Ethical Assessment." *Dao: A Journal of Comparative Philosophy* 6, no. 4: 325–337.
Lai, Shen-chon 賴賢宗. 2010. *Daojia quanshixue* 道家詮釋學. Beijing 北京: Beijing Daxue Chubanshe 北京大學出版社.
Lau, D. C., trans. 1989. *Tao Te Ching*. Rev. ed. Hong Kong: Chinese University Press.
Lefort, Claude. 2012. "Maurice Merleau-Ponty." Translated by Donald A. Landes. In Maurice Merleau-Ponty, *Phenomenology of Perception*, xvii–xxix. New York: Routledge.
Legge, James. 1891. *The Sacred Books of China: The Texts of Taoism*. Oxford: Clarendon Press.

Leibniz, Gottfried Wilhelm. 2004. *Discours de métaphysique suivi de Monadologie et autres textes*. Paris: Gallimard.
Leibniz, Gottfried Wilhelm. 2014. *Leibniz's Monadology: A New Translation and Guide*. Translated by Lloyd Strickland. Edinburgh: Edinburgh University Press.
Levinas, Emmanuel. 1979. *Totality and Infinity: An Essay on Exteriority*. Translated by Alphonso Lingis. The Hague: Martinus Nijhoff.
Levinas, Emmanuel. 1990. *Totalité et infini: Essai sur l'extériorité*. Paris: Kluwer Academic.
Li, Zehou. 1994. *The Path of Beauty: A Study of Chinese Aesthetics*. Hong Kong: Oxford University Press.
Li, Zehou. 2010. *The Chinese Aesthetic Tradition*. Translated by Maija Bell Samei. Honolulu: University of Hawai'i Press.
Liao, Mingchun 廖名春. 2003. *Guodian chujian Laozi jiaoshi* 郭店楚簡老子校釋. Beijing 北京: Qinghua Daxue Chubanshe 清华大学出版社.
Lin, Shuen-Fu. 2003. "Transforming the Dao: A Critique of A. C. Graham's Translation of the Inner Chapters of the *Zhuangzi*." In *Hiding the World in the World: Uneven Discourses on the Zhuangzi*, edited by Scott Cook, 263–290. Albany: State University of New York Press.
Lin, Yutang, trans. 1958. *The Wisdom of Laotse*. London: Michael Joseph.
Lin, Yutang 林語堂. (1942) 2009. *The Wisdom of China, English works of Lin Yutang*. Beijing: Foreign Language Teaching and Research Press.
Linge, David E. 1977. "Editor's Introduction." In Hans-Georg Gadamer, *Philosophical Hermeneutics*. Berkeley: University of California Press.
Liu, Dianjue 劉殿爵, ed. 1995. *A Concordance to the Lunyu* 論語逐字索引. Xianggang 香港: Shangwu Yinshuguan 商務印書館.
Liu, Dianjue 劉殿爵, ed. 1996. *A Concordance to the Liezi* 列子逐字索引. Xianggang 香港: Shangwu Yinshuguan 商務印書館.
Liu, Dianjue 劉殿爵, and Fangzheng Chen, 陳方正, eds. 1992. *A Concordance to the Huainanzi* 淮南子逐字索引. Xianggang 香港: Shangwu Yinshuguan 商務印書館.
Liu, Dianjue 劉殿爵, and Fangzheng Chen, 陳方正, eds. 1995. *A Concordance to the Mengzi* 孟子逐字索引. Xianggang 香港: Shangwu Yinshuguan 商務印書館.
Liu, Xiaogan 劉笑敢. 1986. "From Dialectics to Sophistry: A Brief Analysis of Zhuangzi's 'Qiwulun'" 從辯證法到詭辯論——莊子齊物論淺析. *Journal of Peking University (Humanities and Social Sciences)* 北京大學學報-哲學社會科學版 no. 2: 124–130.
Liu, Xiaogan 劉笑敢. 1987. *The Philosophy of Zhuangzi and Its Evolution* 莊子哲學及其演變. Beijing 北京: Zhongguo Shehui Kexue Chubanshe 中國社會科學出版社.
Liu, Xiaogan. 1994. *Classifying the Zhuangzi Chapters*. Translated by William E. Savage. Ann Arbor, MI: Center for Chinese Studies, University of Michigan.
Liu, Xiaogan 劉笑敢. 1995. "Shilun Laozi zhexue de zhongxin jiazhi" 試論老子哲學的中心價值. *Zhongzhou xue kan* 中州學刊 2: 67–73.

Liu, Xiaogan 劉笑敢. 2006. *Laozi gujin: Wu zhong duikan yu xiping yinlun* 老子古今: 五種對勘與析評引論. Beijing 北京: Zhongguo Shehui Kexue Chubanshe 中國社會科學出版社.

Liu, Xiaogan, ed. 2015. *Dao Companion to Daoist Philosophy*. Dordrecht: Springer.

Llewelyn, John. 1985. *Beyond Metaphysics: The Hermeneutic Circle in Contemporary Continental Philosophy*. Atlantic Highlands, NJ: Humanities Press.

Loy, David. 1985. "Wei-Wu-Wei: Nondual Action." *Philosophy East and West* 35, no. 1: 73–86.

Lynn, Richard John, trans. 1994a. *The Classic of Changes: A New Translation of the I Ching as Interpreted by Wang Bi*. New York: Columbia University Press.

Lynn, Richard John. 1994b. "Introduction." In *The Classic of Changes: A New Translation of the I Ching as Interpreted by Wang Bi*, 1–46. New York: Columbia University Press.

Ma, Lin. 2008. *Heidegger on East-West Dialogue: Anticipating the Event*. New York: Routledge.

Ma, Lin and Jaap van Brakel. 2016. *Fundamentals of Comparative and Intercultural Philosophy*. Albany: State University of New York Press.

Manchester, Martin L. 1985. *The Philosophical Foundations of Humboldt's Linguistic Doctrines*. Amsterdam: J. Benjamins.

Mawangdui Han mu boshu zhengli xiaozu 馬王堆漢墓帛書整理小組. 1976. *Mawangdui Han mu boshu: Laozi* 馬王堆漢墓帛書《老子》. Beijing 北京: Wenwu Chubanshe 文物出版社.

May, Reinhard. 1996. *Heidegger's Hidden Sources: East-Asian Influences on his Work*. Translated by Graham Parkes. New York: Routledge.

Menn, Stephen Philip. 1998. *Descartes and Augustine*. Cambridge: Cambridge University Press.

Merleau-Ponty, Maurice. 2012. *Phenomenology of Perception*. Translated by Donald A. Landes. New York: Routledge.

Meyer, Matthew. 2014. *Reading Nietzsche through the Ancients: An Analysis of Becoming, Perspectivism, and the Principle of Non-Contradiction*. Boston: De Gruyter.

Minford, John, trans. 2019. *Tao Te Ching: The Essential Translation of the Ancient Chinese Book of the Tao*. London: Penguin Classics.

Moeller, Hans-Georg. 2006. *The Philosophy of the Daodejing*. New York: Columbia University Press.

Moeller, Hans-Georg. 2009. *The Moral Fool: A Case for Amorality*. New York: Columbia University Press.

Moran, Dermot. 2007. "Heidegger's Transcendental Phenomenology in the Light of Husserl's Project of First Philosophy." In *Transcendental Heidegger*, edited by Steven Crowell and Jeff Malpas, 135–150. Stanford, CA: Stanford University Press.

Moriarty, Michael. 2008. "Introduction." In René Descartes, *Meditations on First Philosophy: With Selections from the Objections and Replies*, ix–xl. New York: Oxford University Press.
Nancy, Jean-Luc. 2017. *The Banality of Heidegger*. Translated by Jeff Fort. New York: Fordham University Press.
Nehamas, Alexander. 1985. *Nietzsche: Life as Literature*. Cambridge, MA: Harvard University Press.
Nietzsche, Friedrich Wilhelm. (1923) 1962. *Philosophy in the Tragic Age of the Greeks*. Translated by Marianne Cowan. Chicago: Regnery.
Nietzsche, Friedrich Wilhelm. 1967. *The Will to Power*. Translated by Walter Arnold Kaufmann and R. J. Hollingdale. New York: Random House.
Nietzsche, Friedrich Wilhelm. (1889) 1998. *Twilight of the Idols, or, How to Philosophize with a Hammer*. Translated by Duncan Large. Oxford: Oxford University Press.
Nietzsche, Friedrich Wilhelm. (1873) 2000. "On Truth and Lie in an Extra-Moral Sense." In Clive Cazeaux, *The Continental Aesthetics Reader*, 53–62. New York: Routledge.
Nietzsche, Friedrich Wilhelm. (1882) 2001. *The Gay Science: With a Prelude in German Rhymes and an Appendix of Songs*. Translated by Josefine Nauckhoff and Adrian Del Caro. Cambridge: Cambridge University Press.
Nietzsche, Friedrich Wilhelm. (1886) 2002. *Beyond Good and Evil: Prelude to a Philosophy of the Future*. Translated by Judith Norman. Cambridge: Cambridge University Press.
Nietzsche, Friedrich Wilhelm. (1883–85) 2005. *Thus Spoke Zarathustra: A Book for Everyone and Nobody*. Translated by Graham Parkes. New York: Oxford University Press.
Nietzsche, Friedrich Wilhelm. (1887) 2007a. *On the Genealogy of Morality*. Translated by Carol Diethe. Cambridge: Cambridge University Press.
Nietzsche, Friedrich Wilhelm. (1888) 2007b. *Ecce Homo: How to Become What You Are*. Translated by Duncan Large. Oxford: Oxford University Press.
Olafson, Frederick A. 1993. "The Unity of Heidegger's Thought." In *The Cambridge Companion to Heidegger*, edited by Charles B. Guignon, 97–121. Cambridge: Cambridge University Press.
Palmer, Richard E. 1969. *Hermeneutics: Interpretation Theory in Schleiermacher, Dilthey, Heidegger, and Gadamer*. Evanston, IL: Northwestern University Press.
Parkes, Graham. 1983. "The Wandering Dance: Chuang Tzu and Zarathustra." *Philosophy East and West* 33, no. 3: 235–250.
Parkes, Graham, ed. 1987a. *Heidegger and Asian Thought*. Honolulu: University of Hawai'i Press.
Parkes, Graham. 1987b. "Thoughts on the Way: *Being and Time* via Lao-Chuang." In *Heidegger and Asian Thought*, edited by Graham Parkes, 105–144. Honolulu: University of Hawai'i Press.

Parkes, Graham, ed. 1991. *Nietzsche and Asian Thought*. Chicago: University of Chicago Press.
Parkes, Graham. 2013. "Zhuangzi and Nietzsche on the Human and Nature." *Environmental Philosophy* 10, no. 1: 1–24.
Philipse, Herman. 1998. *Heidegger's Philosophy of Being: A Critical Interpretation*. Princeton, NJ: Princeton University Press.
Plato. 1996. *The Dialogues of Plato, Volume 3: Ion, Hippias Minor, Laches, Protagoras*. Translated by Reginald E. Allen. New Haven, CT: Yale University Press.
Plato. 2000. *The Republic*. Translated by Tom Griffith. Cambridge: Cambridge University Press.
Puett, Michael. 2004. "The Ethics of Responding Properly: The Notion of *Qíng* in Early Chinese Thought." In *Love and Emotions in Traditional Chinese Literature*, edited by Halvor Eifring, 37–68. Leiden: Brill.
Pütz, Martin, and Marjolyn Verspoor. 2000. *Explorations in Linguistic Relativity*. Amsterdam: J. Benjamins.
Quine, W. V. 1969. *Ontological Relativity and Other Essays*. New York: Columbia University Press.
Raleigh, Walter. 1829. *The Works of Sir Walter Ralegh: The History of the World*. 8 vols. Vol. 3. Oxford: Oxford University press.
Rancière, Jacques. 2010. *Dissensus: On Politics and Aesthetics*. Translated by Steve Corcoran. London: Continuum.
Raud, Rein. 2006. "Philosophies versus Philosophy: In Defense of a Flexible Definition." *Philosophy East and West* 56, no. 4: 618–625.
Ricci, Matteo. 1985. *The True Meaning of the Lord of Heaven = T'ien-chu shih-i*. Translated by Douglas Lancashire, Kuo-chen Hu and Edward Malatesta. St. Louis: Institute of Jesuit Sources.
Richardson, John. 1996. *Nietzsche's System*. New York: Oxford University Press.
Richardson, John. 2006. "Nietzsche on Time and Becoming." In *A Companion to Nietzsche*, edited by Keith Ansell Pearson, 208–229. Oxford: Blackwell.
Ricoeur, Paul. 1978. *The Rule of Metaphor: Multi-disciplinary Studies of the Creation of Meaning in Language*. Translated by Robert Czerny, Kathleen McLaughlin and John Costello. London: Routledge and Kegan Paul.
Robinet, Isabelle. 1999. "The Diverse Interpretations of the Laozi." In *Religious and Philosophical Aspects of the Laozi*, edited by Mark Csikszentmihalyi and P. J. Ivanhoe, 127–159. Albany: State University of New York Press.
Robinet, Isabelle. 2008. "*daojia*" 道家. In *The Encyclopedia of Taoism*, edited by Fabrizio Pregadio, 5–8. New York: Routledge.
Rorty, Richard. 1991. "Philosophers, Novelists, and Intercultural Comparisons: Heidegger, Kundera, and Dickens." In *Culture and Modernity: East-West Philosophic Perspectives*, edited by Eliot. S. Deutsch, 3–20. Honolulu: University of Hawai'i Press.
Roth, Harold David. 1999. *Original Tao: Inward Training (Nei-yeh) and the Foundations of Taoist Mysticism*. New York: Columbia University Press.

Ryden, Edmund, trans. 2008. *Daodejing*. Oxford: Oxford University Press.
Sapir, Edward. 1929. "The Status of Linguistics as a Science." In *Selected Writings of Edward Sapir in Language, Culture, and Personality*, edited by David Goodman Mandelbaum, 160–166. Berkeley: University of California Press, 1963.
Scharfstein, Ben-Ami. 1978. "Cultures, Contexts, and Comparisons." In *Philosophy East/Philosophy West: A Critical Comparison of Indian, Chinese, Islamic and European Philosophy*, edited by Ben-Ami Scharfstein, 9–47. Oxford: Blackwell.
Schmitt, Carl. 2005. *Political Theology: Four Chapters on the Concept of Sovereignty*. Translated by George Schwab. Chicago: University of Chicago Press.
Sedley, David. 2007. "Philosophy, the Forms, and the Art of Ruling." In *The Cambridge Companion to Plato's Republic*, edited by G. R. F. Ferrari, 256–283. Cambridge: Cambridge University Press.
Shankman, Steven. 2002. " 'These Three Come Forth Together, But are Differently Named': Laozi, Zhuangzi, Plato." In *Early China/Ancient Greece: Thinking through Comparisons*, edited by Steven Shankman and Stephen W. Durrant, 75–92. Albany: State University of New York Press.
Sheehan, Thomas J. 1978. "Heidegger's Interpretation of Aristotle: Dynamis and Ereignis." *Philosophy Research Archives* 4: 278–314.
Shen, Vincent. 2003a. "Laozi (Lao Tzu)." In *Encyclopedia of Chinese Philosophy*, edited by Antonio S. Cua, 355–361. New York: Routledge.
Shen, Vincent. 2003b. "*Ren (Jen)*: Humanity." In *Encyclopedia of Chinese Philosophy*, edited by Antonio S. Cua, 643–646. New York: Routledge.
Simkins, Ronald A. 2014. "The Bible and Anthropocentrism: Putting Humans in Their Place." *Dialectical Anthropology* 38, no. 4: 397–413.
Sivin, N. 1978. "On the Word 'Taoist' as a Source of Perplexity: With Special Reference to the Relations of Science and Religion in Traditional China." *History of Religions* 17, no. 3/4: 303–330.
Slingerland, Edward G. 2003. *Effortless Action: Wu-wei As Conceptual Metaphor and Spiritual Ideal in Early China*. Oxford: Oxford University Press.
Slingerland, Edward. 2013. "Body and Mind in Early China: An Integrated Humanities–Science Approach." *Journal of the American Academy of Religion* 81, no. 1: 6–55.
Sohm, Philip. 2002. "Caravaggio's Deaths." *Art Bulletin* 84, no. 3: 449–468.
Stenstad, Gail. 2006. *Transformations: Thinking after Heidegger*. Madison: University of Wisconsin Press.
Tang, Junyi 唐君毅. 1988a. "Daoyan: Zhongguo wenhua genben jingshen zhi yizhong jieshi" 導言：中國文化根本精神之一種解釋. In *Zhongxi zhexue sixiang zhi bijiao lunwenji* 中西哲學思想之比較論文集, 7–50. Taibei 臺北: Taiwan xuesheng shuju 臺灣學生書局.
Tang, Junyi 唐君毅. 1988b. "Ruhe liaojie Zhongguo zhexueshang tian ren he yi zhi genben guannian" 如何了解中國哲學上天人合一之根本觀念. In *Zhongxi zhexue*

sixiang zhi bijiao lunwenji 中西哲學思想之比較論文集, 128–139. Taibei 臺北: Taiwan xuesheng shuju 臺灣學生書局.

Tang, Junyi 唐君毅. 1988c. "Zhongguo zhexue zhong ziran yuzhouguan zhi tezhi" 中國哲學中自然宇宙觀之特質. In *Zhongxi zhexue sixiang zhi bijiao lunwenji* 中西哲學思想之比較論文集, 95–127. Taibei 臺北: Taiwan xuesheng shuju 臺灣學生書局.

Tang, Junyi 唐君毅. 1988d. "Zhuangzi de bianhua xing'ershangxue yu Heige'er de bianhua xing'ershangxue zhi bijiao" 莊子的變化形而上學與黑格爾的變化形而上學之比較. In *Zhongxi zhexue sixiang zhi bijiao lunwenji* 中西哲學思想之比較論文集, 255–281. Taibei 臺北: Taiwan xuesheng shuju 臺灣學生書局.

Tang, Yijie. 2007. "Constructing 'Chinese Philosophy' in Sino-European Cultural Exchange." *Journal of Chinese Philosophy* 34, Supplement: 33–42.

Tatarkiewicz, Władysław. 1980. *A History of Six Ideas: An Essay in Aesthetics*. Translated by Christopher Kasparek. The Hague: Nijhoff.

Trabant, Jürgen. 2000. "How Relativistic Are Humboldt's 'Weltansichten'?" In *Explorations in Linguistic Relativity*, edited by Martin Pütz and Marjolyn H. Verspoor, 22–44. Amsterdam: J. Benjamins.

Tu, Wei-Ming. 1985. *Confucian Thought: Selfhood as Creative Transformation*. Albany: State University of New York Press.

Van Norden, Bryan W. 1996. "Competing Interpretations of the Inner Chapters of the 'Zhuangzi.'" *Philosophy East and West* 46, no. 2: 247–268.

Vattimo, Gianni. 1981. "La bottiglia, la rete, la rivoluzione e i compiti della filosofia. Un dialogo con 'Lotta continua.'" In Gianni Vattimo, *Al di là del soggetto: Nietzsche, Heidegger e l'ermeneutica*, 11–26. Milano: Feltrinelli.

Vattimo, Gianni. 1987. "'*Verwindung*': Nihilism and the Postmodern in Philosophy." *SubStance* 16, no. 2: 7–17.

Vattimo, Gianni. 1993. "Introduction." Translated by Cyprian Blamires with the assistance of Thomas Harrison. In *The Adventure of Difference: Philosophy after Nietzsche and Heidegger*, 1–8. Baltimore: Johns Hopkins University Press.

Waley, Arthur. 2005. *The Way and Its Power: Lao Tzu's Tao Tê Ching and Its Place in Chinese Thought*. London: Routledge.

Wang, Bo 王博. 1993. *Laozi sixiang de shiguan tese* 老子思想的史官特色. Taibei 臺北: Wenjin Chubanshe 文津出版社.

Wang, Keping. 1998. *The Classic of the Dao: A New Investigation*. Beijing: Foreign Languages Press.

Wang, Robin R. 2012. *Yinyang: The Way of Heaven and Earth in Chinese Thought and Culture*. Cambridge: Cambridge University Press.

Wang, Shumin 王叔岷. 1988. *Collation and Interpretion of the Zhuangzi* 莊子校詮. Taibei 臺北: Zhongyang Yanjiuyuan Lishi Yuyan Yanjiusuo 中央研究院歷史語言研究所.

Watson, Burton, trans. 2013. *The Complete Works of Zhuangzi*. New York: Columbia University Press.
White, Lynn. 1967. "The Historical Roots of Our Ecologic Crisis." *Science* 155, no. 3767: 1203–1207.
Whorf, Benjamin Lee. 1940. "Science and Linguistics." In *Language, Thought, and Reality: Selected Writings of Benjamin Lee Whorf*, edited by John B. Carroll, 207–219. New York: MIT Press and John Wiley & Sons, 1959.
Wu, Charles, trans. 2016. *Thus Spoke Laozi: A New Translation with Commentaries of Daodejing*. Honolulu: University of Hawai'i Press.
Wu, Kuang-ming. 1982. *Chuang Tzu: World Philosopher at Play*. New York: Crossroad.
Wu, Kuang-ming. 1990. *The Butterfly as Companion: Meditations on the First Three Chapters of the Chuang-Tzu*. Albany: State University of New York Press.
Wu, Xiao-ming. 1998. "Philosophy, Philosophia, and Zhe-xue." *Philosophy East and West* 48, no. 3: 406–452.
Xu, Kangsheng 許抗生. 1985. *Boshu Laozi zhu yi yu yanjiu* 帛書老子注譯與研究. Hangzhou 杭州: Zhejiang Renmin Chubanshe 浙江人民出版社.
Ye, Lang 葉朗. 1985. *Zhongguo meixueshi dagang* 中國美學史大綱. Shanghai 上海: Shanghai Renmin Chubanshe 上海人民出版社.
Zarader, Marlène. 2006. *The Unthought Debt: Heidegger and the Hebraic Heritage*. Translated by Bettina Bergo. Stanford, CA: Stanford University Press.
Zhang, Dainian 張岱年. 2002. *Key Concepts in Chinese Philosophy* 中國古典哲學概念範疇要論. Translated by Edmund Ryden. Beijing: Foreign Lauguages Press.
Zhang, Longxi 1998. *Mighty Opposites: From Dichotomies to Differences in the Comparative Study of China*. Stanford, CA: Stanford University Press.
Zhang, Weiyi 張瑋儀. 2007. "Lun Zhuangzi churu shi de jingshen—Jian ping Chen Guying yu Liu Xiaogan xiansheng zhi quanshi" 論莊子出入世的精神——兼評陳鼓應與劉笑敢先生之詮釋. *Beijing Ligong Daxue Xuebao: Shehuikexue ban* 北京理工大學學報：社會科學版 9, no. 2: 21–25.
Zhu, Rui. 2002. "Wu-Wei: Lao-zi, Zhuang-zi and the aesthetic judgement." *Asian Philosophy* 12, no. 1: 53–63.
Zhuo, Dawei 卓達維. 2010. "Dao shui chuan liu: Chalasitutela yu Zhuangzi yangyi de linghun" 蹈水穿流：查拉斯圖特拉與莊子洋溢的靈魂. *Xiandai Zhexue* 現代哲學 no. 5: 111–120.
Ziporyn, Brook. 2003. "How Many Are the Ten Thousand Things and I? Relativism, Mysticism, and the Privileging of Oneness in the 'Inner Chapters.'" In *Hiding the World in the World: Uneven Discourses on the Zhuangzi*, edited by Scott Cook, 33–63. Albany: State University of New York Press.

Index

action of non-action (*weiwuwei* 為無為), 152–153
æterna Ratio, 19
aesthetic attunement, to world, 9, 112, 147, 153
aesthetic awareness, 111–112, 127–128, 132–133
 in self-other relationship, 7
aesthetic configuration, 136, 142–144, 148
 of *Lao-Zhuang* 老莊, 4, 148
aesthetic encounter, with the other, 48, 111
aesthetic encounter, with world, 9, 91, 111–112, 125–127, 146
 aesthetic awareness, 7, 111–112, 127–128, 132–134
 aesthetic ethos, 75, 132–134
aesthetic ethos, 75, 132–134
aesthetic gesture, 6, 10, 78, 151–152, 155
 world as, 10, 152, 155
aesthetic judgment, 2, 140–141
 Kant on, 2, 157n3
 no cognition in, 2
 "Qiwulun" 齊物論 and, 140–141
Aesthetica (Baumgarten), 2
aesthetics
 Baumgarten conception of, 2
 derived from *aísthēsis* αἴσθησις, 2
 ethics link to, 2
 Goethe on Chinese, 148–149
 as lower knowledge, 2
 as theory of beauty, 3
 Weltanschauung and problem of, 8
 Western metaphysics on ethics and, 3
"The Age of the World Picture" (AWP), of Heidegger, 40–42
aisthánomai αἰσθάνομαι (to perceive), 2
aísthēsis αἴσθησις, 2
alḗtheia ἀλήθεια, 42, 46
Allen, Reginald, 136–137
Ames, Rogers, 25, 83, 85–86, 89, 104, 114, 126, 159n2, 160nn9–10, 161nn15–16, 165n9, 165nn1–2, 167n36, 170n9, 170n12, 171n18, 172n25
 on *hun* 混 translation, 165n10
 on *ming* 名, 167n36
 on way-making 道, 21–23, 79
 on *you* 有 and *wu* 無, 81
 on *Zhuangzi* 莊子, 174n15
amor fati, 74–75, 78
an-aesthetic, 136–137, 139, 148
Anwesen (presencing), 41–43, 44, 46, 163n5
 as metaphor, 43, 44
 from *parousía* παρουσία, 41
 Sein and, 42

appropriation, event, happening
    (*Ereignis*), 55, 56, 164n6
  avoidance of direct reference to
    Being, 5–6, 52
  Geschick relation to, 51–52,
    163nn2–3
Aquinas, Thomas, 19
Aristotle, 1, 15, 57
Art, 3, 136–138, 147, 148, 152–153,
    175n17
  as child's play, Nietzsche on, 68–74,
    77
  Heidegger on, 152
l'Autre (the Other), 6, 158n13
AWP. See "The Age of the World
    Picture"

The Basic Problems of Phenomenology
    (BPP) lecture course, of
    Heidegger, 33–34, 162nn4–6
Baumgarten, Alexander Gottlieb, 2
beauty
  aesthetics as theory of, 3
  Sedley on metaphysical aspect of, 139
  Zhu on truth and, 141
becoming, 6, 8–9, 25–26, 65–66, 73,
    86, 108, 123
  Being-beings structure differing
    from, 9
  constant, 74, 75
  of myriad things, 100, 123
  Nietzschean idea of, 8, 65–66,
    68–75, 77
  will to power and, 69–70
Being, 5–9, 19, 20, 24–26, 34–37, 43,
    47, 60, 63, 66, 68–73, 78–81,
    84–85, 94, 107–108, 123, 126,
    139, 150, 153, 158nn12–13,
    160n9, 162n23, 163n9, 164n7,
    173n23
  Ereignis avoidance of direct reference
    to, 5–6, 52

Heidegger on language spoken
    through, 53, 78
Heidegger on philosophy and, 14–
    15, 34–35
language relation to, 9, 49–56
as metaphor, 55–56
Minford, Ryden, and Wu translation
    of *you* 有 as, 17–18
sayers and, 52–55
Being-beings structure, of Western
    metaphysics, 7–9, 15, 123,
    126–127
beingless, Nonbeing, Non-Being
  Minford, Ryden, and Wu translation
    of *wu* 無 as, 17–18, 160n9
be-wëgen, 21–25
Beyond Good and Evil (Nietzsche), 62,
    63–64, 148
bian 變, 79, 80, 85
bianhua 變化, 172n23
Blumenberg, Hans, 55, 57, 60, 95
BPP. See *The Basic Problems of*
    Phenomenology
bu gai 不改, 84–86
Burik, Steven, 5–6, 48, 157n10,
    159n4
butterfly dream, in "Qiwulun" 齊物論,
    125–126, 144–145, 173n8

cause in sense of motion, *dao* 道 as,
    87–89
chang 常, 20, 77–87, 99, 161n11
chang dao 常道, 18, 78, 80, 87
chang ming 常名, 79, 80, 87, 98, 99
character (*ēthos* ἦθος), 1
Chen Guying, 84, 86, 91, 120, 121,
    124–125, 129, 130, 161n17,
    166n17, 166n21, 167n35,
    170n10, 170n15, 171n18,
    172n27
  on *da tong* 大通, 130
  on "Qiwulun" 齊物論, 120

on *wuming* 無名, 167n35
on *yi*, 121
Chen Shaoming, 112, 114, 120
Chuang-tzu 莊子. See *Zhuangzi*
circularity
  of knowledge, 59–61, 63
  of metaphors, 58–60
cogito, 42, 50, 135, 136
"Comments on Karl Jaspers's *Psychology of Worldviews*" (Heidegger), 35–36
comparative studies, translation problem in, 11–14, 159n1
concepts, 1, 7, 9
  metaphor relations with, 57–59
  in philosophy of comparisons, transformation of, 26–27
  translation problem of, 13, 14
constant becoming, 25, 68, 74, 75, 86, 100, 108
constant change, 22, 77–87, 97, 99, 161n11
continuity, 83, 87, 121–123, 129, 135, 149, 170n12, 171n19. See also *yi* 一
  revolving transformations and, 124–125
Contributions to Philosophy (Heidegger), 38
Cook Ding, 127–130, 132, 150–151, 172nn29–30
corresponding
  dreamer and dreamed, 145
  other, 6, 7, 135
  pluralties, 114, 116
  things, 116, 126
  with and to world, 7, 141
Coutinho, Steve, 142, 171n19
cravings, 99, 102–103, 105, 109
Critique of Judgment (Kant), 3
Critique of Pure Reason (Kant), 62
cross-cultural interpretations, of concepts, 7, 12

da tong 大通, 128–130
dao 道, 18, 24–26, 158n17, 161n11
  as *æterna Ratio*, 19
  Ames on, 161n16
  as *be-wëgen*, 21–26
  as cause in sense of motion, 87–89
  chang 常 relation to, 87, 99
  movement of, 80–84
  myriad things relationship with, 87–91
  unchanging process of, 84–87
  wanwu 萬物 relationship with, 87–91
  as way-making, 21–23
  yin 陰 and *yang* 陽 revolving process in, 22–23
  ziran 自然 relation to, 9, 88–89, 154
Daodejing (*Tao te ching* 道德經), 3, 7, 8, 9, 17–21, 26, 27, 46, 78–80, 82, 85, 87, 89, 90–91, 94–95, 98, 103–105, 107, 108, 109, 128, 133, 143–144, 157nn5–6, 160n9, 161n15, 161n17, 161nn11–12, 166n13, 167n25, 167n29, 168n2, 168n38, 170n13, 171n19, 173n5, 173n11
  on knowledge, 104
  on language, 113
  onto-theology in relation to, 5
  on rulership, 90
Daoism, 3–4, 5, 6, 8, 9, 16, 26, 28, 29, 48, 53, 78, 79, 85, 112, 141–142, 150, 155, 157n5, 157n8, 160n8, 161nn12–13, 162n22, 168n38. See also *Lao-Zhuang* 老莊
  aesthetic configuration of, 143–144
  Coutinho on, 142, 171n19
  Froese and Heideggerian reinterpretation of, 5, 162n22
  Heidegger divergence from, 6
daojia 道家, 3, 157n8

daojiao 道教, 157n8
Dasein, 24, 34, 35, 51
Dazhuan 大傳 (*Xici* 繫辭), on *yin* 陰 and *yang* 陽, 22
Derrida, Jacques, 20, 41, 44, 45, 54
   on concept of metaphor, 59
   on Heidegger, 41, 164n12
   on translation and representation, 45
Descartes, René, 10, 19, 45, 108, 138
   AWP attack of, 42–43
   on dream, 144–146
   metaphysics of, 40
   on sense perception, 145–146, 173n4
   subject/object dichotomy of, 97–98
"A Dialogue on Language" (Heidegger), 38
differentiation, 30, 109, 112, 113, 114, 121, 123, 124, 126, 127, 151, 152
   "Qiwulun" 齊物論 on, 115, 117
domination, *ziran* 自然 and avoidance of, 106–109
dream
   Descartes on, 144–146
   Nietzsche on, 151–152
   "Qiwulun" 齊物論 butterfly, 125–126, 144–145, 173n8
duli 獨立, 84–85, 165n12

Ecce Homo (Nietzsche), 69–70, 74, 164n16
eidos εἶδος, 137
Eight Powers, 116–117
Ereignis (appropriation, event, happening), 55, 56, 164n6
   Being direct reference avoidance, 5–6, 52
   Geschick relation to, 51–52, 163nn2–3
es gibt, 24, 161n20
   Geschick relation to, 51, 52, 163nn2–3

esse, 14. See also Being
Essence, 14, 15, 53, 57–58, 62, 66–68, 84, 88, 107, 123–124, 125, 151. See also Being
essentia, Heidegger on, 14
essential translation, of Heidegger, 51–53, 56
ethical, 1, 6, 9
ethical implications
   of Nietzsche and metaphors, 65–75
   of *wuwei* 無為 and *ziran* 自然, 87–98
ethics, 2–3
ēthikḗ ἠθική, 1, 6, 9
ethos, 1, 2
   aesthetic, 75, 132–134
éthos ἔθος (habit), 1
ēthos ἦθος (character), 1

fa ziran 法自然, 88–90, 109, 154
fa 法, 89–90
fan 反, 81, 86
fan 返, 82
forgetting, 72–73, 147
   of *Sein*, 34
   sitting and (*zuowang* 坐忘), 50, 102, 128–131, 134
forgotten, in sitting and forgetting (*zuowang* 坐忘), 102, 128–132
Froese, Katrin, 5, 18, 24, 162n22
   on Cook Ding, 172n29
   wu 無 translation of non-being by, 18
fu tong wei yi 復通為一, 121, 123
The Fundamental Concepts of Metaphysics lecture course, of Heidegger, 38
fusion, of worldview, 31–33

Gadamer, Hans-Georg, 3, 12, 31, 32–33
gai 改, 84–85

Index | 197

Gao Ming, 100–101
The Gay Science (Nietzsche), 70, 72–74, 151–152
genealogy, Nietzsche on, 61, 62, 71
Geschick, 51–53, 56, 163n1
   Ereignis in relation to, 51–52, 163nn2–3
   es gibt relation to, 51, 52, 163nn2–3
   Sein defined by, 52
Goethe, Johann Wolfgang von, 148–149
Graham, Angus, 17, 94, 119, 157n6, 165n6, 168nn1–2, 170nn11–12, 171n16, 172n28, 172n31
   on "Qiwulun" 齊物論, 169n5
grounding, 22, 56, 60, 91, 150. See *also* re-grounding grounds
   subiectus and, 16, 24, 47, 135
guan 觀, 141–142
Guo Xiang 郭象, *Zhuangzi* edited by, 157n6, 168n3, 170n14

habit (*éthos* ἔθος), 1
Hall, David, 13, 21–23, 25, 79, 83, 104, 114, 160n9, 161n15, 165nn1–2, 166n20, 167n29, 170n9, 171n18, 172n25
   on *hun* 混 translation, 165n10
   on *ming* 名, 167n36
   on way-making 道, 21–23
   on *you* 有 and *wu* 無, 81
Hansen, Chad, 4, 12–13, 79, 168n38, 170n7
   on Cook Ding, 172n30
   on dictionary for translation problem, 12
   on "Qiwulun" 齊物論, 112, 171n19
Heidegger, Martin, 158n12
   on art, 152
   on Being and philosophy, 14–15
   on Being speaking through language, 53
   on *be-wëgen*, 21, 22
   on *dao* 道 as *be-wëgen*, 21–24
   Daoism divergence from, 6
   Derrida on, 41, 164n12
   on *essentia*, 14
   essential translation, 51–53
   on *Geschick*, 51, 163n1
   Ma on, 5, 159n4, 163n8
   metaphors rejection by, 53
   metatheory of, 44, 47–49
   on modernity, 41
   onto-theology critique by, 5
   representation critique by, 43
   on *Sein*, 15, 24, 50, 54, 160n6
   universal ontology of, 29, 36–39, 50
   Verwindung and, 6, 158n11
   Weltanschauung critique by, 33–36
   on will to power, 68
   worldview philosophy and, 5, 29–30, 157n10
heng 恆, 99
Heraclitus, 16, 73–74, 108, 160n7
historicism, 12
hua 化, 80, 85, 87
Huainanzi 淮南子, 4, 133, 157n7, 172n33
   Lao-Zhuang 老莊 term in, 3–4
Huang-Lao 黃老 philosophy
   Hansen on superstitious dogmatic ideology of, 4
   Mawangdui 馬王堆 excavated texts on, 4, 157n5
humanity, *as subiectus*, 40–41
Humboldt, Wilhelm von, 30, 49, 162n2
hun 混, 84
   Ames and Hall translation of, 165n10
Husserl, Edmund, 34, 38, 162n6, 163n7
hypokeímenon ὑποκείμενον, *subiectum* as translation of, 40

illusion, Nietzsche on truth as, 57, 66
imitation (*mimesis* μίμησις), 137
incomparability, of philosophy, 38–39
infinite regression (*regressus ad infinitum*), 59
    of "Qiwulun" 齊物論, 116–119, 123
interpretations
    across boundaries, 12
    Nietzsche on *amor fati* and limits of, 75
    will to power and, 69–70
    worldview objective world, 30–31
in-venire, 25, 28, 48, 79
Ion (Plato), 136–137, 173n2

Jaspers, Karl, 35–36

Kant, Immanuel, 62
    on aesthetic judgment, 2, 157n4
    Zhu Rui comparison of *Zhuangzi* 莊子 to, 140
Kearney, Richard, 31–32, 91
Key Concepts in Chinese Philosophy (Zhang Dainian), 17
knowledge, 41, 151
    aesthetics as lower, 2
    circularity of, 59–61, 63
    Daodejing on, 104
    Nietzsche on metaphorical, 60
    teleological expectation of, 32

Lai, Karyn, 91
language
    Being relation to, 9, 49–56
    Daodejing on, 113
    Heidegger on Being speaking through, 53
    Humboldt on means to understand world through, 30
    as interpretation of world, 30–31, 49–50
    Sein and, 53
    transformation from re-grounding grounds, 7–8
    worldview and, 29–33, 49
Lao-Zhuang 老莊, 78, 89, 140. *See also* Daoism
    aesthetic configuration of, 4, 148
    in *Huainanzi* 淮南子, 3–4
    Roth criticism of philosophy of, 4
Laozi (*Lao-tzu, Lao-tze* 老子). See *Daodejing* (*Tao te ching* 道德經)
Levinas, Emmanuel, 6, 24, 56, 158n13
limit-concept, *ziran* 自然 as, 97–98, 111
Liu Xiagan, 89–90, 168n3, 169n6
lógos λόγος, 163n2
Loy, David, 152–153

Ma Lin, on Heidegger philosophy, 5, 159n4, 163n8
Mawangdui 馬王堆, 93, 98–99, 102–104, 161n15, 166n20
    Huang-Lao 黃老 excavated texts in, 4, 157n5
Meditations on First Philosophy (Descartes), 145
metaphérō μεταφέρω, 32
metaphorá μεταφορά, 32
metaphorical circle, Nietzsche on inside and outside of, 58–59, 61–65
metaphorical existence within metaphysics, 58
metaphorical knowledge, Nietzsche on, 60
metaphors, 9
    Anwesen as, 43, 44
    Aristotle on concept and, 57
    Being as, 55–56
    Blumenberg on absolute, 55, 57
    circularity of, 58–60
    Derrida on, 59
    ethical implications of Nietzsche, 65–75

Heidegger metatheory and, 44, 47–49
Heidegger rejection of, 53
Nietzsche on concepts relation with, 57–59
Nietzsche on truth and, 56–65
as process of translation, 32, 56
representations as, 42–47
Ricoeur on Derrida and, 59, 66
Vorstellen as, 43, 45, 46
of world as will to power, 66–68
metaphysics. *See* overcoming metaphysics; Western metaphysics
metatheory, 64
of *dao* 道, 48
of Heidegger, 44, 47–49
universal ontology as, 39
mimesis μίμησις (imitation), 137
Minford, John, 17
ming 名, 78–80, 161n11
Ames and Hall on, 167n36
wuming 無名 relation with, 111–112
modernity, 41
movement, of *dao* 道, 80–84
myriad things (*wanwu* 萬物), 17, 22, 66, 79, 81–84, 85, 92–93, 101–104, 106, 112, 116, 119–124, 127, 129–131, 133, 144, 148–150, 153–154, 165n11, 169n4, 170n12
becoming of, 100
dao 道 relationship with, 86–91
revolving transformation and, 124–125, 127, 133, 150, 154
transformation of, 27–28, 94, 96–97, 99, 109, 122–123

"The Nature of Language" (Heidegger), 23
Nicomachean Ethics (Aristotle), 1
Nietzsche, Friedrich, 3, 47
on *amor fati*, 74–75
on art as child play, 68–74
becoming idea of, 8, 74
on concepts and metaphors relations, 57–59
on dream, 151–152
ethical implications of metaphor of, 65–75
on genealogy, 61, 62, 71
inside and outside metaphorical circle, 58–59, 61–65
knowledge circularity and, 59–61
on truth and metaphor, 56–65
on value of circularity, 63
on values transvaluation, 64–65
on will to truth, 98
Noëlas, Jean-François, 19
non-metaphysics, for Chinese philosophy description, 126

object. *See* subject/object dichotomy
object present-at-hand, 22, 24, 29
objective knowledge, representation and, 41
Olafson, Frederick, 164n7
ontology, 56, 84, 170n9
universal, 29, 50
worldview and, 33–39
onto-theology, 4, 7, 20, 80, 107, 123, 126
Heidegger critique of, 5, 50
of metaphysics, 16, 126–127
in relation to *Daodejing* and *Zhuangzi*, 5
self vision in, 136
the other
aesthetic encounter with, 9, 48, 49, 111
ethical values development through encounter with, 9
language and perspective interpretation of, 8
philosophy interpretation of, 47–48
self definition and, 8

the Other (*l'Autre*), 6, 158n13
overcoming metaphysics, 16, 37, 39.
 See also Western metaphysics
 Vattimo on, 158n11

Parkes, Graham, 147, 173n8, 174n12
parousía παρουσία, 41
phenomenology
 Burik on, 48
 Heidegger on, 33–34, 50, 162nn4–5
Philipse, Herman, 53, 161n20, 163n10
philósophía φιλόσοφία, 159n3
 philosophy and, 13, 14–16
 as pseudo-problem, 26–28
philosophy, 158n12
 of Descartes, 40–42
 getting under way of metaphysics, 15–16
 Heidegger on worldview product and object of, 35
 incomparability of, 39
 non-metaphysics to describe Chinese, 126
 the other interpretation and, 47–48
 philósophía φιλόσοφία and, 13, 14–16
 Platonic-Cartesian, 138–139
 Richardson on metaphysics and, 66
Philosophy in the Tragic Age of the Greeks (Nietzsche), 73
philosophy of comparisons, 8, 13–14, 39–40, 48
 in-venire and, 28
 transformation of concepts and, 26–27
Plato, 136–138, 143–144
Platonic-Cartesian philosophy, 138–139
polarity
 "Qiwulun" 齊物論 self-other, 120
 of *shifei* 是非, 115–116, 120–121
 Zhuangzi 莊子 relational, 111–120

presence-at-hand, 41–42, 67. *See also* object present-at-hand
 Gadamer on world reduction to, 33
presencing (*Anwesen*), 46
 as metaphor, 43, 44
 from *parousía* παρουσία, 41
 Sein and, 42
The Principle of Reason (Heidegger), 51, 58
pseudo-problem, *philósophía* φιλόσοφία as, 26–28
Psychologie der Weltanschauungen (Jaspers), 35–36
psychology, of worldview, 35–36

"Qiwulun" 齊物論, 28–29
 butterfly dream in, 125–126, 144, 173n8
 Chen Guying on, 120
 Chen Shaoming on, 112, 114, 120
 on differentiation, 115, 117
 Graham on, 169n5
 Hansen on, 112, 171n19
 infinite regression of, 116–119, 123
 Liu on, 169n6
 preliminary remarks on, 112–114
 self-other polarities in, 120
 shifei 是非 and, 9, 112–116, 119–121, 125–126, 135
question of Being, 6, 15, 53, 54. *See also* Being

Ratio, 19
re-evaluative value, 39, 73–75, 77
regressus ad infinitum (infinite regression), 59
 of "Qiwulun" 齊物論, 116–119, 123
re-grounding grounds, 16, 21, 28, 39, 46
 language transformation possibility from, 7–8

relational polarities, in *Zhuangzi* 莊子, 111–120
ren 仁, 100, 167n29
representation (*repræsentatio*), 41, 173n1
   Derrida on translation and, 45
   Heidegger critique against, 43
   as metaphors, 42–47
   objective knowledge and, 41
   problem of, 8
   worldview and, 39–48
Republic (Plato), 137
reversal process, 103–106
revolving transformation, 124–125
   wanwu 萬物 and, 124–125, 127, 133, 150, 154
Ricci, Matteo, 161n12
Richards, John, 66
Ricoeur, Paul, 24–25
   on Derrida and metaphor, 59, 66
Roth, Harold, 4
Rule of Metaphor (Ricoeur), 24–25
rulership, 167n33
   Daodejing on, 90
Ryden, Edmund, 17, 20, 160n9

sayers
   Being and, 52–55
   Daodejing on, 113
   Zhuangzi on, 114
Schmitt, Carl, 109–109
Sedley, David, 139
Sein, 5, 6, 25, 29, 35, 43, 51–56, 61, 160n6. *See also* Being
   Anwesen and, 42
   forgetting of, 34, 37
   Geschick and, 52
   Heidegger on, 15, 24, 34, 50, 54, 160n6
   language and, 53
self, onto-theology and vision of, 136
self-other relationship, 7, 119–120
   aesthetic awareness in, 7

self-renewing, 73
self-renewing re-evaluative value, 73, 75, 77
self-transformation, 26, 68, 91. *See also zihua* 自化
self-understanding, 31–32, 102
sense perception, 2–3, 136–140, 143–144, 150–151
   Descartes on, 145–146, 173n4
Shen, Vincent, 173n11
sheng 生, 87
   Gao on, 100–101
shifei 是非, 109, 112, 141, 159n20, 169n6
   dao 道 on, 123–124
   polarity of, 115–116, 120–121
   "Qiwulun" 齊物論 and, 9, 112–116, 119–121, 125–126, 135
si 死, Gao on, 100–101
Sima Tan 司馬談, 3
Simkins, Ronald, 107
sitting and forgetting (*zuowang* 坐忘), 50, 102, 128–132, 134
skill
   of Cook Ding, 127–128, 172n30
   Zhuangzi 莊子 stories of, 127, 140–142
Slingerland, Edward, 166n22, 167n25
   on *wuwei* 無為, 93–99
Socrates, 136–137
spontaneity, spontaneously (*ziran* 自然)
   dao 道 relation to, 9, 88–89, 154
   domination avoidance and, 106–109
   ethical implications of, 87–98
   Lai on, 91
   as limit-concept, 97–98, 111
   Liu on, 89–90
   wuming 無名 and unassertive definitions, 98–103
   wuwei 無為 relationship with, 91–98, 111

spontaneous transformation, 9, 103, 106, 109, 153, 171n22
"*Die Sprache spricht*" (Heidegger), 53
Stenstad, Gail, 23–24
subiectus (lying under), 22, 25, 45, 97
   cogito and, 42, 135
   grounding and, 16, 24, 47, 135
   humanity as, 40–41
   hypokeímenon ὑποκείμενον translation for, 40
subject/object dichotomy, 8
   of Descartes, 97–98
   Weltbild and, 40–42
Summa Theologiæ (Aquinas), 19
supreme will to power, 69, 73, 75

Tang Junyi, 122–123, 149, 165nn12–13, 172n23
Tao te ching 道德經. See *Daodejing*
Taoism. See Daoism
teleological expectation, of knowledge, 32
theory of beauty, aesthetics as, 3
tian xia 天下, 17, 160n9
tian 天, 95
tiandi 天地, 100, 120, 167n29
time, shape of, 122–124
to perceive (*aisthánomai* αἰσθάνομαι), 2
transformation
   myriad things and, 27–28, 122–123
   you 有 and *wu* 無 revolving, 27
transformation of things, 105, 145. See also *wuhua* 物化
   butterfly dream and, 145
   continuity and revolving, 124–125
   of *wanwu* 萬物, 27–28, 122–123
   yi description of continuity of, 121–123
translatio, 32
translation problems
   in comparative studies, 11–14, 159n1
   of concepts, 13, 14
   Hansen on dictionary for, 12
   for *wu* 無, 17, 18, 160n9, 165n1, 169n4
   for *you* 有, 17, 18, 160n9, 165n1
translations, 30
   dependence on own worldview, 32
   Derrida on representation and, 45
   Gadamer on, 31, 32–33
   as metaphor for translation process, 32, 56
transvaluation of values, of Nietzsche, 64–65
truth
   Nietzsche on metaphor and, 56–65
   Nietzsche on will to, 98
   as unconcealment, 47
   Zhu on beauty is, 141
Twilight of the Idols (Nietzsche), 60, 65
twisting (*Verwindung*), 6, 158n11

unchanging (*bu gai* 不改), 84–86
unchanging process, of *dao* 道, 84–87
unconcealment, 42, 46, 47, 153, 163n9
undiscriminative, 127
un-education, 101
universal ontology, 29, 50
   as metatheory, 39
   worldview and, 33, 36–39, 50
unnaming, 99–103, 167n35
unobstructive, 89, 90, 92, 93, 98–99, 101, 105–106, 111–112, 153–154, 174n15. See also *wuwei* 無為

values
   embedded in metaphors, 9
   Nietzsche on transvaluation of, 64–65
   Nietzsche philosophy of, 61
   the other encounter development of ethical, 9

problem of, 8
re-evaluative, 39, 73–75, 77
Vattimo, Gianni, 150, 158n11
Verwindung (twisting), 6, 158n11
Vorstellen, 40
as metaphor, 43, 45, 46

walking both ways, 120–121, 124, 154
Wang Bi 王弼, 173n11
Daodejing version by, 18, 99, 161n15
Wang Bo, on *wuming* 無名 and *youming* 有名, 99
wanwu 萬物 (myriad things), 17, 22, 66, 79, 81–84, 85, 92–93, 101–104, 106, 112, 116, 119–124, 127, 129–131, 133, 144, 148–150, 153–154, 165n11, 169n4, 170n12
becoming of, 100
dao 道 relationship with, 86–91
revolving transformation and, 124–125, 127, 133, 150, 154
transformation of, 27–28, 94, 96–97, 99, 109, 122–123
Watson, Burton, 112, 175n16
way (*dao* 道), 18, 24–26, 158n17, 161n11
as *æterna Ratio*, 19
Ames on, 161n16
as *be-wëgen*, 21–26
as cause in sense of motion, 87–89
chang 常 relation to, 87, 99
movement of, 80–84
myriad things relationship with, 87–91
unchanging process of, 84–87
wanwu 萬物 relationship with, 87–91
as way-making, 21–23
yin 陰 and *yang* 陽 revolving process in, 22–23

ziran 自然 relation to, 9, 88–89, 154
way-making, 21–26, 79–80, 83, 87. See also *dao* 道
weiwuwei 為無為 (action of non-action), 152–153
Weltanschauung (worldview), 43–44, 58, 158n15
aesthetics problem and, 8
fusion of, 31–33
Heidegger critique of, 33–36, 33–38, 41
Heidegger on production and object of philosophy, 35
Humboldt on, 30
language and, 29–33, 49–50
as modernity product, 41
objective world interpretations in, 30–31
ontology and, 33–39
psychology of, 35–36
representations and, 39–48
translation dependence on own, 32
universal ontology compared to, 33, 36–39, 50
Weltanschauungsphilosophie (worldview philosophy), 5, 34–38, 46, 50, 159n4
Weltbild (world picture), 8, 135
as modernity product, 41
subject/object dichotomy, 40–42
Western metaphysics
on aesthetics and ethics, 3
Being-beings structure of, 7, 9, 15, 126–127
Verwindung and, 6
you 有 and *wu* 無 interpretations in, 7
What Is Philosophy? (Heidegger), 14, 15
will to power
becoming and, 69–70

will to power *(continued)*
  Heidegger on, 68
  interpretations and, 69–70
  metaphor of world as, 66–68
  supreme, 69, 73, 75
The Will to Power (WP) (Nietzsche), 62, 63, 67–69, 72, 152
will to truth, Nietzsche on, 98
world. *See also* aesthetic encounter, with world
  aesthetic attunement to, 9, 112, 147, 153
  as aesthetic gesture, 10, 152, 155
  experiencing of, 9
  Gadamer on presence-at-hand and reduction of, 33
  Humboldt on language means to understand, 30
  metaphor of world as will to power, 66–68
  shape of time in, 122–124
  Tang on one, 122
  worldview interpretations of objective, 30–31
world picture (*Weltbild*), 8, 135
  as modernity product, 41
  subject/object dichotomy, 40–42
worldview (*Weltanschauung*), 43–44, 58, 158n15
  aesthetics problem and, 8
  fusion of, 31–33
  Heidegger critique of, 33–36, 33–38, 41
  Heidegger on production and object of philosophy, 35
  Humboldt on, 30
  language and, 29–33, 49–50
  as modernity product, 41
  objective world interpretations in, 30–31
  ontology and, 33–39
  psychology of, 35–36

  representations and, 39–48
  translation dependence on own, 32
  universal ontology compared to, 33, 36–39, 50
worldview philosophy (*Weltanschauungsphilosophie*), 5, 34–38, 46, 50, 159n4
WP. See *The Will to Power*
Wu, Charles, 17
Wu Kuang-ming, 131, 142
wu 無, 84, 105–106, 109, 113, 117, 123, 148
  revolving transformation and, 27
  Ricci on concept of, 161n12
  Slingerland on, 94
  translation problems for, 17, 18, 160n9, 165n1, 169n4
  Western metaphysics interpretation of, 7
wuhua 物化, 9, 66, 83, 133
wuming 無名, 9, 109, 134
  aesthetic attunement link to, 112
  Chen Guying and Xu Kangsheng on, 167n35
  ming 名 relation with, 111–112
  as part of *wuwei* 無為, 105
  unassertive definitions and, 98–103
  Wang Bo on, 99
wuqing 無情, 9, 134
  differentiations assimilation and, 127
  Zhuangzi 莊子 on, 109, 127
wushi 無事, 105–106
wuwei 無為, 9, 102, 109, 134, 153
  ethical implications of, 87–98
  problem of, 93–97
  Slingerland on, 93–99
  unobstructive actions of, 111–112, 174n15
  wuming 無名 as part of, 105
  ziran 自然 relationship with, 91–93, 111

wuyu 無欲, 9, 105–106

Xici 繫辭 (*Dazhuan* 大傳), on *yin* 陰 and *yang* 陽, 22
Xu Kangsheng, on *wuming* 無名, 167n35

yang 陽. See *yin* 陰 and *yang* 陽
yi 一, 83, 120–124, 165n7, 171n19. *See also* continuity
   Chen Guying on, 121
   process and wholeness of, 123
yin 陰 and *yang* 陽, 114, 173n11
   dao 道 revolving process of, 22–23
yixiang 意象, 149
you 有, 7, 16–18, 20, 29, 81, 113, 117–118
   revolving transformation and, 27
   translation problems of, 17, 18, 160n9, 165n1
   Western metaphysics interpretation of, 7
youming 有名, Wang Bo on, 99

Zhu Rui
   on beauty is truth, 141
   Zhuangzi 莊子 comparison to Kant, 140
Zhuangzi 莊子 (*Chuang-tzu* 莊子), 135, 171n22
   Ames on, 174n15
   analysis of, 25
   constant formation and division in, 27
   continuity of *yi* 一, 121–122
   corresponding pluralities in, 114–116, 121
   Daoism foundation, 3
   Guo Xiang 郭象 editing of, 157n6, 168n3, 170n14
   infinite regression of relations in, 59, 116–119, 123
   onto-theology in relation to, 5
   relational polarities in, 111–120
   revolving transformations in, 124–125
   on sayers, 114
   self-other relationship, 119–120
   shape of time and, 122–123
   on *shifei* 是非, 109, 112
   skill stories of, 127, 140–142
   Wu Kuang-ming on, 131, 142
   on *wuqing* 無情, 109, 127
   Zhu Rui comparison to Kant, 140
Zhuo Dawei, 147–148
zihua 自化, 105–106, 153, 171n22, 172n27
ziran 自然 (spontaneity, spontaneously)
   dao 道 relation to, 9, 88–89, 154
   domination avoidance and, 106–109
   ethical implications of, 87–98
   Lai on, 91
   as limit-concept, 97–98, 111
   Liu on, 89–90
   wuming 無名 and unassertive definitions, 98–103
   wuwei 無為 relationship with, 91–93, 111
zuowang 坐忘 (sitting and forgetting), 50, 102, 128–132, 134

www.ingramcontent.com/pod-product-compliance
Lightning Source LLC
Chambersburg PA
CBHW020332240426
43665CB00043B/441